Wok & Stir Fry

Wok
& Stir Fry

𝑝

This is a Parragon Publishing Book
This edition published in 2004

Parragon Publishing
Queen Street House
4 Queen Street
Bath BA1 1HE, UK

ISBN: 0-75258-327-1

Printed in China

NOTE
Cup measurements in this book are for American cups.
Tablespoons are assumed to be 15ml. Unless otherwise stated,
milk is assumed to be full fat, eggs are medium
and pepper is freshly ground black pepper.

Recipes using uncooked eggs should be
avoided by infants, the elderly, pregnant women, and anyone
suffering from an illness.

Contents

Introduction 8–9 Regional Cooking 10–13
Cooking Techniques 14–15 How to Use This Book 17

Soups & Appetizers

Poultry & Meat

Savory Meals (continued)

Fish & Seafood

Vegetables

Vegetarian & Vegan

Rice & Noodles

Introduction

One of the quickest, easiest, and most versatile methods of cooking is to cook in a wok. It takes only a few minutes to assemble the ingredients—a selection of vegetables, to which may be added meat, fish, seafood, bean curd, nuts, rice, or noodles. The possibilities are endless for ringing the changes with different oils, seasonings, and sauces, and the result is a colorful, delicious, healthy meal that is as pleasing to the eye as it is to the tastebuds.

A wok is a metal cooking implement in the shape of a shallow, curved bowl, with either one long wooden handle or two looped handles. The wok comes in a variety of sizes—one approximately 30–35cm/12–14 inches in diameter is suitable for the average family—and, as with most kitchen equipment, it is worth investing in the best you can. Woks are made from stainless steel, copper, or cast iron, and the latter is ideal as it retains heat more efficiently, especially once it has become well-seasoned.

Although it is possible to cook in a skillet, there are several good reasons to use a wok. The key to successful cooking is to move and toss the ingredients constantly as they go in, and this is much easier to achieve in the convex shape of a wok. The curved sides allow the heat to rise, so that the whole wok becomes hot, speeding up the cooking process; and as the food cannot become lodged in corners or edges, it is extremely easy to clean the wok after use.

A useful addition in the Western kitchen is a metal collar, shaped like a crown, with angled sides and a hollow in which to sit the wok. The collar aids heat convection from the stove or burner, and the wok heats up more evenly than if it were placed directly on the heat source.

A palette knife with a long wooden handle is ideal for cooking and removing foods, as the curved edge follows the curve of the wok.

By adding a frying strainer or shallow wire-meshed basket, the wok may be used for deep-frying, while a steaming trivet and a domed, tight-fitting lid will convert the wok to a very efficient steamer. These extra items are often supplied with the wok when it is first purchased.

Before using the wok, it is essential to season it properly. Use oiled paper towels to wipe the wok both inside and out, then heat it to a high temperature in the stove or on the burner. Remove the wok from the heat, allow it to cool, then repeat the process several times to create a good, non-stick coating. After the initial seasoning, the wok can simply be wiped clean, or washed in soapy water—but if the wok is made of cast iron, it is essential to dry it thoroughly immediately after washing, to prevent rusting.

Regional cooking

Although its popularity is now far more wide-ranging, wok cooking originated in Asia and the Far East, where variations of this useful implement are commonly used in the preparation of many dishes. In India, the curry derives its name from *karahi*, a large pan that sits over a hole in a brick or earth stove and is used for braising and cooking, while in Mongolia the convex iron griddle used for barbecueing meat, especially lamb, is very similar in shape to a wok.

It was the Chinese, however, who devised cooking in a wok. There are regional variations in ingredients throughout this vast country, but fresh vegetables play a very important role in all Chinese cooking. This rapid and efficient method of cooking the vegetables ensures that they retain their individual flavors, their vibrant colors, and their crisp texture, as well as preserving their vitamin content. Poultry, lamb, beef, and pork are also cooked in the wok —either deep-fried or steamed—and are combined with sauces and seasonings. Long- or short-grain rice is often added or served as an accompaniment, and noodles made from wheat, buckwheat, or rice flours are also widely used.

Chinese influence has spread to its neighboring countries as well. Throughout Indonesia, Japan, Thailand, Singapore, and Malaysia the wok is used over wood or charcoal for curries and rice dishes as well as stir-fries, with variations in the addition of different meat, fish, spices, and sauces.

Regional cooking

A style of cuisine that has enjoyed a huge rise in popularity in recent years is Thai. For the people of Thailand, the preparation and eating of good food, beautifully served, is taken very seriously. The ingredients, locally grown and very fresh, are carefully chosen and skilfully balanced for texture and flavor, combining bitter, salt, sour, hot, and sweet tastes.

The monsoon climate and abundant rainfall in Thailand produce ideal conditions for growing rice, so it's not surprising that Thai cuisine is centered around this, the country's most important staple. Thai fragrant rice is a long-grain, fluffy white rice, delicately scented, while glutinous rice is short-grain with a high starch content, which makes it sticky when cooked. Rice flour is also used to make noodles, usually in the shape of flat ribbons or thin vermicelli.

The warm Gulf seas around Thailand, and the inland waterways, produce a wide variety of fish in abundance, and in all the coastal towns fresh seafood is sold from thatch-roofed beach kiosks—

barbecued or sautéed fish with ginger, shrimp with coconut milk and coriander, or steamed crab. Meat is often combined with seafood such as shrimp or crab meat.

Other essentials in Thai cooking are coconut (almost as important as rice), lime, chili, garlic, lemongrass, ginger root, and cilantro, as well as seasonings such as soy sauce, rice vinegar, and fish sauce. All of these ingredients are now readily available in your local food store.

Cooking techniques

Although the wok can be used for steaming and deep-frying, its main use is for cooking. In China, where this is the most widely used method of cooking, it is called Ch'au, a term that describes cooking a number of ingredients, thinly sliced, in oil. As it cooks, the food is tossed and turned with long bamboo chopsticks.

There are two basic types of cooking, known as Pao and Liu. Pao, or "explosion", is a method where the food is stirred rapidly in a dry wok over the highest heat for about one minute. Foods cooked in this way are often

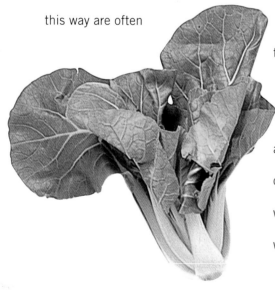

marinated beforehand for flavor and tenderness. Liu is wet frying, where the foods are constantly turned until cooked. Peanut or corn oil are usually used for such cooking. Sesame oil burns easily, but can be drizzled over the finished dish as a seasoning.

Some foods need a slightly longer cooking time than others and, for this reason, cooking is often done in stages. This also allows the individual ingredients to retain their distinct flavors. As they cook, the foods are removed from the wok, but they are always combined once everything is cooked, and served as a whole dish. In Liu, a mixture of cornstarch and stock is added to the wok at the end of cooking, together with sugar, vinegar, and soy sauce, to

make a delicious, almost sticky coating sauce.

There is plenty of scope for creativity when choosing ingredients, even for the simplest stir-fry. A combination of onions, carrots, bell peppers (green, red, yellow, and orange), broccoli and snow peas will provide the basis for a colorful dish. Add beansprouts at the end of cooking and toss quickly for texture, or some canned water chestnuts, which add a delicious crunch. A few cashew nuts or almonds, some cubed bean curd or chicken breast, or a handful of shrimp provide protein, while adding some pre-cooked rice or noodles makes a gutsy stir-fry. A ready-made sauce—perhaps oyster, or yellow bean—will finish off the dish.

Ginger, garlic, and chilies are wonderful for flavoring stir-fries. Chilies come in a wide variety, ranging in heat from very mild to fiery hot. Red chilies are slightly sweeter and milder than green, and larger chilies also tend to be milder. Crushed dried chilies are useful for seasoning. The Thais favor the small red or green "bird-eye" chilies, which are very fiery, and their curries are flavoured with ferociously hot chili pastes.

Some of the "kick" can be taken out of a hot chili by removing the seeds, but this must be done very carefully as they can cause a nasty reaction. Cut fresh chilies in half, and scrape out the seeds with the point of a knife, and with dried chilies, simply cut off the end and shake out the seeds. Always remember to wash your hands!

How to Use This Book

Each recipe contains a wealth of useful information, including a breakdown of nutritional quantities, preparation, and cooking times, and level of difficulty. All of this information is explained in detail below.

The nutritional information provided for each recipe is per serving or per portion. Optional ingredients, variations or serving suggestions have not been included in the calculations.

The number of chef's hats represents the difficulty of each recipe, ranging from easy (1 chef's hat) to difficult (5 chef's hats).

This amount of time represents the preparation of ingredients, including cooling, chilling and soaking times.

This represents the cooking time.

The ingredients for each recipe are listed in the order that they are used.

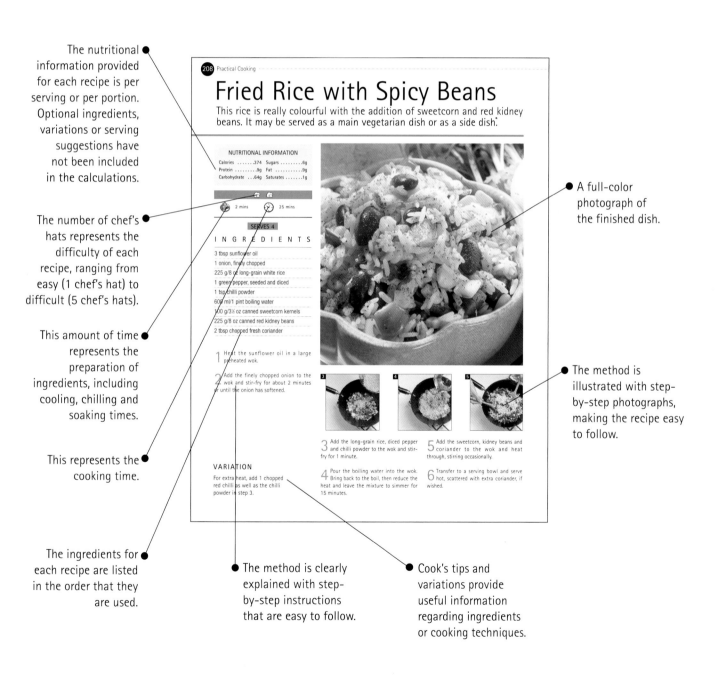

A full-color photograph of the finished dish.

The method is illustrated with step-by-step photographs, making the recipe easy to follow.

The method is clearly explained with step-by-step instructions that are easy to follow.

Cook's tips and variations provide useful information regarding ingredients or cooking techniques.

Soups & Appetizers

Soup is indispensable at Asian tables, especially in China, Japan, Korea, and South-East Asia. It is generally eaten part way through a main meal to clear the palate for further dishes. There are many different types of delicious

soups, both thick and thin and, of course, the clear soups which are often served with wontons or dumplings.

Appetizers or snacks are drier foods in general; the spring roll is a well-known Chinese snack and these come in many variations and shapes across the Far East. Other delights are wrapped in pastry, bread, and rice paper or are skewered for ease of eating; vegetables, fish, and meat are also deep-fried for a crispy coating. These dishes are served as starters in Westernized restaurants to animate the tastebuds for the main course.

Hot & Sour Mushroom Soup

Hot and sour soups are found across South East Asia in different forms.
Reduce the number of chilies added if you prefer a milder dish.

NUTRITIONAL INFORMATION

Calories 87	Sugars 7g
Protein 4g	Fat 5g
Carbohydrate 8g	Saturates 1g

   10 mins 🕐 20 mins

SERVES 4

INGREDIENTS

2 tbsp tamarind paste

4 red chilies, very finely chopped

2 cloves garlic, crushed

2 tsp finely chopped Thai ginger

4 tbsp fish sauce

2 tbsp palm sugar or superfine sugar

8 lime leaves, roughly torn

5 cups vegetable bouillon

1 large carrot, thinly sliced

8 oz/225 g white mushrooms, halved

12 oz/350 g shredded white cabbage

3½ oz/100 g fine green beans, halved

3 tbsp coarsely chopped fresh cilantro

3½ oz/100 g cherry tomatoes, halved

COOK'S TIP

Tamarind is the dried fruit of
the tamarind tree. Sold as a pulp
or paste, it is used to give a
special sweet and sour flavor to
Asian dishes.

1 Place the tamarind paste, red chilies,
garlic, ginger, fish sauce, palm
or superfine sugar, lime leaves, and
vegetable bouillon in a large preheated
wok or heavy-based skillet. Bring the
mixture to a boil, stirring occasionally.

2 Reduce the heat and add the carrots,
mushrooms, white cabbage, and
green beans. Let the soup simmer,
uncovered, for about 10 minutes, or until
the vegetables are tender, but not soft.

3 Stir the fresh cilantro and cherry
tomatoes into the mixture in the wok
and heat through for another 5 minutes.

4 Transfer the soup to a warm tureen or
individual serving bowls and serve
immediately.

Crab & Corn Soup

Crab and corn are classic ingredients in Chinese cooking.
Here egg noodles are added for a filling dish.

NUTRITIONAL INFORMATION

Calories 324   Sugars 6g
Protein . . . . .27g   Fat 8g
Carbohydrate . . .39g   Saturates 2g

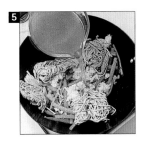

5 mins   20 mins

SERVES 4

I N G R E D I E N T S

1 tbsp sunflower oil

1 tsp Chinese five-spice powder

3 small carrots, cut into sticks

½ cup canned or frozen corn kernels

¾ cup peas

6 scallions, trimmed and sliced

1 red chili, seeded and very thinly sliced

14 oz/400 g can white crab meat

6 oz/175 g egg noodles

7½ cups fish bouillon

3 tbsp soy sauce

1 Heat the sunflower oil in a large preheated wok or heavy-based skillet.

2 Add the Chinese five-spice powder, carrots, corn, peas, scallions, and red chili to the wok and cook for about 5 minutes, stirring constantly.

3 Add the crab meat to the wok and cook the mixture for 1 minute, distributing the crab meat evenly.

4 Roughly break up the egg noodles and add to the wok.

5 Pour the fish bouillon and soy sauce into the mixture in the wok and bring to a boil.

6 Cover the wok or skillet and let the soup simmer for 5 minutes.

7 Stir once more, then transfer the soup to a warm soup tureen or individual serving bowls and serve at once.

COOK'S TIP

Chinese five-spice powder is a mixture of star anise, fennel, cloves, cinnamon and Szechuan pepper. It has an unmistakeable flavor. Use it sparingly, as it is very pungent.

Spicy Shrimp Soup

Lime leaves are used as a flavoring in this soup to add tartness.

NUTRITIONAL INFORMATION

Calories . . . . .217 Sugars 16g
Protein . . . . .16g Fat 4g
Carbohydrate . . .31g Saturates 1g

 10 mins   🕐 20 mins

SERVES 4

I N G R E D I E N T S

2 tbsp tamarind paste

4 red chilies, very finely chopped

2 cloves garlic, crushed

2 tsp finely chopped Thai ginger

4 tbsp fish sauce

2 tbsp palm sugar or superfine sugar

5 cups fish bouillon

8 lime leaves

1 large carrot, very thinly sliced

2 cups diced sweet potatoes

3½ oz/100 g halved baby corn cobs

3 tbsp fresh cilantro, coarsely chopped

3½ oz/100g cherry tomatoes, halved

8 oz/225 g fan-tail shrimp

1 Place the tamarind paste, red chilies, garlic, ginger, fish sauce, sugar, and fish bouillon in a preheated wok or large, heavy skillet. Tear the lime leaves and add to the wok. Bring to the boil, stirring constantly to blend the flavors.

2 Reduce the heat and add the carrot, sweet potatoes, and baby corn cobs to the mixture in the wok.

3 Leave the soup to simmer, uncovered, for about 10 minutes, or until the vegetables are just tender.

4 Stir the cilantro, cherry tomatoes, and shrimp into the soup and heat through for 5 minutes.

5 Transfer the soup to a warm soup tureen or individual serving bowls and serve hot.

COOK'S TIP

Thai ginger or galangal is a member of the ginger family, but it is yellow in color with pink sprouts. The flavor is aromatic and less pungent than ginger.

Coconut & Crab Soup

Thai red curry paste is quite fiery, but adds a superb flavor to this dish. It is available from most large food stores.

NUTRITIONAL INFORMATION

Calories	122	Sugar	.........9g
Protein	........11g	Fats	...........4g
Carbohydrates	...11g	Saturates	......1g

 5 mins   10 mins

SERVES 4

INGREDIENTS

1 tbsp peanut oil

2 tbsp red curry paste

1 red bell pepper, seeded and sliced

2½ cups coconut milk

2½ cups fish bouillon

2 tbsp fish sauce

8 oz/225 g canned or fresh white crab meat

8 oz/225 g fresh or frozen crab claws

2 tbsp chopped fresh cilantro

3 scallions, trimmed and sliced

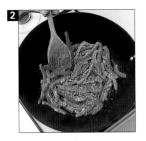

1 Heat the oil in a large preheated wok.

2 Add the red curry paste and red bell pepper to the wok and cook for 1 minute.

3 Add the coconut milk, fish bouillon, and fish sauce and bring to a boil.

4 Add the crab meat, crab claws, cilantro, and scallions to the wok.

5 Stir the mixture well and heat thoroughly for 2–3 minutes or until everything is warmed through.

6 Transfer the soup to warm bowls and serve hot.

COOK'S TIP

Clean the wok after use by washing it with water, using a mild detergent if necessary, and a soft cloth or brush. Do not scrub or use any abrasive cleaner as this will scratch the surface. Dry thoroughly then wipe the surface all over with a little oil to protect the surface.

Chili Fish Soup

Chinese mushrooms add an intense flavor to this soup which is unique. If they are unavailable, use open-cap mushrooms, sliced.

NUTRITIONAL INFORMATION

Calories 166	Sugars 1g	
Protein 23g	Fat 7g	
Carbohydrate 4g	Saturates 1g	

15 mins   15 mins

SERVES 4

I N G R E D I E N T S

½ oz/15 g dried Chinese mushrooms

2 tbsp sunflower oil

1 onion, sliced

1½ cups snow peas

3½ oz/100 g canned, drained bamboo shoots

3 tbsp sweet chili sauce

5 cups fish or vegetable bouillon

3 tbsp light soy sauce

2 tbsp fresh cilantro, plus extra to garnish

1 lb/450 g cod fillet, skinned and cubed

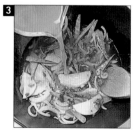

COOK'S TIP

Cod is used in this recipe as it is a meaty white fish. For real luxury, use monkfish tail instead.

There are many different varieties of dried mushrooms, but shiitake are best. They are not cheap, but a small amount will go a long way.

1 Place the mushrooms in a large bowl. Pour over enough boiling water to cover and let stand for 5 minutes. Drain the mushrooms thoroughly in a strainer. Using a sharp knife, roughly chop the mushrooms.

2 Heat the sunflower oil in a preheated wok or large skillet. Add the sliced onion to the wok and cook for 5 minutes, or until softened.

3 Add the snow peas, bamboo shoots, chili sauce, bouillon, and soy sauce to the wok and bring to a boil.

4 Add the cilantro and cod and let simmer for 5 minutes or until the fish is cooked through.

5 Transfer the soup to warm bowls, garnish with extra cilantro, if wished, and serve hot.

Fish Soup with Wontons

This soup is topped with small wontons filled with shrimp, making it both very tasty and satisfying.

NUTRITIONAL INFORMATION

Calories 115   Sugars 0g
Protein . . . . .16g   Fat 5g
Carbohydrate . . . .1g   Saturates 1g

10 mins   15 mins

SERVES 4

INGREDIENTS

4½ oz/125 g large, cooked, peeled shrimp

1 tsp chopped fresh chives

1 small garlic clove, finely chopped

1 tbsp vegetable oil

12 wonton wrappers

1 small egg, beaten

3½ cups fish bouillon

6 oz/175 g white fish fillet, diced

dash of chili sauce

TO GARNISH

sliced fresh red chili

snipped chives

1 Roughly chop a quarter of the shrimp and mix together with the chopped chives and garlic.

2 Heat the oil in a preheated wok or large skillet until it is really hot.

3 Cook the shrimp mixture for 1–2 minutes. Remove from the heat and let cool completely.

4 Spread out the wonton wrappers on a counter. Spoon a little of the shrimp filling into the center of each wrapper. Brush the edges of the wrappers with beaten egg and press the edges together, scrunching them to form a "moneybag" shape. Set aside while you are preparing the soup.

5 Pour the fish bouillon into a large pan and bring to a boil. Add the diced white fish and the remaining shrimp and cook for 5 minutes.

6 Season to taste with the chili sauce. Add the wontons and cook for a further 5 minutes.

7 Spoon into warmed serving bowls, garnish with sliced red chili and chives and serve immediately.

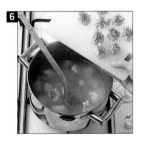

VARIATION

Replace the shrimp with cooked crabmeat for an alternative flavor.

Fish & Vegetable Soup

A chunky fish soup with strips of vegetables, all flavored with ginger and lemon, makes a meal in itself.

NUTRITIONAL INFORMATION

Calories 88	Sugars 1g
Protein 12g	Fat 3g
Carbohydrate 3g	Saturates 0.5g

40 mins   20 mins

SERVES 4

I N G R E D I E N T S

9 oz/250 g white fish fillets (cod, halibut, haddock, sole)

½ tsp ground ginger

½ tsp salt

1 small leek, trimmed

2–4 crab sticks, thawed if frozen (optional)

1 tbsp sunflower oil

1 large carrot, cut into very thin sticks

8 canned water chestnuts, thinly sliced

5 cups fish or vegetable bouillon

1 tbsp lemon juice

1 tbsp light soy sauce

1 large zucchini, cut into very thin sticks

black pepper

1 Remove any skin from the fish and cut into cubes of about 1 inch/2.5 cm. Combine the ground ginger and salt and use to rub into the pieces of fish. Let the fish marinate for at least 30 minutes.

2 Meanwhile, divide the green and white parts of the leek. Cut each part into 1-inch/2.5-cm lengths and then into very thin strips down the length of each piece, keeping the two parts separate. Slice the crab sticks into ½-inch/1-cm pieces.

3 Heat the oil in the wok, swirling it around so it is really hot. Add the white part of the leek and cook for a couple of minutes, then add the carrots and water chestnuts and continue to cook for 1–2 minutes, stirring thoroughly.

4 Add the bouillon and bring to a boil, then add the lemon juice and soy sauce and simmer for 2 minutes.

5 Add the fish and continue to cook for about 5 minutes until the fish begins to break up a little, then add the green part of the leek and the zucchini and simmer for about 1 minute. Add the sliced crab sticks, if using, and season to taste with black pepper. Simmer for a further minute or so and serve piping hot.

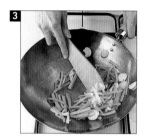

COOK'S TIP

To skin fish, place the fillet skin-side down and insert a sharp, flexible knife at one end between the flesh and the skin. Hold the skin tightly at the end and push the knife along, keeping the blade flat against the skin.

Shrimp Soup

This soup is an interesting mix of colors and textures. The egg may be made into a flat omelet and added as thin strips if preferred.

NUTRITIONAL INFORMATION

Calories	123	Sugars	.......0.2g
Protein	........13g	Fat	..........8g
Carbohydrate	....1g	Saturates	.......1g

🕐 20 mins

SERVES 4

INGREDIENTS

2 tbsp sunflower oil

2 scallions, thinly sliced diagonally

1 carrot, coarsely grated

4½ oz/125 g large closed cup mushrooms, thinly sliced

4 cups fish or vegetable bouillon

½ tsp Chinese five-spice powder

1 tbsp light soy sauce

4½ oz/125 g large peeled shrimp or peeled jumbo shrimp, thawed if frozen

½ bunch arugula leaves, coarsely chopped

1 egg, well beaten

salt and pepper

4 large shrimp in shells, to garnish (optional)

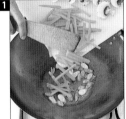
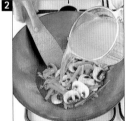

1 Heat the oil in a wok, swirling it around until really hot. Add the scallions and cook for 1 minute then add the carrots and mushrooms and continue to cook for about 2 minutes.

2 Add the bouillon and bring to a boil then season to taste with salt and pepper, Chinese five-spice powder, and soy sauce, and simmer for 5 minutes.

3 If the shrimp are really large, cut them in half before adding to the wok and simmer for 3–4 minutes.

4 Add the arugula leaves to the wok and mix well, then slowly pour in the beaten egg in a circular movement so that it cooks in threads in the soup. Adjust the seasoning and serve each portion topped with a whole shrimp.

COOK'S TIP

Large open mushrooms with black gills give the best flavor but they tend to spoil the color of the soup, making it very dark. Oyster mushrooms can also be used.

Spicy Chicken Noodle Soup

This filling soup is filled with spicy flavors and bright colors for a really attractive and hearty dish.

NUTRITIONAL INFORMATION

Calories .... .286 Sugars .... .21g
Protein .... .22g Fat 6g
Carbohydrate ...37g Saturates 1g

15 mins   20 mins

SERVES 4

I N G R E D I E N T S

2 tbsp tamarind paste

4 red chilies, finely chopped

2 cloves garlic, crushed

2 tsp finely chopped Thai ginger

4 tbsp fish sauce

2 tbsp palm sugar or superfine sugar

8 lime leaves, roughly torn

5 cups chicken bouillon

12 oz/350 g boneless chicken breast

1 large carrot, thinly sliced

2 cups diced sweet potatoes

3½ oz/100 g halved baby corn cobs

3 tbsp coarsely chopped cilantro

3½ oz/100 g cherry tomatoes, halved

5½ oz/150 g flat rice noodles

chopped fresh cilantro to garnish

1 Preheat a large wok or skillet. Place the tamarind paste, chilies, garlic, ginger, fish sauce, sugar, lime leaves, and chicken bouillon in the wok and bring to a boil, stirring constantly. Reduce the heat and cook for about 5 minutes.

2 Using a sharp knife, thinly slice the chicken. Add the chicken to the wok and cook for a further 5 minutes, stirring the mixture well.

3 Reduce the heat and add the carrots, sweet potatoes, and baby corn cobs to the wok. Let simmer, uncovered, for 5 minutes, or until the vegetables are just tender and the chicken is completely cooked through.

4 Stir in the chopped fresh cilantro, cherry tomatoes, and flat rice noodles.

5 Leave the soup to simmer for about 5 minutes, or until the noodles are tender.

6 Garnish the spicy chicken noodle soup with chopped fresh cilantro and serve hot.

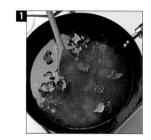

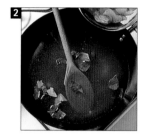

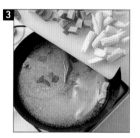

Chicken Noodle Soup

Quick to make, this hot and spicy soup is hearty and warming. If you like your food really fiery, add a chopped dried or fresh chili with its seeds.

NUTRITIONAL INFORMATION

Calories	196	Sugars	........4g
Protein	........16g	Fat	..........11g
Carbohydrate	....8g	Saturates	.......2g

  10 mins   25 mins

SERVES 4–6

INGREDIENTS

1 sheet of dried egg noodles
from a 9 oz/250 g pack

1 tbsp oil

4 skinless, boneless chicken thighs, diced

1 bunch scallions, sliced

2 garlic cloves, chopped

2 tsp finely chopped fresh root ginger

3½ cups chicken bouillon

scant 1 cup coconut milk

3 tsp red curry paste

3 tbsp peanut butter

2 tbsp light soy sauce

1 small red bell pepper, chopped

½ cup frozen peas

salt and pepper

1 Put the noodles in a shallow dish and soak in boiling water as instructed on the package.

2 Heat the oil in a large preheated pan or wok.

3 Add the diced chicken to the pan or wok and cook for 5 minutes, stirring until lightly browned.

4 Add the white part of the scallions, garlic, and ginger, and cook for 2 minutes, stirring.

5 Stir in the chicken bouillon, coconut milk, red curry paste, peanut butter, and soy sauce.

6 Season with salt and pepper to taste. Bring to a boil, stirring, then simmer for 8 minutes, stirring occasionally.

7 Add the red bell pepper, peas, and green scallion tops and cook for 2 minutes.

8 Add the drained noodles and heat through. Spoon the chicken noodle soup into warmed bowls and serve with a spoon and fork.

VARIATION

Green curry paste can be used instead of red curry paste for a less fiery flavor.

Spicy Corn Fritters

Cornmeal can be found in most supermarkets or health food shops.
Yellow in color, it acts as a binding agent in this recipe.

NUTRITIONAL INFORMATION

Calories 213	Sugars 6g
Protein 5g	Fat 8g
Carbohydrate . . .30g	Saturates 1g

 5 mins   15 mins

SERVES 4

INGREDIENTS

¾ cup canned or frozen corn kernels

2 red chilies, seeded and very finely chopped

2 cloves garlic, crushed

10 lime leaves, finely chopped

2 tbsp chopped fresh cilantro

1 large egg

½ cup cornmeal

3½ oz/100 g fine green beans, finely sliced

peanut oil

1 Place the corn, chilies, garlic, lime leaves, cilantro, egg, and cornmeal in a large mixing bowl, and stir to combine.

2 Add the green beans to the ingredients in the bowl and mix well, using a wooden spoon.

3 Divide the mixture into small, evenly sized balls. Flatten the balls of mixture between the palms of your hands to form rounds.

4 Heat a little peanut oil in a preheated wok or large skillet until really hot. Cook the fritters, in batches, until brown and crispy on the outside, turning occasionally.

5 Leave the fritters to drain on paper towels while cooking the remaining fritters.

6 Transfer the drained fritters to warm serving plates and serve immediately.

COOK'S TIP

Kaffir lime leaves are dark green, glossy leaves that have a lemony-lime flavor. They can be bought from specialist Asian stores either fresh or dried. Fresh leaves impart the most delicious flavor.

Vegetable Spring Rolls

There are many different versions of spring rolls throughout the Far East, a vegetable filling being the classic.

NUTRITIONAL INFORMATION

Calories 189   Sugars 4g
Protein . . . . .2g   Fat 16g
Carbohydrate . . . .11g   Saturates 5g

10 mins   15 mins

SERVES 4

INGREDIENTS

3 small carrots

1 red bell pepper

2 tbsp sunflower oil

¾ cup bean sprouts

finely grated zest and juice of 1 lime

1 red chili, seeded and very finely chopped

1 tbsp soy sauce

½ tsp arrowroot

2 tbsp chopped fresh cilantro

8 sheets phyllo pastry

2 tbsp butter

2 tsp sesame oil

TO SERVE

chili sauce

scallion tassels

1 Using a sharp knife, cut the carrots into thin sticks. Seed the bell pepper and cut into thin slices.

2 Heat the sunflower oil in a large preheated wok.

3 Add the carrot, red bell pepper, and beansprouts and cook, stirring, for 2 minutes, or until softened. Remove the wok from the heat and toss in the lime zest and juice, and the red chili.

4 Mix the soy sauce with the arrowroot. Stir the mixture into the wok, return to the heat and cook for 2 minutes or until the juices thicken.

5 Add the chopped fresh cilantro to the wok and mix well.

6 Lay the sheets of phyllo pastry out on a board. Melt the butter and sesame oil and brush each sheet with the mixture.

7 Spoon a little of the vegetable filling at the top of each sheet, fold over each long side, and roll up.

8 Add a little oil to the wok and cook the spring rolls in batches, for 2–3 minutes, or until crisp and golden.

9 Transfer the spring rolls to a serving dish, garnish, and serve hot with chili dipping sauce.

Seven-Spice Eggplants

This is a really simple dish which is perfect served with a chili dip.

NUTRITIONAL INFORMATION

Calories	169	Sugars	.........2g
Protein	.........2g	Fat	..........12g
Carbohydrate	...15g	Saturates	.......1g

35 mins   20 mins

SERVES 4

I N G R E D I E N T S

1 lb/450 g eggplants, wiped

1 egg white

3½ tbsp cornstarch

1 tsp salt

1 tbsp seven-spice seasoning

oil, for deep-frying

1 Using a sharp knife, thinly slice the eggplants. Place the eggplant in a strainer, sprinkle with salt, and let stand for 30 minutes. This will remove all the bitter juices.

2 Rinse the eggplant thoroughly and pat dry with paper towels.

3 Place the egg white in a small bowl and whip until light and foamy.

4 Using a spoon, mix together the cornstarch, salt, and seven-spice seasoning on a large plate.

5 Heat the oil for deep-frying in a large preheated wok or heavy-based skillet.

6 Dip the eggplants into the egg white, and then into the cornstarch and seven-spice mixture to coat evenly.

7 Deep-fry the coated eggplant slices, in batches, for 5 minutes, or until pale golden and crispy.

8 Transfer the eggplants to paper towels and let drain. Transfer the seven-spice eggplants to serving plates and serve hot.

COOK'S TIP

The best oil to use for deep-frying is peanut oil which has a high smoke point and mild flavor, so it will neither burn or taint the food. About 2½ cups of oil is sufficient.

Bean Curd with Peanut Sauce

This is a very sociable dish if put in the center of the table where people can help themselves with cocktail sticks.

NUTRITIONAL INFORMATION

Calories	338	Sugars	........9g
Protein	........16g	Fat	..........22g
Carbohydrate	...21g	Saturates	.......4g

  5 mins   20 mins

SERVES 4

INGREDIENTS

1 lb 2 oz/500 g marinated or plain, firm
  bean curd

2 tbsp rice vinegar

2 tbsp sugar

1 tsp salt

3 tbsp smooth peanut butter

½ tsp chili flakes

3 tbsp barbecue sauce

4 cups sunflower oil

2 tbsp sesame oil

BATTER

4 tbsp all-purpose flour

2 eggs, beaten

4 tbsp milk

½ tsp baking powder

½ tsp chili powder

1 Cut the bean curd into 1-inch/2.5-cm triangles. Set aside until required.

2 Combine the rice vinegar, sugar, and salt in a pan. Bring to a boil and then simmer for 2 minutes.

3 Remove the sauce from the heat and add the smooth peanut butter, chili flakes, and barbecue sauce, stirring well until thoroughly blended.

4 To make the batter, sift the all-purpose flour into a bowl, make a well in the center and add the eggs. Draw in the flour, adding the milk slowly. Stir in the baking powder and chili powder.

5 Heat both the sunflower oil and sesame oil in a deep-fryer or large pan until a light haze appears on top.

6 Dip the bean curd triangles into the batter and deep-fry until golden brown. You may need to do this in batches. Drain on paper towels.

7 Transfer the bean curd triangles to a serving dish and serve with the peanut sauce.

COOK'S TIP

Bean curd is made from puréed soy beans. It is white, with a soft cheese-like texture, and is sold in blocks, either fresh or vacuum-packed. Although it has a bland flavor, it blends well with other ingredients, and absorbs the flavors of spices and sauces.

Chicken Balls with Sauce

Serve these bite-sized chicken appetizers warm as a snack, with drinks, or packed cold for a picnic or lunch-time treat.

NUTRITIONAL INFORMATION

Calories 214	Sugars 2g	
Protein 20g	Fat 13g	
Carbohydrate 5g	Saturates 2g	

 10 mins   25 mins

SERVES 4

I N G R E D I E N T S

2 large boneless, skinless chicken breasts

3 tbsp vegetable oil

2 shallots, finely chopped

1 celery stalk, finely chopped

1 garlic clove, crushed

2 tbsp light soy sauce

1 small egg, beaten

1 bunch scallions

salt and pepper

scallion tassels, to garnish

D I P P I N G   S A U C E

3 tbsp dark soy sauce

1 tbsp rice wine

1 tsp sesame seeds

1 Cut the chicken into ¾-inch/2-cm pieces. Heat half of the oil in a skillet or wok and cook the chicken over a high heat for 2–3 minutes until golden. Remove from the pan with a perforated spoon; set aside.

2 Add the shallots, celery, and garlic to the pan and cook for 1–2 minutes until softened but not browned.

3 Place the chicken, shallots, celery, and garlic in a food processor and process until finely ground. Add 1 tablespoon of the light soy sauce, just enough egg to make a fairly firm mixture, and salt and pepper.

4 Trim the scallions and cut into 2-inch/5-cm lengths. Make the dipping sauce by mixing together the dark soy sauce, rice wine, and sesame seeds; set aside.

5 Shape the chicken mixture into 16–18 walnut-sized balls. Heat the remaining oil in the skillet or wok and cook the balls in small batches for 4–5 minutes until golden brown. As each batch is cooked drain on paper towels and keep hot.

6 Cook the scallions for 1–2 minutes until they begin to soften, then stir in the remaining light soy sauce. Serve with the chicken balls and dipping sauce on a platter, garnished with the scallion tassels.

Crispy Pork & Peanut Baskets

These tasty little appetite-teasers are an adaptation of a traditional recipe made with a light batter, but phyllo pastry is just as good.

NUTRITIONAL INFORMATION

Calories	243	Sugars	.........1g
Protein	........12g	Fat	..........16g
Carbohydrate	...12g	Saturates	.......3g

🍲 10 mins   🕐 15 mins

SERVES 4

I N G R E D I E N T S

2 sheets phyllo pastry, each about
  16½ x 11 inches/42 x 28 cm

2 tbsp vegetable oil

1 garlic clove, crushed

125 g/4½ oz ground pork

1 tsp red curry paste

2 scallions, finely chopped

3 tbsp crunchy peanut butter

1 tbsp light soy sauce

1 tbsp chopped fresh cilantro

salt and pepper

fresh cilantro sprigs, to garnish

1 Cut each sheet of phyllo pastry into squares 2¾-inches/7-cm across, to make a total of 48 squares. Brush each square lightly with oil, and arrange the squares in stacks of 4 in 12 small muffin pans, pointing outward. Press the pastry down into the muffin pans.

2 Bake the pastry cases in the oven preheated to 400°F/200°C for 6–8 minutes until golden brown.

3 Meanwhile, heat 1 tablespoon of oil in a wok. Add the garlic and cook for 30 seconds, then stir in the pork and cook over a high heat for 4–5 minutes until the meat is golden brown.

4 Add the red curry paste and scallions and continue cooking for a further 1 minute, then stir in the peanut butter, soy sauce, and cilantro. Season to taste with salt and pepper.

5 Spoon the pork mixture into the phyllo baskets and serve hot, garnished with cilantro.

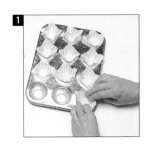

COOK'S TIP

When using phyllo pastry, remember that it dries out very quickly and becomes brittle and difficult to handle. Work quickly and keep any sheets of pastry you're not using covered with plastic wrap and a dampened cloth.

Crispy Seaweed

This tasty Chinese appetizer is not all that it seems—the "seaweed" is in fact bok choy which is then fried, salted, and tossed with pine nuts.

NUTRITIONAL INFORMATION

Calories . . . . .214 Sugars 14g
Protein . . . . .6g Fat 15g
Carbohydrate . . .15g Saturates 2g

10 mins   5 mins

SERVES 4

I N G R E D I E N T S

2 lb 4 oz/1 kg bok choy

3½ cups peanut oil, for deep-frying

1 tsp salt

1 tbsp superfine sugar

2½ tbsp toasted pine nuts

1 Rinse the bok choy leaves under cold running water and then pat dry thoroughly with paper towels.

2 Discarding any tough outer leaves, roll each bok choy leaf up, then slice through thinly so that the leaves are finely

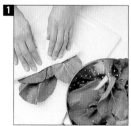

shredded. Alternatively, use a food processor to shred the bok choy.

COOK'S TIP

The tough, outer leaves of bok choy are discarded as these will spoil the overall taste and texture of the dish.

Use savoy cabbage instead of the bok choy if it is unavailable, drying the leaves thoroughly before frying.

3 Heat the peanut oil in a large wok or heavy-based skillet.

4 Carefully add the shredded bok choy leaves to the wok or skillet and cook for about 30 seconds or until they shrivel up and become crispy (you will probably need to do this in several batches,

depending on the size of your wok).

5 Remove the crispy seaweed from the wok with a slotted spoon and drain on paper towels.

6 Transfer the crispy seaweed to a large bowl and toss with the salt, sugar, and pine nuts. Serve immediately on warm serving plates.

Thai-Stuffed Omelet

This makes a substantial appetizer, or a light lunch or supper dish. Serve with a colorful, crisp salad to accompany the dish.

NUTRITIONAL INFORMATION

Calories	250	Sugars	.........1g
Protein	........21g	Fat	..........18g
Carbohydrate	....2g	Saturates	.......4g

 5–10 mins   25 mins

SERVES 4

I N G R E D I E N T S

2 garlic cloves, chopped

4 black peppercorns

4 sprigs fresh cilantro

2 tbsp vegetable oil

7 oz/200 g ground pork

2 scallions, chopped

1 large, firm tomato, chopped

6 large eggs

1 tbsp fish sauce

¼ tsp turmeric

mixed salad greens, tossed, to serve

1 Place the garlic, peppercorns, and cilantro in a pestle and mortar and crush until a smooth paste forms.

2 Heat 1 tablespoon of the oil in a wok over a medium heat. Add the paste and cook for 1–2 minutes until it just changes color.

3 Stir in the pork and cook until it is lightly browned. Add the scallions and tomato, and cook for a further minute, then remove from the heat.

4 Heat the remaining oil in a small, heavy-based skillet. Beat the eggs with the fish sauce and turmeric, then pour a quarter of the egg mixture into the pan. As the mixture begins to set, stir lightly to ensure that all the liquid egg is set.

5 Spoon a quarter of the pork mixture down the center of the omelet, then fold the sides inward toward the center, enclosing the filling. Make 3 more omelets with the remaining egg and fill with the remaining pork mixture.

6 Slide the omelets on to a serving plate and serve with mixed salad greens.

COOK'S TIP

If you prefer, spread half the pork mixture evenly over one omelet, then place a second omelet on top, without folding. Cut into slim wedges to serve.

Thai-Style Fish Cakes

These small fish cakes are quick to make and are delicious served with a chili dip.

NUTRITIONAL INFORMATION

Calories ....240 Sugars 1g
Protein ....23g Fat 14g
Carbohydrate ....7g Saturates 3g

 10 mins   20 mins

SERVES 4

INGREDIENTS

1 lb/450 g cod fillets, skinned

2 tbsp fish sauce

2 red Thai chilies, seeded and very finely chopped

2 cloves garlic, crushed

10 lime leaves, finely chopped

2 tbsp chopped fresh cilantro

1 large egg

scant ¼ cup all-purpose flour

3½ oz/100 g fine green beans, finely sliced

peanut oil

1 Using a sharp knife, roughly cut the cod fillets into bite-sized pieces.

COOK'S TIP

Fish sauce is a salty, brown liquid which is a must for authentic flavor. It is used to salt dishes but is milder in flavor than soy sauce. It is available from Asian food stores or health food shops.

2 Place the cod pieces in a food processor together with the fish sauce, chilies, garlic, lime leaves, cilantro, egg, and all-purpose flour. Process until finely chopped and turn out into a large mixing bowl.

3 Add the green beans to the cod mixture and combine.

4 Divide the mixture into small balls. Flatten the balls between the palms of your hands to form rounds.

5 Heat a little oil in a preheated wok. Cook the fish cakes on both sides until brown and crispy on the outside.

6 Transfer the fish cakes to serving plates and serve hot.

Chili & Peanut Shrimp

Peanut flavors are widely used in Far East and South East Asian cooking and complement many ingredients.

NUTRITIONAL INFORMATION

Calories 478	Sugars 2g	
Protein 32g	Fat 30g	
Carbohydrate ...19g	Saturates 11g	

15 mins   10 mins

SERVES 4

INGREDIENTS

1 lb/450 g jumbo shrimp, peeled apart from tail end

3 tbsp crunchy peanut butter

1 tbsp chili sauce

10 sheets phyllo pastry

2 tbsp butter, melted

1¾ oz/50 g fine egg noodles

oil, for cooking

1 Using a sharp knife, make a small horizontal slit across the back of each shrimp. Press down on the shrimps so that they lie flat.

2 Mix together the peanut butter and chili sauce in a small bowl until well blended. Using a pastry brush, spread a little of the sauce on to each shrimp so they are evenly coated.

3 Cut each pastry sheet in half and brush with melted butter.

4 Wrap each shrimp in a piece of pastry, tucking the edges under to fully enclose the shrimp.

5 Place the fine egg noodles in a bowl, pour over enough boiling water to cover and let stand for 5 minutes. Drain the noodles thoroughly. Use 2–3 cooked noodles to tie around each shrimp parcel.

6 Heat the oil in a preheated wok. Cook the shrimp for 3–4 minutes, or until golden and crispy.

7 Remove the shrimp with a slotted spoon, transfer to paper towels, and let drain. Transfer to serving plates and serve warm.

COOK'S TIP

When using phyllo pastry, keep any unused pastry covered to prevent it drying out and becoming brittle.

Shrimp Parcels

These small shrimp bites are packed with the flavor of lime and cilantro for a quick and tasty appetizer.

NUTRITIONAL INFORMATION

Calories 305	Sugars 2g	
Protein 15g	Fat 21g	
Carbohydrate . . .14g	Saturates 8g	

15 mins   20 mins

SERVES 4

I N G R E D I E N T S

1 tbsp sunflower oil

1 red bell pepper, seeded and thinly sliced

¾ cup beansprouts

finely grated zest and juice of 1 lime

1 red chili, seeded and very finely chopped

1 tsp grated fresh root ginger

8 oz/225 g peeled shrimp

1 tbsp fish sauce

½ tsp arrowroot

2 tbsp chopped fresh cilantro

8 sheets phyllo pastry

2 tbsp butter

2 tsp sesame oil

3 tbsp vegetable oil

scallion tassels, to garnish

chili sauce, to serve

1 Heat the sunflower oil in a large preheated wok. Add the red bell pepper and beansprouts and cook for 2 minutes, or until the vegetables have softened.

2 Remove the wok from the heat and toss in the lime zest and juice, red chili, ginger, and shrimp, stirring well.

3 Mix the fish sauce with the arrowroot and stir the mixture into the wok juices. Return the wok to the heat and cook, stirring, for 2 minutes, or until the juices thicken. Toss in the cilantro and mix well.

4 Lay the sheets of phyllo pastry out on a board. Melt the butter and sesame oil and brush each pastry sheet with the mixture.

5 Spoon a little of the shrimp filling on to the top of each sheet, fold over each end, and roll up to enclose the filling.

6 Heat the oil in a large wok. Cook the parcels, in batches, for 2–3 minutes, or until crisp and golden. Garnish with scallion tassels and serve hot with a chili dipping sauce.

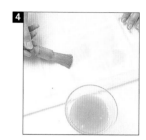

COOK'S TIP

If using cooked shrimp, cook for 1 minute only, otherwise the shrimp will toughen.

Chinese Shrimp Salad

Noodles and beansprouts form the basis of this refreshing salad which combines the flavors of fruit and shrimp.

NUTRITIONAL INFORMATION

Calories	359	Sugars	........4g
Protein	........31g	Fat	..........15g
Carbohydrate	...25g	Saturates	.......2g

🍲 15 mins   🕐 5 mins

SERVES 4

I N G R E D I E N T S

9 oz/250 g fine egg noodles

3 tbsp sunflower oil

1 tbsp sesame oil

1 tbsp sesame seeds

1½ cups beansprouts

1 ripe mango, sliced

6 scallions, sliced

75 g/2¾ oz radishes, sliced

12 oz/350 g peeled, cooked shrimp

2 tbsp light soy sauce

1 tbsp sherry

1 Place the egg noodles in a large bowl and pour over enough boiling water to cover. Let stand for 10 minutes.

2 Drain the noodles thoroughly and pat dry with paper towels.

COOK'S TIP

If fresh mango is unavailable, use canned mango slices, rinsed and drained, instead.

3 Heat the sunflower oil in a large wok or skillet and cook the noodles for 5 minutes, tossing frequently.

4 Remove the wok from the heat and add the sesame oil, sesame seeds, and beansprouts, tossing to mix well.

5 In a separate bowl, mix together the sliced mango, scallions, radishes, and shrimp. Stir in the light soy sauce and sherry and mix until thoroughly combined.

6 Toss the shrimp mixture with the noodles and transfer to a serving dish. Alternatively, arrange the noodles around the edge of a serving plate and pile the shrimp mixture into the center. Serve immediately as this salad is best eaten warm.

Shrimp Omelet

This is called *Foo Yung* in China and is a classic dish which may be flavored with any ingredients you have to hand.

NUTRITIONAL INFORMATION

Calories 320	Sugars 1g
Protein 31g	Fat 18g
Carbohydrate 8g	Saturates 4g

5 mins   10 mins

SERVES 4

INGREDIENTS

3 tbsp sunflower oil

2 leeks, trimmed and sliced

12 oz/350 g raw jumbo shrimp

4 tbsp cornstarch

1 tsp salt

6 oz/175 g mushrooms, sliced

1¾ cups beansprouts

6 eggs

deep-fried leeks, to garnish (optional)

1 Heat the sunflower oil in a preheated wok or large skillet. Add the sliced leeks and cook for 3 minutes.

2 Rinse the shrimp under cold running water and then pat them dry with paper towels.

3 Mix together the cornstarch and salt in a large bowl.

4 Add the shrimp to the cornstarch and salt mixture and toss to coat all over.

5 Add the shrimp to the wok or skillet and cook for 2 minutes, or until the shrimp are almost cooked through.

6 Add the mushrooms and beansprouts to the wok and cook for a further 2 minutes.

7 Beat the eggs with 3 tablespoons of cold water. Pour the egg mixture into the wok and cook until the egg sets, carefully turning over once. Turn the omelet out on to a clean board, divide into 4 and serve hot, garnished with deep-fried leeks (if using).

VARIATION

If liked, divide the mixture into 4 once the initial cooking has taken place in step 6 and cook 4 individual omelets.

Salt & Pepper Shrimp

Szechuan peppercorns are very hot, adding heat and a red color to the shrimp. They are effectively offset by the sugar in this recipe.

NUTRITIONAL INFORMATION

Calories ....174 Sugars 1g
Protein ....25g Fat 8g
Carbohydrate ....1g Saturates 1g

5 mins   10 mins

SERVES 4

INGREDIENTS

2 tsp salt

1 tsp black pepper

2 tsp Szechuan peppercorns

1 tsp sugar

1 lb/450 g peeled raw jumbo shrimp

2 tbsp peanut oil

1 red chili, seeded and finely chopped

1 tsp freshly grated root ginger

3 cloves garlic, crushed

sliced scallions, to garnish

shrimp crackers, to serve

1 Grind the salt, black pepper, and Szechuan peppercorns with a pestle and mortar.

2 Mix the salt and pepper mixture with the sugar and set aside until required.

3 Rinse the jumbo shrimp under cold running water and pat dry with paper towels.

4 Heat the oil in a preheated wok or large skillet.

5 Add the shrimp, chopped red chili, ginger, and garlic to the wok or skillet and cook for 4–5 minutes, or until the shrimp are cooked through.

6 Add the salt and pepper mixture to the wok and cook for 1 minute, stirring constantly so it does not burn on the base of the wok.

7 Transfer the shrimp to warm serving bowls and garnish with scallions. Serve hot with shrimp crackers.

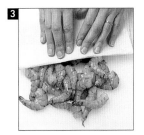

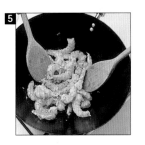

COOK'S TIP

Jumbo shrimp are widely available and have a lovely meaty texture. If using cooked shrimp, add them with the salt and pepper mixture in step 5—if the cooked shrimp are added any earlier they will toughen up and be inedible.

Sesame Shrimp Toasts

These are one of the most recognized and popular appetizers in Chinese restaurants in the Western world. They are also quick and easy to make.

NUTRITIONAL INFORMATION

Calories 237   Sugars 1g
Protein ....18g   Fat 12g
Carbohydrate ...15g   Saturates 2g

🍤 5 mins   🕙 10 mins

SERVES 4

INGREDIENTS

4 slices medium, thick-sliced white bread

8 oz/225 g cooked, peeled shrimp

1 tbsp soy sauce

2 cloves garlic, crushed

1 tbsp sesame oil

1 egg

2 tbsp sesame seeds

oil, for deep-frying

sweet chili sauce, to serve

1 Remove the crusts from the bread, if desired, then set aside until required.

2 Place the peeled shrimp, soy sauce, crushed garlic, sesame oil, and egg into a food processor and blend until a smooth paste has formed.

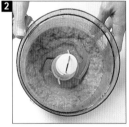 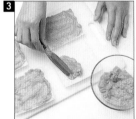 

3 Spread the shrimp paste evenly over the 4 slices of bread. Sprinkle the sesame seeds over the top of the shrimp mixture and press the seeds down with your hands so that they stick to the mixture. Cut each slice in half and in half again to form 4 triangles.

4 Heat the oil in a large wok or skillet and deep-fry the toasts, sesame seed-side up, for 4–5 minutes, or until they are golden and crispy.

5 Remove the toasts with a slotted spoon and transfer to paper towels and let drain thoroughly.

6 Serve the sesame shrimp toasts warm with sweet chili sauce for dipping.

VARIATION

Add 2 chopped scallions to the mixture in step 2 for added flavor and crunch.

Sweet & Sour Shrimp

Shrimp are marinated in a soy sauce mixture then coated in a light batter and served with a delicious sweet-and-sour dip.

NUTRITIONAL INFORMATION

Calories 294	Sugars 11g
Protein 14g	Fat 12g
Carbohydrate ...34g	Saturates 2g

40 mins   20 mins

SERVES 4

INGREDIENTS

16 large raw shrimp, peeled

1 tsp grated fresh root ginger

1 garlic clove, crushed

2 scallions, sliced

2 tbsp dry sherry

2 tsp sesame oil

1 tbsp light soy sauce

vegetable oil, for deep-frying

shredded scallion, to garnish

BATTER

4 egg whites

4 tbsp cornstarch

2 tbsp all-purpose flour

SAUCE

2 tbsp tomato paste

3 tbsp white wine vinegar

4 tsp light soy sauce

2 tbsp lemon juice

3 tbsp light brown sugar

1 green bell pepper, seeded and cut into very thin sticks

½ tsp chili sauce

1¼ cups vegetable bouillon

2 tsp cornstarch

1 Using tweezers, de-vein the shrimp, then flatten them with a large knife.

2 Place the shrimp in a dish and add the ginger, garlic, scallions, dry sherry, sesame oil, and soy sauce. Cover them with plastic wrap and let them marinate for 30 minutes.

3 Make the batter by beating the egg whites until thick. Fold in the cornstarch and all-purpose flour to form a light batter.

4 Place all of the sauce ingredients in a pan and bring to a boil. Reduce the heat and let simmer for 10 minutes.

5 Remove the shrimp from the marinade and dip them into the batter to coat.

6 Heat the vegetable oil in a preheated wok or large skillet until almost smoking. Reduce the heat and cook the shrimp for 3–4 minutes, until crisp and golden brown.

7 Garnish the shrimp with shredded scallion and serve with the sauce.

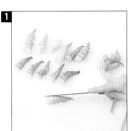

Rice Paper Parcels

These special rice paper wrappers are available in Chinese food stores and health stores. Do not use the rice paper sold for making cakes.

NUTRITIONAL INFORMATION

Calories	133	Sugars 2g
Protein	........10g	Fat 8g
Carbohydrate	....5g	Saturates 1g

5 mins   15 mins

SERVES 4

INGREDIENTS

1 egg white

2 tsp cornstarch

2 tsp dry sherry

1 tsp superfine sugar

2 tsp hoisin sauce

8 oz/225 g peeled, cooked shrimp

4 scallions, sliced

1 oz/25 g canned water chestnuts, drained, rinsed, and chopped

8 Chinese rice paper wrappers

vegetable oil, for deep-frying

hoisin sauce or plum sauce, to serve

1 Lightly beat the egg white in a bowl. Mix in the cornstarch, dry sherry, sugar, and hoisin sauce. Add the shrimp, scallions, and water chestnuts, mixing thoroughly.

COOK'S TIP

Use this filling inside wonton wrappers (see page 47) if the rice paper wrappers are unavailable.

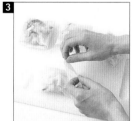

2 Soften the rice papers first by dipping them in a bowl of water one at a time. Spread them out on a clean counter.

3 Using a dessert spoon, place a little of the shrimp mixture into the center of each rice paper. Carefully wrap the rice paper around the filling to make a secure parcel. Repeat to make 8 parcels.

4 Heat the oil in a wok until it is almost smoking. Reduce the heat slightly, add the parcels, in batches if necessary, and deep-fry for 4–5 minutes, until crisp. Remove from the oil with a slotted spoon and drain on paper towels.

5 Transfer the parcels to a warmed serving dish and serve immediately with a little hoisin or plum sauce.

Crispy Crab Wontons

These delicious wontons are a superb appetizer. Deep-fried until crisp
and golden, they are delicious with a chili dipping sauce.

NUTRITIONAL INFORMATION

Calories	266	Sugars	.......0.4g
Protein	........10g	Fat	..........17g
Carbohydrate	...18g	Saturates	.......5g

10 mins   15 mins

SERVES 4

I N G R E D I E N T S

6 oz/175 g white crabmeat, flaked

1¾ oz/50 g canned water chestnuts,
    drained, rinsed, and chopped

1 small fresh red chili, chopped

1 scallion, chopped

1 tbsp cornstarch

1 tsp dry sherry

1 tsp light soy sauce

½ tsp lime juice

24 wonton wrappers

vegetable oil, for deep-frying

sliced lime, to garnish

1 To make the filling, mix together the
crabmeat, water chestnuts, chili,
scallion, cornstarch, sherry, soy sauce, and
lime juice.

2 Spread out the wonton wrappers on a
counter and spoon one portion of the
filling into the center of each wonton
wrapper.

3 Dampen the edges of the wonton
wrappers with a little water and fold
them in half to form triangles. Fold the
two pointed ends in towards the center,
moisten with a little water to secure and
then pinch together to seal to prevent the
wontons unwrapping.

4 Heat the oil for deep-frying
in a wok or deep-fryer to
350°F–375°F/180°C–190°C, or until a cube
of bread browns in 30 seconds. Cook the
wontons, in batches, for 2–3 minutes,
until golden brown and crisp. Remove the
wontons from the oil and let them drain
on paper towels.

5 Serve the wontons hot, garnished
with slices of lime.

COOK'S TIP

Handle wonton wrappers
carefully as they can be easily
damaged. Make sure that the
wontons are sealed well and
secured before deep-frying to
prevent the filling coming out
and the wontons unwrapping.

Crab Ravioli

These small parcels are made from wonton wrappers, filled with mixed vegetables and crabmeat for a melt-in-the-mouth appetizer.

NUTRITIONAL INFORMATION

Calories	292	Sugars	.........1g
Protein	........25g	Fat	..........17g
Carbohydrate	....11g	Saturates	.......5g

 20 mins   25 mins

SERVES 4

I N G R E D I E N T S

450 g/1 lb fresh or canned crabmeat, drained

½ red bell pepper, seeded and finely diced

4½ oz/125 g Napa cabbage, shredded

¼ cup beansprouts, roughly chopped

1 tbsp light soy sauce

1 tsp lime juice

16 wonton wrappers

1 small egg, beaten

2 tbsp peanut oil

1 tsp sesame oil

salt and pepper

1 Mix together the crabmeat, bell pepper, Napa cabbage, beansprouts, soy sauce, and lime juice. Season and let stand for 15 minutes.

2 Spread out the wonton wrappers on a counter. Spoon a little of the crabmeat mixture into the center of each wrapper. Brush the edges with egg and fold in half, pushing out any air. Press the edges together to seal.

3 Heat the peanut oil in a preheated wok or skillet. Cook the ravioli, in batches, for 3–4 minutes, turning, until browned. Remove with a slotted spoon and drain on paper towels.

4 Heat any remaining filling in the wok or skillet over a gentle heat until hot. Serve the ravioli with the hot filling and sprinkled with sesame oil.

COOK'S TIP

Make sure that the edges of the ravioli are sealed well and that all of the air is pressed out to prevent them from opening during cooking.

Spicy Chicken Livers

This is a richly flavored dish with a dark, slightly tangy sauce which is popular in China.

NUTRITIONAL INFORMATION

Calories ....195 Sugars 2g
Protein ....20g Fat 8g
Carbohydrate ....9g Saturates 1g

5 mins   5–10 mins

SERVES 4

I N G R E D I E N T S

12 oz/350 g chicken livers

2 tbsp sunflower oil

1 red chili, seeded and finely chopped

1 tsp grated fresh root ginger

2 cloves garlic, crushed

2 tbsp tomato catsup

3 tbsp sherry

3 tbsp soy sauce

1 tsp cornstarch

1 lb/450 g bok choy

egg noodles, to serve

1 Using a sharp knife, trim the fat from the chicken livers and slice into small pieces.

2 Heat the oil in a large wok. Add the chicken liver pieces and cook over a high heat for 2–3 minutes.

3 Add the chili, ginger, and garlic and cook for about 1 minute.

4 Mix together the tomato catsup, sherry, soy sauce, and cornstarch in a small bowl and set aside.

5 Add the bok choy to the wok and cook until it just wilts.

6 Add the reserved tomato catsup mixture to the wok and cook, stirring to mix, until the juices start to bubble.

7 Transfer to serving bowls and serve hot with noodles.

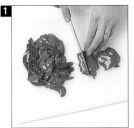  

COOK'S TIP

Fresh ginger root will keep for several weeks in a dry, cool place.

Chicken livers are available fresh or frozen from most food stores.

Honeyed Chicken Wings

Chicken wings are ideal for an appetizer as they are small and perfect for eating with the fingers.

NUTRITIONAL INFORMATION

Calories 131	Sugars 4g	
Protein 10g	Fat 8g	
Carbohydrate 4g	Saturates 2g	

2 hrs 5 mins   40 mins

SERVES 4

INGREDIENTS

1 lb/450 g chicken wings

2 tbsp peanut oil

2 tbsp light soy sauce

2 tbsp hoisin sauce

2 tbsp clear honey

2 garlic cloves, crushed

1 tsp sesame seeds

MARINADE

1 dried red chili

$\frac{1}{2}$–1 tsp chili powder

$\frac{1}{2}$–1 tsp ground ginger

finely grated zest of 1 lime

1 To make the marinade, crush the dried chili with a pestle and mortar. Mix together the crushed dried chili, chili powder, ground ginger, and lime zest in a small mixing bowl.

2 Thoroughly rub the spice mixture into the chicken wings with your fingertips. Let stand for at least 2 hours to allow the flavors to penetrate the chicken wings.

3 Heat the peanut oil in a large wok or skillet.

4 Add the chicken wings and cook, turning frequently, for about 10–12 minutes, until golden and crisp. Drain off any excess oil.

5 Add the soy sauce, hoisin sauce, honey, garlic, and sesame seeds to the wok, turning the chicken wings to coat.

6 Reduce the heat and cook for 20–25 minutes, turning the chicken wings frequently, until completely cooked through. Serve hot.

COOK'S TIP

Make the dish in advance and freeze the chicken wings. Thaw thoroughly, cover with foil, and heat right through in a moderate oven.

Steamed Duck Buns

The dough used in this recipe may also be wrapped around chicken, pork, or shrimp, or sweet fillings, as an alternative.

NUTRITIONAL INFORMATION

Calories 307   Sugars 11g
Protein . . . . .17g   Fat 6g
Carbohydrate . . .50g   Saturates 1g

1½ hours   1 hour

SERVES 4

I N G R E D I E N T S

D U M P L I N G   D O U G H

generous 2 cups all-purpose flour

½ oz/15 g dry yeast

1 tsp superfine sugar

2 tbsp warm water

¾ cup warm milk

F I L L I N G

10½ oz/300 g duck breast

1 tbsp brown sugar

1 tbsp light soy sauce

2 tbsp clear honey

1 tbsp hoisin sauce

1 tbsp vegetable oil

1 leek, finely chopped

1 garlic clove, crushed

1 tsp grated fresh root ginger

1 Place the duck breast in a large bowl. Mix together the brown sugar, soy sauce, honey, and hoisin sauce. Pour the mixture over the duck and marinate for 20 minutes.

2 Remove the duck from the marinade and cook on a rack set over a roasting pan in a preheated oven, at 400°F/200°C

for 35–40 minutes, or until cooked through. Let cool, remove the meat from the bones, and cut into small cubes.

3 Heat the vegetable oil in a preheated wok or skillet until really hot.

4 Add the leek, garlic, and ginger to the wok and cook for 3 minutes. Mix with the duck meat.

5 Strain the all-purpose flour into a large bowl. Mix the yeast, superfine sugar, and warm water in a separate bowl and let stand in a warm place for 15 minutes.

6 Pour the yeast mixture into the flour, together with the warm milk, mixing to form a firm dough. Knead the dough on a floured counter for 5 minutes. Roll into a sausage shape, 1 inch/2.5 cm in diameter. Cut into 16 pieces, cover, and let stand for 20–25 minutes.

7 Flatten the dough pieces into 4-inch/10-cm circles. Place a spoonful of filling in the center of each, draw up the sides to form a "moneybag" shape and twist to seal.

8 Place the dumplings on a clean, damp dish cloth in the base of a steamer, cover, and steam for 20 minutes. Serve immediately.

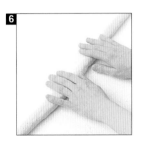

Spring Rolls

This classic Chinese dish is very popular in the West. Serve hot or chilled with a soy sauce or hoisin dip.

NUTRITIONAL INFORMATION

Calories 442	Sugars 4g	
Protein 23g	Fat 21g	
Carbohydrate ...42g	Saturates 3g	

45 mins   45 mins

SERVES 4

INGREDIENTS

6 oz/175 g cooked pork, chopped

2¾ oz/75 g cooked chicken, chopped

1 tsp light soy sauce

1 tsp brown sugar

1 tsp sesame oil

1 tsp vegetable oil

2¼ cups beansprouts

1 oz/25 g canned bamboo shoots, drained, rinsed, and chopped

1 green bell pepper, seeded and chopped

2 scallions, sliced

1 tsp cornstarch

2 tsp water

vegetable oil, for deep-frying

SKINS

scant 1 cup all-purpose flour

5 tbsp cornstarch

2 cups water

3 tbsp vegetable oil

1 Mix the pork, chicken, soy sauce, sugar, and sesame oil. Cover and marinate for 30 minutes.

2 Heat the vegetable oil in a preheated wok. Add the beansprouts, bamboo shoots, bell pepper, and scallions to the wok and cook for 2–3 minutes. Add the meat and the marinade to the wok and cook for 2–3 minutes.

3 Blend the cornstarch with the water and stir the mixture into the wok. Let cool completely.

4 To make the skins, mix the flour and cornstarch and gradually stir in the water, to make a smooth batter.

5 Heat a small, oiled skillet. Swirl one-eighth of the batter over the bottom and cook for 2–3 minutes. Repeat with the remaining batter. Cover the skins with a damp dish cloth while cooking the remaining skins.

6 Spread out the skins and spoon one-eighth of the filling along the center of each. Brush the edges with water and fold in the sides, then roll up.

7 Heat the oil for deep-frying in a wok to 350°F/180°C. Cook the spring rolls, in batches, for 2–3 minutes, or until golden and crisp. Remove from the oil with a slotted spoon, drain and serve immediately.

Pancake Rolls

This classic dim sum dish is adaptable to almost any filling of your choice. Here the traditional mixture of pork and bok choy is used.

NUTRITIONAL INFORMATION

Calories ....488 Sugars 19g
Protein ....16g Fat 24g
Carbohydrate ...55g Saturates 4g

 20 mins   20 mins

SERVES 4

I N G R E D I E N T S

4 tsp vegetable oil

1–2 garlic cloves, crushed

8 oz/225 g ground pork

8 oz/225 g bok choy, shredded

4½ tsp light soy sauce

½ tsp sesame oil

8 spring roll skins, 10 inches/25 cm square, thawed if frozen

oil, for deep-frying

CHILI SAUCE

generous ¼ cup superfine sugar

scant ¼ cup rice vinegar

2 tbsp water

2 red chilies, finely chopped

1 Heat the oil in a preheated wok. Add the garlic and cook for 30 seconds. Add the pork and cook for 2–3 minutes, until lightly colored.

2 Add the bok choy, soy sauce, and sesame oil to the wok and cook for 2–3 minutes. Remove from the heat and let cool.

3 Spread out the spring roll skins on a counter and spoon 2 tablespoons of the pork mixture along one edge of each. Roll the skin over once and fold in the

sides. Roll up completely to make a sausage shape, brushing the edges with a little water to seal. Set the pancake rolls aside for 10 minutes to seal firmly.

4 To make the chili sauce, heat the sugar, vinegar, and water in a small pan, stirring until the sugar dissolves. Bring the mixture to a boil and boil rapidly until a light syrup forms. Remove from the heat and stir in the chopped red chilies.

Let the sauce cool before serving.

5 Heat the oil for deep-frying in a wok until almost smoking. Reduce the heat slightly and cook the pancake rolls, in batches if necessary, for 3–4 minutes, until golden brown. Remove from the oil with a slotted spoon and drain on paper towels. Serve on a warm serving plate with the chili sauce.

Poultry & Meat

Meat is expensive in Far Eastern countries and is eaten in smaller proportions than in the Western world. However, when meat is used, it is done so to its full potential—it is marinated or spiced and combined with other delicious native flavorings to create a wide array of mouthwatering dishes.

In Malaysia, a wide variety of spicy meats is offered, reflecting the many ethnic origins of the population. In China, poultry, lamb, beef, or pork are cooked or steamed in the wok and combined with sauces and seasonings such as soy, black bean, and oyster sauce. In Japan, meat is usually marinated and quickly cooked in a wok over a very high heat or simmered in miso bouillon. Thai dishes use meat that is leaner and more flavorsome due to its "free-range" rearing.

Stir-Fried Ginger Chicken

The oranges add color and piquancy to this refreshing dish, which complements the chicken well.

NUTRITIONAL INFORMATION

Calories	289	Sugars	........15g
Protein	........20g	Fat	..........9g
Carbohydrate	...17g	Saturates	.......2g

 5 mins   🕐 20 mins

SERVES 4

I N G R E D I E N T S

2 tbsp sunflower oil

1 onion, sliced

2 carrots, cut into thin sticks

1 clove garlic, crushed

12 oz/350 g boneless skinless chicken breasts

2 tbsp grated fresh root ginger

1 tsp ground ginger

4 tbsp sweet sherry

1 tbsp tomato paste

1 tbsp raw brown sugar

generous ⅓ cup orange juice

1 tsp cornstarch

1 orange, peeled and segmented

fresh snipped chives, to garnish

1 Heat the oil in a large preheated wok. Add the onion, carrots, and garlic and cook over a high heat for 3 minutes or until the vegetables begin to soften.

2 Slice the chicken into thin strips. Add to the wok with the fresh and ground ginger. Cook for a further 10 minutes, or until the chicken is well cooked through and golden in color.

3 Mix together the sherry, tomato paste, sugar, orange juice, and cornstarch in a bowl. Stir the mixture into the wok and heat through until the mixture bubbles and the juices start to thicken.

4 Add the orange segments and carefully toss to mix.

5 Transfer the stir-fried chicken to warm serving bowls and garnish with freshly snipped chives. Serve immediately.

COOK'S TIP

Make sure that you do not continue cooking the dish once the orange segments have been added in step 4, otherwise they will break up.

Coconut Chicken Curry

Okra, or ladies fingers, are slightly bitter in flavor. The pineapple and coconut in this recipe offsets them in both color and flavor.

NUTRITIONAL INFORMATION

Calories 456	Sugars 21g
Protein 29g	Fat 29g
Carbohydrate ...22g	Saturates 17g

5 mins   45 mins

SERVES 4

INGREDIENTS

2 tbsp sunflower oil

1 lb/450 g boneless, skinless chicken
    thighs or breasts

1 cup okra

1 large onion, sliced

2 cloves garlic, crushed

3 tbsp mild curry paste

1¼ cups chicken bouillon

1 tbsp fresh lemon juice

½ cup coarsely grated creamed coconut

1¼ cups cubed fresh or canned pineapple

⅔ cup thick, unsweetened yogurt

2 tbsp chopped fresh cilantro

freshly boiled rice, to serve

TO GARNISH

lemon wedges

fresh cilantro sprigs

 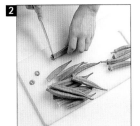 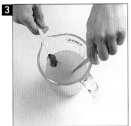

1 Heat the oil in a wok. Cut the chicken into bite-sized pieces, add to the wok, and cook until evenly browned.

2 Using a sharp knife, trim the okra. Add the onion, garlic, and okra to the wok and cook for a further 2–3 minutes, stirring constantly.

3 Mix the curry paste with the chicken bouillon and lemon juice and pour into the wok. Bring to a boil, cover, and let simmer for 30 minutes.

4 Stir the grated coconut into the curry and cook for about 5 minutes.

5 Add the pineapple, yogurt, and cilantro and cook for 2 minutes, stirring. Garnish and serve.

COOK'S TIP

Score around the top of the okra with a knife before cooking to release the sticky glue-like substance which is bitter in taste.

Cashew Chicken

Yellow bean sauce is available from large food stores. Try to buy a chunky sauce rather than a smooth sauce for texture.

NUTRITIONAL INFORMATION

Calories	398	Sugars	........2g
Protein	........31g	Fat	..........27g
Carbohydrate	....8g	Saturates	.......4g

   10 mins   15 mins

SERVES 4

I N G R E D I E N T S

1 lb/450 g boneless chicken breasts

2 tbsp vegetable oil

1 red onion, sliced

6 oz/175 g flat mushrooms, sliced

1 cup cashew nuts

2¾ oz/75 g jar yellow bean sauce

fresh cilantro, to garnish

egg fried rice or plain boiled rice,
    to serve

1 Using a sharp knife, remove the excess skin from the chicken breasts, if desired. Cut the chicken into small, bite-sized chunks.

2 Heat the vegetable oil in a preheated wok or skillet.

VARIATION

Chicken thighs could be used instead of the chicken breasts for a more economical dish.

3 Add the chicken to the wok and cook for 5 minutes.

4 Add the red onion and mushrooms to the wok and continue to stir-fry for a further 5 minutes.

5 Place the cashew nuts on a cookie sheet and toast under a preheated medium broiler until just browning—toasting nuts brings out their flavor.

6 Toss the toasted cashew nuts into the wok together with the yellow bean sauce and heat through.

7 Allow the sauce to bubble for 2–3 minutes.

8 Transfer the chop suey to warm serving bowls and garnish with fresh cilantro. Serve hot with egg fried rice or plain boiled rice.

Lemon Chicken

This is on everyone's list of favorite Chinese dishes, and it is so simple to make. Serve with lightly cooked vegetables for a truly delicious meal.

NUTRITIONAL INFORMATION

Calories	272	Sugars	.........1g
Protein	........36g	Fat	...........11g
Carbohydrate	....5g	Saturates	.......2g

 5 mins 15 mins

SERVES 4

INGREDIENTS

vegetable oil, for deep-frying

1 lb 7 oz/650 g skinless, boneless
chicken, cut into strips

SAUCE

1 tbsp cornstarch

6 tbsp cold water

3 tbsp fresh lemon juice

2 tbsp sweet sherry

½ tsp superfine sugar

TO GARNISH

lemon slices

shredded scallion

1 Heat the oil for deep-frying in a preheated wok or skillet to 350°F/180°C or until a cube of bread browns in 30 seconds.

2 Reduce the heat and cook the chicken strips for 3–4 minutes, until cooked through.

3 Remove the chicken with a slotted spoon, set aside, and keep warm. Drain the oil from the wok.

4 To make the sauce, mix the cornstarch with 2 tablespoons of the water to form a paste.

5 Pour the lemon juice and remaining water into the mixture in the wok.

6 Add the sweet sherry and superfine sugar and bring to a boil, stirring until the sugar has completely dissolved.

7 Stir in the cornstarch mixture and return to a boil. Reduce the heat and simmer, stirring constantly, for 2–3 minutes, until the sauce is thickened and clear.

8 Transfer the chicken to a warm serving plate and pour the sauce over the top.

9 Garnish the chicken with the lemon slices and shredded scallion and serve immediately.

COOK'S TIP

If you would prefer to use chicken portions rather than strips, cook them in the oil, covered, over a low heat for about 30 minutes, or until cooked through.

Sweet Mango Chicken

The sweet, scented flavor of mango gives this dish its characteristic sweetness.

NUTRITIONAL INFORMATION

Calories 244   Sugars 18g
Protein . . . . .27g   Fat 7g
Carbohydrate . . .2.1g   Saturates 2g

10 mins   15 mins

SERVES 4

I N G R E D I E N T S

1 tbsp sunflower oil

6 skinless, boneless chicken thighs

1 ripe mango

2 cloves garlic, crushed

8 oz/225 g leeks, shredded

3½ oz/100 g beansprouts

⅔ cup mango juice

1 tbsp white wine vinegar

2 tbsp clear honey

2 tbsp tomato catsup

1 tsp cornstarch

COOK'S TIP

Mango juice is available in jars from most supermarkets and is quite thick and sweet. If it is unavailable, purée and sieve a ripe mango and add a little water to make up the required quantity.

1 Heat the sunflower oil in a large preheated wok.

2 Cut the chicken into bite-sized cubes, add to the wok and cook over a high heat for 10 minutes, tossing frequently until the chicken is cooked through and golden in color.

3 Peel and slice the mango and add to the wok with the garlic, leeks, and beansprouts. Cook for a further 2–3 minutes, or until softened.

4 Mix together the mango juice, white wine vinegar, honey, tomato catsup, and cornstarch. Pour into the wok and cook for a further 2 minutes, or until the juices start to thicken.

5 Transfer to a warmed serving dish and serve immediately.

Chicken with Cashew Nuts

This is a popular dish in Chinese restaurants in the West, although nothing beats making it yourself.

NUTRITIONAL INFORMATION

Calories .... .330	Sugars 5g
Protein .... .22g	Fat .... .18g
Carbohydrate ...19g	Saturates 3g

  5 mins   15 mins

SERVES 4

I N G R E D I E N T S

10½ oz/300 g boneless, skinless chicken breasts

1 tbsp cornstarch

1 tsp sesame oil

1 tbsp hoisin sauce

1 tsp light soy sauce

3 garlic cloves, crushed

2 tbsp vegetable oil

¾ cup unsalted cashew nuts

1 oz/25 g snow peas

1 celery stalk, sliced

1 onion, cut into 8 pieces

generous ½ cup beansprouts

1 red bell pepper, seeded and diced

S A U C E

2 tsp cornstarch

2 tbsp hoisin sauce

generous ¾ cup chicken bouillon

1 Trim any fat from the chicken breasts and cut the meat into thin strips. Place the chicken in a large mixing bowl. Sprinkle with the cornstarch and toss to coat the chicken strips in it, shaking off any excess. Mix together the sesame oil, hoisin sauce, soy sauce, and 1 garlic clove. Pour this mixture over the chicken, turning to coat thoroughly. Let marinate for 20 minutes.

2 Heat half of the vegetable oil in a preheated wok. Add the cashew nuts and cook for 1 minute, until browned. Add the snow peas, celery, the remaining garlic, the onion, beansprouts, and red bell pepper, and cook, stirring occasionally, for 2–3 minutes. Remove the vegetables from the wok with a slotted spoon, set aside and keep warm.

3 Heat the remaining oil in the wok. Remove the chicken from the marinade and cook for 3–4 minutes. Return the vegetables to the wok.

4 To make the sauce, mix the cornstarch, hoisin sauce, and chicken bouillon together and pour into the wok. Bring to a boil, stirring until thickened and clear. Serve immediately on warm serving plates.

Chicken Chop Suey

Chop suey is a well known and popular dish based on beansprouts and soy sauce with a meat or vegetable flavoring.

NUTRITIONAL INFORMATION

Calories 337	Sugars 7g
Protein 32g	Fat 18g
Carbohydrate . . .14g	Saturates 3g

25 mins 15 mins

SERVES 4

I N G R E D I E N T S

4 tbsp light soy sauce

2 tsp brown sugar

1 lb 2 oz /500 g skinless, boneless chicken breasts

3 tbsp vegetable oil

2 onions, quartered

2 garlic cloves, crushed

3½ cups beansprouts

3 tsp sesame oil

1 tbsp cornstarch

3 tbsp water

scant 2 cups chicken bouillon

shredded leek, to garnish

VARIATION

This recipe may be made with strips of lean steak, pork, or with mixed vegetables. Change the type of bouillon accordingly.

1 Mix the soy sauce and sugar together, stirring until the sugar has dissolved.

2 Trim any fat from the chicken and cut into thin strips. Place the meat in a shallow dish and spoon the soy mixture over them, turning to coat. Marinate in the refrigerator for 20 minutes.

3 Heat the oil in a wok and cook the chicken for 2–3 minutes, until golden brown. Add the onions and garlic and cook for a further 2 minutes. Add the beansprouts, cook for 4–5 minutes, then add the sesame oil.

4 Mix the cornstarch and water to form a smooth paste. Pour the bouillon into the wok, add the cornstarch paste and bring to a boil, stirring until the sauce is thickened and clear. Serve, garnished with shredded leek, on warm serving plates.

Chicken with Chili & Basil

Chicken drumsticks are cooked in a delicious sauce and served with deep-fried basil for color and flavor.

NUTRITIONAL INFORMATION

Calories 196   Sugars 2g
Protein . . . . .23g   Fat 10g
Carbohydrate . . . .3g   Saturates 2g

5 mins   30 mins

SERVES 4

INGREDIENTS

8 chicken drumsticks

2 tbsp soy sauce

1 tbsp sunflower oil

1 red chili

1 large carrot, cut into thin sticks

6 celery stalks, cut into sticks

3 tbsp sweet chili sauce

oil, for cooking

about 50 fresh basil leaves

1 Remove the skin from the chicken drumsticks if desired. Make 3 slashes in each drumstick. Brush the drumsticks with the soy sauce.

2 Heat the sunflower oil in a preheated wok and cook the drumsticks for 20 minutes, turning frequently, until they are cooked through.

3 Seed and finely chop the chili. Add the chili, carrot, and celery to the wok and cook for a further 5 minutes. Stir in the chili sauce, cover and allow to bubble gently whilst preparing the basil leaves.

4 Heat a little oil in a heavy based pan. Carefully add the basil leaves—stand well away from the pan and protect your hand with a dish cloth as they may spit a little. Cook the basil leaves for about 30 seconds or until they begin to curl up but not brown. Let the leaves drain on paper towels.

5 Arrange the cooked chicken, vegetables, and pan juices on a warm serving plate, garnish with the deep-fried crispy basil leaves and serve immediately.

COOK'S TIP

Basil has a very strong flavor which is perfect with chicken and Chinese flavorings. You could use baby spinach instead of the basil, if you prefer.

Crispy Chicken

In this recipe, the chicken is brushed with a syrup and deep-fried until golden. It is a little time consuming, but well worth the effort.

NUTRITIONAL INFORMATION

Calories 283	Sugars 8g
Protein 29g	Fat 15g
Carbohydrate 8g	Saturates 3g

 15 hours   35 mins

SERVES 4

INGREDIENTS

3 lb 5 oz/1.5 kg oven-ready chicken

2 tbsp clear honey

2 tsp Chinese five-spice powder

2 tbsp rice wine vinegar

3 ½ cups vegetable oil, for deep-frying

chili sauce, to serve

1 Rinse the chicken inside and out under cold running water and pat dry with paper towels.

2 Bring a large pan of water to a boil and remove from the heat. Place the chicken in the water, cover, and set aside for 20 minutes.

3 Remove the chicken from the water and pat dry with paper towels. Cool

the chicken and let chill in the refrigerator overnight.

4 To make the glaze, mix the honey, Chinese five-spice powder, and rice wine vinegar.

5 Brush some of the glaze all over the chicken and return to the refrigerator for 20 minutes.

6 Repeat this process of glazing and refrigerating the chicken until all of the glaze has been used up. Return the chicken to the refrigerator for at least 2 hours after the final coating.

7 Using a cleaver or heavy knife, open the chicken out by splitting it through the center through the breast, and then cut each half into 4 pieces.

8 Heat the oil for deep-frying in a wok until almost smoking. Reduce the heat and cook each piece of chicken for 5–7 minutes, until golden and cooked through. Remove from the oil with a slotted spoon and drain on paper towels.

9 Transfer to a serving dish and serve hot with a little chili sauce.

COOK'S TIP

If it is easier, use chicken portions instead of a whole chicken. You could also use chicken legs for this recipe, if you prefer.

Spicy Peanut Chicken

This quick dish has many variations, but this version includes the classic combination of peanuts, chicken, and chilies.

NUTRITIONAL INFORMATION

Calories	342	Sugars	.........3g
Protein	........25g	Fat	..........24g
Carbohydrate	....6g	Saturates	.......5g

5 mins   10 mins

SERVES 4

INGREDIENTS

10½ oz/300 g skinless, boneless chicken breast

2 tbsp peanut oil

1 cup shelled peanuts

1 fresh red chili, sliced

1 green bell pepper, seeded and cut into strips

fried rice, to serve

SAUCE

⅔ cup chicken bouillon

1 tbsp Chinese rice wine or dry sherry

1 tbsp light soy sauce

1½ tsp light brown sugar

2 garlic cloves, crushed

1 tsp grated fresh root ginger

1 tsp rice wine vinegar

1 tsp sesame oil

1 Trim any fat from the chicken and cut the meat into 1-inch/2.5-cm cubes. Set aside until required.

2 Heat the peanut oil in a preheated wok or skillet.

3 Add the peanuts to the wok and cook for 1 minute. Remove the peanuts with a slotted spoon and set aside.

4 Add the chicken to the wok and cook for 1–2 minutes.

5 Stir in the chili and green bell pepper and cook for 1 minute. Remove from the wok with a slotted spoon and set aside.

6 Put half of the peanuts in a food processor and process until almost smooth. If necessary, add a little bouillon to form a softer paste. Alternatively, place them in a plastic bag and crush them with a rolling pin.

7 To make the sauce, add the chicken bouillon, Chinese rice wine or dry sherry, light soy sauce, light brown sugar, crushed garlic cloves, grated fresh root ginger, and rice wine vinegar to the wok.

8 Heat the sauce without boiling and stir in the peanut paste, remaining peanuts, chicken, sliced red chili, and green bell pepper strips. Mix well until all the ingredients are thoroughly combined.

9 Sprinkle the sesame oil into the wok, stir and cook for 1 minute. Transfer the spicy peanut chicken to a warm serving dish and serve hot with fried rice.

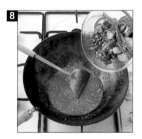

Chinese Chicken Salad

This is a refreshing dish suitable for a summer meal or light lunch.

NUTRITIONAL INFORMATION

Calories . . . . . . .162 Sugars 3g
Protein . . . . .15g Fat 10g
Carbohydrate . . . .5g Saturates 2g

25 mins   10 mins

SERVES 4

INGREDIENTS

8 oz/225 g skinless, boneless chicken breasts

2 tsp light soy sauce

1 tsp sesame oil

1 tsp sesame seeds

2 tbsp vegetable oil

1¼ cups beansprouts

1 red bell pepper, seeded and thinly sliced

1 carrot, cut into very thin sticks

3 baby corn cobs, sliced

SAUCE

2 tsp rice wine vinegar

1 tbsp light soy sauce

dash of chili oil

TO GARNISH

snipped chives and carrot sticks

1 Place the chicken breasts in a shallow glass dish.

2 Mix together the soy sauce and sesame oil and pour over the chicken. Sprinkle with the sesame seeds and let stand for 20 minutes, turning the chicken over occasionally.

3 Remove the chicken from the marinade and cut the meat into thin slices.

4 Heat the vegetable oil in a preheated wok or large skillet. Add the chicken and fry for 4–5 minutes, until cooked through and golden brown on both sides. Remove the chicken from the wok with a slotted spoon, set aside and let cool.

5 Add the beansprouts, bell pepper, carrot, and baby corn cobs to the wok and cook for 2–3 minutes. Remove from the wok with a slotted spoon, set aside and let the mixture cool.

6 To make the sauce, mix together the rice wine vinegar, light soy sauce, and chili oil.

7 Arrange the chicken and vegetables together on a serving plate. Spoon the sauce over the salad, garnish with chives and carrot sticks and serve.

Speedy Peanut Pan-Fry

Thread egg noodles are the ideal accompaniment to this quick dish because they can be cooked quickly and easily while the pan-fry sizzles.

NUTRITIONAL INFORMATION

Calories 563	Sugars 7g	
Protein 45g	Fat 33g	
Carbohydrate . . .22g	Saturates 7g	

5 mins   15 mins

SERVES 4

I N G R E D I E N T S

10½ oz/300 g zucchini

9 oz/250 g baby corn cobs

9 oz/250 g thread egg noodles

2 tbsp corn oil

1 tbsp sesame oil

8 boneless, skinless chicken thighs or 4
  breasts, thinly sliced

10½ oz/300 g white mushrooms

3½ cups beansprouts

4 tbsp smooth peanut butter

2 tbsp soy sauce

2 tbsp lime or lemon juice

generous ½ cup roasted peanuts

salt and pepper

fresh cilantro, to garnish

1 Using a sharp knife, trim and thinly slice the zucchini and baby corn. Set the vegetables aside until required.

2 Cook the noodles in lightly salted boiling water for 3–4 minutes.

3 Meanwhile, heat the corn oil and sesame oil in a large wok or skillet and fry the chicken over a fairly high heat for 1 minute.

4 Add the zucchini, corn, and mushrooms, and cook them all for 5 minutes.

5 Add the beansprouts, peanut butter, soy sauce, lime or lemon juice, and pepper, then cook for a further 2 minutes.

6 Drain the noodles thoroughly. Scatter with the roasted peanuts and serve with the zucchini and mushroom mixture. Garnish with fresh cilantro.

COOK'S TIP

Try serving this pan-fry with flat rice noodles. These are broad, pale, translucent ribbon noodles made from ground rice.

Chicken & Corn Sauté

Stir-fries are quick and healthy dishes because you need use only the minimum of fat.

NUTRITIONAL INFORMATION

Calories 280   Sugars 7g
Protein ....31g   Fat 11g
Carbohydrate ....9g   Saturates 2g

 5 mins   🕐 10 mins

SERVES 4

INGREDIENTS

4 skinless, boneless chicken breasts

9 oz/250 g baby corn cobs

9 oz/250 g snow peas

2 tbsp sunflower oil

1 tbsp sherry vinegar

1 tbsp honey

1 tbsp light soy sauce

1 tbsp sunflower seeds

pepper

rice or Chinese egg noodles, to serve

1 Using a sharp knife, slice the chicken breasts into long, thin strips.

2 Cut the baby corn cobs in half lengthwise and then top and tail the snow peas.

3 Heat the sunflower oil in a preheated wok or a wide skillet.

4 Add the chicken and cook over a fairly high heat, stirring, for 1 minute.

5 Add the baby corn cobs and snow peas and cook over a moderate heat for 5–8 minutes, until evenly cooked. The vegetables should still be slightly crunchy.

6 Mix together the sherry vinegar, honey, and soy sauce in a small bowl.

7 Stir the vinegar mixture into the pan with the sunflower seeds.

8 Season well with pepper. Cook, stirring, for 1 minute.

9 Serve the dish hot with rice or Chinese egg noodles.

VARIATION

Rice vinegar or balsamic vinegar makes a good substitute for the sherry vinegar.

Spicy Chicken Tortillas

The chicken filling for these easy-to-prepare tortillas has a mild, mellow, spicy heat, and a fresh salad makes a perfect accompaniment.

NUTRITIONAL INFORMATION

Calories ....650 Sugars 15g
Protein ....48g Fat 31g
Carbohydrate ...47g Saturates 10g

 10 mins   35 mins

SERVES 4

I N G R E D I E N T S

2 tbsp oil

8 skinless, boneless chicken thighs, sliced

1 onion, chopped

2 garlic cloves, chopped

1 tsp cumin seeds, roughly crushed

2 large dried chilies, sliced

14 oz/400 g canned tomatoes

14 oz/400 g canned red kidney beans, drained

⅔ cup chicken bouillon

2 tsp sugar

salt and pepper

lime wedges, to garnish

TO SERVE

1 large ripe avocado

1 lime

8 soft tortillas

1 cup thick yogurt

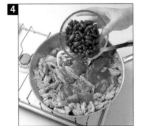

1 Heat the oil in a large wok, add the chicken and cook for 3 minutes.

2 Add the chopped onion and cook for 5 minutes, stirring until browned.

3 Add the chopped garlic, cumin, and chilies, with their seeds, and cook for about 1 minute.

4 Add the tomatoes, kidney beans, bouillon, sugar, and salt and pepper. Bring to a boil, breaking up the tomatoes. Cover and simmer for 15 minutes. Remove the lid and cook for 5 minutes, stirring occasionally until the sauce has thickened.

5 Halve the avocado, discard the stone and scoop out the flesh onto a plate. Mash the avocado with a fork.

6 Cut half of the lime into 8 thin wedges. Now squeeze the juice from the remaining lime over the mashed avocado.

7 Warm the tortillas according to the directions on the package. Put two tortillas on each serving plate, fill with the chicken mixture and top with spoonfuls of avocado and yogurt. Garnish the tortillas with lime wedges.

Chicken & Mango Stir-Fry

A colorful, exotic mix of flavors that works surprisingly well, this dish is easy and quick to cook—ideal for a mid-week family meal.

NUTRITIONAL INFORMATION

Calories 200	Sugars 5g
Protein 23g	Fat 6g
Carbohydrate 7g	Saturates 1g

5 mins   12 mins

SERVES 4

INGREDIENTS

6 boneless, skinless chicken thighs

2 tsp fresh root ginger, grated

1 garlic clove, crushed

1 small red chili, seeded

1 large red bell pepper

4 scallions

7 oz/200 g snow peas

3½ oz/100 g baby corn cobs

1 large, firm, ripe mango

2 tbsp sunflower oil

1 tbsp light soy sauce

3 tbsp rice wine or sherry

1 tsp sesame oil

salt and pepper

snipped chives, to garnish

1 Cut the chicken into long, thin strips and place in a bowl. Mix together the ginger, garlic, and chili, then stir in to the chicken strips to coat them evenly.

2 Slice the bell pepper thinly, cutting diagonally. Trim and diagonally slice the scallions. Cut the snow peas and corn cobs in half diagonally. Peel the mango, remove the pit and slice thinly.

3 Heat the oil in a large skillet or wok over a high heat. Add the chicken and cook for 4–5 minutes until just turning golden brown. Add the bell peppers and cook over a medium heat for 4–5 minutes to soften them.

4 Add the scallions, snow peas, and corn cobs and cook for another minute.

5 Mix together the soy sauce, rice wine or sherry, and sesame oil, and stir it into the wok. Add the mango and stir gently for 1 minute to heat thoroughly.

6 Adjust the seasoning with salt and pepper to taste and serve immediately. Garnish with chives.

Thai Stir-Fried Chicken

Coconut adds a creamy texture and delicious flavour to this Thai-style stir-fry, which is spiked with green chili.

NUTRITIONAL INFORMATION

Calories 184   Sugars 6g
Protein ....24g   Fat 5g
Carbohydrate ....8g   Saturates 2g

15 mins   10 mins

SERVES 4

I N G R E D I E N T S

3 tbsp sesame oil

12 oz/350 g skinless, boneless chicken breast, sliced thinly

2 shallots, sliced

2 garlic cloves, finely chopped

2 tsp grated fresh root ginger

1 green chili, finely chopped

1 each red and green (bell) pepper, sliced thinly

3 zucchini, thinly sliced

2 tbsp ground almonds

1 tsp ground cinnamon

1 tbsp oyster sauce

¼ cup grated creamed coconut

salt and pepper

1 Heat the sesame oil in a wok, add the chicken, season with salt and pepper, and cook for about 4 minutes.

2 Add the shallots, garlic, ginger and chili, and cook for 2 minutes.

3 Add the bell peppers and zucchini and cook for about 1 minute.

4 Finally, add the remaining ingredients and seasoning. Cook for 1 minute and serve immediately on warm serving plates.

COOK'S TIP

Creamed coconut is sold in blocks by supermarkets and Asian stores. It is a useful store-cupboard standby as it adds richness and depth of flavor.

Chicken with Black Bean Sauce

This tasty chicken stir-fry is quick and easy to make and is full of fresh flavors and crunchy vegetables.

NUTRITIONAL INFORMATION

Calories 205	Sugars 4g
Protein 25g	Fat 9g
Carbohydrate 6g	Saturates 2g

 40 mins   10 mins

SERVES 4

I N G R E D I E N T S

15 oz/425 g skinless, boneless chicken breasts, thinly sliced

pinch of salt

pinch of cornstarch

2 tbsp oil

1 garlic clove, crushed

1 tbsp black bean sauce

1 each small red and green bell pepper, seeded and cut into strips

1 red chili, finely chopped

2¾ oz/75 g mushrooms, sliced

1 onion, chopped

6 scallions, chopped

salt and pepper

S E A S O N I N G

½ tsp salt

½ tsp sugar

3 tbsp chicken bouillon

1 tbsp dark soy sauce

2 tbsp beef bouillon

2 tbsp rice wine

1 tsp cornstarch, blended with a little rice wine

1 Put the chicken strips in a bowl. Add a pinch of salt and a pinch of cornstarch and cover with water. Let stand for 30 minutes.

2 Heat 1 tablespoon of the oil in a wok or deep-sided skillet and cook the chicken for 4 minutes.

3 Remove the chicken to a warm serving dish and clean the wok.

4 Add the remaining oil to the wok and add the garlic, black bean sauce, red and green bell peppers, chili, mushrooms, onion, and scallions. Cook for 2 minutes then return the chicken to the wok.

5 Add the seasoning ingredients, cook for 3 minutes and thicken with a little of the cornstarch blend. Serve immediately with fresh noodles.

Chili Coconut Chicken

This tasty dish combines the flavors of lime, peanut, coconut, and chili. You'll find coconut cream in most large food stores or delicatessens.

NUTRITIONAL INFORMATION

Calories 348	Sugars 2g
Protein 36g	Fat 21g
Carbohydrate 3g	Saturates 8g

5 mins 15 mins

SERVES 4

INGREDIENTS

⅔ cup hot chicken bouillon

⅓ cup creamed coconut

1 tbsp sunflower oil

8 skinless, boneless chicken thighs, cut into long, thin strips

1 small red chili, thinly sliced

4 scallions, thinly sliced

4 tbsp smooth or crunchy peanut butter

finely grated zest and juice of 1 lime

boiled rice, to serve

TO GARNISH

1 fresh red chili

scallion tassel

1 Pour the chicken bouillon into a measuring jug or small bowl. Crumble the creamed coconut into the chicken bouillon and stir the mixture until the coconut dissolves.

2 Heat the oil in a preheated wok or large heavy pan.

3 Add the chicken strips and cook, stirring, until the chicken turns a golden color.

4 Stir in the chopped red chili and scallions and cook the mixture gently for a few minutes.

5 Add the peanut butter, coconut and chicken bouillon mixture, lime zest, and lime juice, and simmer, uncovered, for about 5 minutes, stirring frequently to prevent the mixture sticking to the bottom of the wok or pan.

6 Transfer the chili coconut chicken to a warm serving dish, garnish with the red chili and scallion tassel and serve with boiled rice.

COOK'S TIP

Serve jasmine rice with this spicy dish. It has a fragrant aroma that is well-suited to the flavors in this dish.

Turkey with Cranberry Glaze

Traditional Thanksgiving ingredients are given a Chinese twist in this stir-fry which contains cranberries, ginger, chestnuts, and soy sauce!

NUTRITIONAL INFORMATION

Calories 167	Sugars 11g	
Protein 8g	Fat 7g	
Carbohydrate ...20g	Saturates 1g	

  5 mins   15 mins

SERVES 4

INGREDIENTS

1 turkey breast

2 tbsp sunflower oil

2 tbsp preserved ginger

½ cup fresh or frozen cranberries

3½ oz/100 g canned chestnuts

4 tbsp cranberry sauce

3 tbsp light soy sauce

salt and pepper

1 Remove any skin from the turkey breast. Using a sharp knife, thinly slice the turkey breast.

2 Heat the sunflower oil in a large preheated wok or heavy-based skillet.

3 Add the turkey to the wok and cook for 5 minutes, or until cooked through.

4 Using a sharp knife, finely chop the preserved ginger.

5 Add the ginger and the cranberries to the wok or skillet and cook for 2–3 minutes or until the cranberries have started to become soft.

6 Add the chestnuts, cranberry sauce, and soy sauce, season to taste with salt and pepper, and allow to bubble for 2–3 minutes.

7 Transfer the turkey stir-fry to warm serving dishes and serve immediately.

COOK'S TIP

It is very important that the wok is very hot before you cook. Test by by holding your hand flat about 3 inches/7.5 cm above the bottom of the interior—you should be able to feel the heat radiating from it.

Duck in Spicy Sauce

Chinese five-spice powder gives a lovely flavor to this sliced duck, and the chili adds a little subtle heat.

NUTRITIONAL INFORMATION

Calories	162	Sugars	.........2g
Protein	........20g	Fat	...........7g
Carbohydrate	....3g	Saturates	.......2g

5 mins   25 mins

SERVES 4

INGREDIENTS

1 tbsp vegetable oil

1 tsp grated fresh root ginger

1 garlic clove, crushed

1 fresh red chili, chopped

12 oz/350 g skinless, boneless duck meat, cut into strips

4½ oz/125 g cauliflower, cut into florets

2 oz/60 g snow peas

2 oz/60 g baby corn cobs, halved lengthwise

1¼ cups chicken bouillon

1 tsp Chinese five-spice powder

2 tsp Chinese rice wine or dry sherry

1 tsp cornstarch

2 tsp water

1 tsp sesame oil

1 Heat the oil in a wok. Lower the heat slightly, add the ginger, garlic, chili and duck, and cook for 2–3 minutes. Remove from the wok and set aside.

2 Add the vegetables to the wok and cook for 2–3 minutes. Pour off any excess oil from the wok and push the vegetables to one side.

3 Return the duck to the wok and pour in the bouillon. Sprinkle the Chinese five-spice powder over the top, stir in the wine or sherry, and cook over a low heat for 15 minutes or until the duck is tender.

4 Blend the cornstarch with the water to form a paste and stir into the wok with the sesame oil. Bring to a boil, stirring until the sauce has thickened and cleared. Transfer the duck and spicy sauce to a warm serving dish and serve immediately.

COOK'S TIP

Omit the chili for a milder dish, or seed the chili before adding it to remove some of the heat.

Duck with Mangoes

Use fresh mangoes in this recipe for a terrific flavor and color. If they are unavailable, use canned mangoes and rinse them before using.

NUTRITIONAL INFORMATION

Calories ....235 Sugars 6g
Protein ....23g Fat 14g
Carbohydrate ....6g Saturates 2g

 5 mins   35 mins

SERVES 4

I N G R E D I E N T S

2 ripe mangoes

1¼ cups chicken bouillon

2 garlic cloves, crushed

1 tsp grated fresh root ginger

3 tbsp vegetable oil

2 large skinless duck breasts,
    8 oz/225 g each

1 tsp wine vinegar

1 tsp light soy sauce

1 leek, sliced

chopped fresh parsley, to garnish

1 Peel the mangoes and cut the flesh from each side of the pits. Cut the flesh into strips.

2 Put half of the mango pieces and the chicken bouillon in a food processor and process until smooth. Alternatively, press half of the mangoes through a fine strainer and mix with the bouillon.

3 Rub the garlic and ginger over the duck. Heat the vegetable oil in a preheated wok and cook the duck breasts, turning, until sealed. Reserve the oil in the wok and remove the duck.

4 Place the duck on a rack set over a roasting pan and cook in a preheated

oven, 425°F/220°C for 20 minutes, until the duck is cooked through.

5 Meanwhile, place the mango and bouillon mixture in a pan and add the wine vinegar and light soy sauce.

6 Bring the mixture in the pan to a boil and cook over a high heat, stirring, until reduced by half.

7 Heat the oil reserved in the wok and cook the sliced leek and remaining mango for 1 minute. Remove from the wok, transfer to a serving dish and keep warm until required.

8 Slice the cooked duck breasts and arrange the slices on top of the leek and mango mixture. Pour the sauce over the duck slices, garnish and serve.

Duck with Broccoli

This is a colorful dish using different colored bell peppers and broccoli to make it both tasty and appealing to the eye.

NUTRITIONAL INFORMATION

Calories 261	Sugars 3g
Protein 26g	Fat 13g
Carbohydrate 11g	Saturates 2g

35 mins   15 mins

SERVES 4

I N G R E D I E N T S

1 egg white

2 tbsp cornstarch

1 lb/450 g skinless, boneless duck meat

vegetable oil, for deep-frying

1 red bell pepper, seeded and diced

1 yellow bell pepper, seeded and diced

4½ oz/125 g small broccoli florets

1 garlic clove, crushed

2 tbsp light soy sauce

2 tsp Chinese rice wine or dry sherry

1 tsp light brown sugar

½ cup chicken bouillon

2 tsp sesame seeds

1 In a mixing bowl, beat together the egg white and cornstarch.

2 Using a sharp knife, cut the duck into 1-inch/2.5-cm cubes and stir into the egg white mixture. Let stand for 30 minutes.

3 Heat the oil for deep-frying in a preheated wok or heavy-based skillet until almost smoking.

4 Remove the duck from the egg white mixture, add to the wok and cook in the oil for 4–5 minutes, until crisp.

Remove the duck from the oil with a slotted spoon and drain on paper towels.

5 Add the bell peppers and broccoli to the wok and cook for 2–3 minutes. Remove with a slotted spoon and drain on paper towels.

6 Pour all but 2 tablespoons of the oil from the wok and return to the heat. Add the garlic and cook for 30 seconds.

Stir in the soy sauce, Chinese rice wine or sherry, sugar, and chicken bouillon and bring to a boil.

7 Stir in the duck and reserved vegetables and cook for 1–2 minutes.

8 Carefully spoon the duck and vegetables on to a warmed serving dish and sprinkle with the sesame seeds. Serve immediately.

Duck with Leek & Cabbage

Duck is a strongly-flavored meat which benefits from the added citrus peel to counteract this rich taste.

NUTRITIONAL INFORMATION

Calories	192	Sugars	.........5g
Protein	........26g	Fat	...........7g
Carbohydrate	....6g	Saturates	.......2g

10 mins   40 mins

SERVES 4

INGREDIENTS

4 duck breasts

12 oz/350 g green cabbage, thinly shredded

8 oz/225 g leeks, sliced

finely grated zest of 1 orange

6 tbsp oyster sauce

1 tsp toasted sesame seeds, to serve

1 Heat a large wok and dry-cook the duck breasts, with the skin on, for about 5 minutes on each side (you may need to do this in 2 batches).

2 Remove the duck breasts from the wok and transfer to a clean board.

3 Using a sharp knife, cut the duck breasts into thin slices.

4 Remove all but 1 tablespoon of the fat from the duck left in the wok; discard the rest.

5 Using a sharp knife, thinly shred the green cabbage.

6 Add the leeks, green cabbage, and orange zest to the wok and cook for about 5 minutes, or until the vegetables have softened.

7 Return the duck to the wok and heat through for 2–3 minutes.

8 Drizzle the oyster sauce over the mixture in the wok, toss well until all the ingredients are combined and then heat through.

9 Scatter the stir-fry with toasted sesame seeds, transfer to a warm serving dish and serve hot.

VARIATION

Use Napa cabbage for a lighter, sweeter flavor instead of the green cabbage, if you prefer.

Fruity Duck Stir-Fry

The pineapple and plum sauce add a sweetness and fruity flavor
to this colorful recipe which blends well with the duck.

NUTRITIONAL INFORMATION

Calories 241	Sugars 7g	
Protein 26g	Fat 8g	
Carbohydrate . . .16g	Saturates 2g	

🕐 5 mins   🕐 25 mins

SERVES 4

INGREDIENTS

4 duck breasts

1 tsp Chinese five-spice powder

1 tbsp cornstarch

1 tbsp chili oil

8 oz/225 g pearl onions, peeled

2 cloves garlic, crushed

3½ oz/100 g baby corn cobs

1¼ cups canned pineapple chunks

6 scallions, sliced

1 cup beansprouts

2 tbsp plum sauce

1 Remove any skin from the duck breasts. Cut the duck into thin slices.

2 Mix the Chinese five-spice powder and the cornstarch. Toss the duck in the mixture until well coated.

3 Heat the oil in a preheated wok. Cook the duck for 10 minutes, or until just beginning to crispen around the edges. Remove from the wok and set aside.

4 Add the onions and garlic to the wok and cook for 5 minutes, or until softened. Add the baby corn cobs and cook for a further 5 minutes. Add the pineapple, scallions, and beansprouts and cook for 3–4 minutes. Stir in the plum sauce.

5 Return the cooked duck to the wok and toss until well mixed. Transfer to warm serving dishes and serve hot.

COOK'S TIP

Buy pineapple chunks in natural juice rather than syrup for a fresher flavor. If you can only obtain pineapple in syrup, rinse it in cold water and drain thoroughly before using.

Pork Satay Stir-Fry

Satay sauce is easy to make and is one of the best known and loved sauces in Asian cooking. It is perfect with beef, chicken, or pork.

NUTRITIONAL INFORMATION

Calories ....506 Sugars 11g

Protein ....31g Fat 36g

Carbohydrate ...15g Saturates 8g

10 mins   15 mins

SERVES 4

INGREDIENTS

2 small carrots

2 tbsp sunflower oil

12 oz/350 g pork tenderloin, thinly sliced

1 onion, sliced

2 cloves garlic, crushed

1 yellow bell pepper, seeded and sliced

5½ oz/150 g snow peas

2¾ oz/75 g fine asparagus

chopped salted peanuts, to serve

SATAY SAUCE

6 tbsp crunchy peanut butter

6 tbsp coconut milk

1 tsp chili flakes

1 clove garlic, crushed

1 tsp tomato paste

COOK'S TIP

Cook the sauce just before serving as it tends to thicken very quickly and will not be spoonable if you cook it too far in advance.

1 Using a sharp knife, slice the carrots into thin sticks.

2 Heat the oil in a large, preheated wok. Add the pork, onion, and garlic and cook for 5 minutes or until the lamb is cooked through.

3 Add the carrots, bell pepper, snow peas and asparagus to the wok, and cook for 5 minutes.

4 To make the satay sauce, place the peanut butter, coconut milk, chili flakes, garlic, and tomato paste in a small pan and heat gently, stirring, until well combined. Be careful not to let the sauce stick to the bottom of the pan.

5 Transfer the stir-fry to warm serving plates. Spoon the satay sauce over the stir-fry and scatter with chopped peanuts. Serve immediately.

Spicy Pork & Rice

Pork is coated in a spicy mixture before being fried until crisp in this recipe and then stirred into a delicious egg rice for a very filling meal.

NUTRITIONAL INFORMATION

Calories 599	Sugars 11g	
Protein 30g	Fat 22g	
Carbohydrate . . .76g	Saturates 7g	

10 mins   35 mins

SERVES 4

I N G R E D I E N T S

1¼ cups long-grain white rice

2½ cups cold water

12 oz/350 g pork tenderloin

2 tsp Chinese five-spice powder

4 tbsp cornstarch

3 large eggs, beaten (one kept separate raw)

2 tbsp brown sugar

2 tbsp sunflower oil

1 onion

2 cloves garlic, crushed

1 large carrot, diced

1 red bell pepper, seeded and diced

¾ cup peas

1 tbsp butter

salt and pepper

1 Rinse the rice under cold running water. Place the rice in a large pan, add the cold water and a pinch of salt. Bring to a boil, cover, then reduce the heat and let simmer for about 9 minutes, or until all of the liquid has been absorbed and the rice is tender.

2 Meanwhile, slice the pork tenderloin into very thin even-sized pieces, using a sharp knife or meat cleaver. Set the pork strips aside until required.

3 Whisk together the Chinese five-spice powder, cornstarch, 1 egg and the raw brown sugar. Toss the pork in the mixture until coated.

4 Heat the sunflower oil in a large wok or skillet. Add the pork and cook over a high heat until the pork is cooked through and crispy. Remove the pork from the wok with a slotted spoon and set aside until required.

5 Using a sharp knife, cut the onion into dice.

6 Add the onion, garlic, carrot, bell pepper, and peas to the wok and cook for 5 minutes.

7 Return the pork to the wok together with the cooked rice and cook for 5 minutes.

8 Heat the butter in a skillet. Add the remaining beaten eggs and cook until set. Turn out on to a clean board and slice thinly. Toss the strips of egg into the rice mixture and serve immediately.

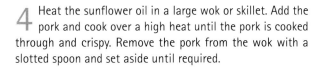

Spicy Pork Balls

These small meatballs are packed with flavor and cooked in a crunchy tomato sauce for a very quick dish.

NUTRITIONAL INFORMATION

Calories 299	Sugars 3g
Protein 28g	Fat 15g
Carbohydrate ...14g	Saturates 4g

 10 mins   40 mins

SERVES 4

I N G R E D I E N T S

1 lb/450 g ground pork

2 shallots, finely chopped

2 cloves garlic, crushed

1 tsp cumin seeds

½ tsp chili powder

½ cup fresh whole-wheat breadcrumbs

1 egg, beaten

2 tbsp sunflower oil

14 oz/400 g canned chopped tomatoes, flavoured with chili

2 tbsp soy sauce

7 oz/200 g canned water chestnuts, drained

3 tbsp chopped fresh cilantro

COOK'S TIP

Add a few teaspoons of chili sauce to a tin of chopped tomatoes, if you can't find the flavored variety.

1 Place the ground pork in a large mixing bowl. Add the shallots, garlic, cumin seeds, chili powder, breadcrumbs, and beaten egg, and mix together well.

2 Form the mixture into balls between the palms of your hands.

3 Heat the oil in a large preheated wok. Add the pork balls and cook, in batches, over a high heat for about 5

minutes or until sealed on all sides.

4 Add the tomatoes, soy sauce, and water chestnuts and bring to a boil. Return the pork balls to the wok, reduce the heat and let simmer for 15 minutes.

5 Scatter with chopped fresh cilantro and serve hot.

Sweet & Sour Pork

In this classic Chinese dish, tender pork pieces are fried and served in a crunchy sauce. This dish is perfect served with plain rice.

NUTRITIONAL INFORMATION

Calories 357	Sugars 25g	
Protein 28g	Fat 14g	
Carbohydrate ...30g	Saturates 4g	

 10 mins   20 mins

SERVES 4

I N G R E D I E N T S

1 lb/450 g pork tenderloin

2 tbsp sunflower oil

8 oz/225 g zucchini

1 red onion, cut into thin wedges

2 cloves garlic, crushed

3 carrots, cut into thin sticks

1 red bell pepper, seeded and sliced

3½ oz/100 g baby corn cobs

3½ oz/100 g white mushrooms, halved

1¼ cups fresh cubed pineapple

1 cup beansprouts

⅔ cup pineapple juice

1 tbsp cornstarch

2 tbsp soy sauce

3 tbsp tomato catsup

1 tbsp white wine vinegar

1 tbsp clear honey

1 Using a sharp knife, thinly slice the pork tenderloin into even-sized pieces.

2 Heat the sunflower oil in a large preheated wok. Add the pork to the wok and cook for 10 minutes, or until the pork is completely cooked through and beginning to turn crispy at the edges.

3 Meanwhile, cut the zucchini into thin sticks.

4 Add the onion, garlic, carrots, zucchini, bell pepper, corn cobs, and mushrooms to the wok, and cook for a further 5 minutes.

5 Add the pineapple cubes and beansprouts to the wok and cook for 2 minutes.

6 Mix together the pineapple juice, cornstarch, soy sauce, tomato catsup, white wine vinegar, and honey.

7 Pour the sweet and sour mixture into the wok and cook over a high heat, tossing frequently, until the juices thicken. Transfer the sweet and sour pork to serving bowls and serve hot.

COOK'S TIP

If you prefer a crisper coating, toss the pork in a mixture of cornstarch and egg white and deep fry in the wok in step 2.

Twice-Cooked Pork

Twice-cooked is a popular way of cooking meat in China. The meat is first boiled to tenderize it, then cut into strips or slices and stir-fried.

NUTRITIONAL INFORMATION

Calories . . . . . . .199 Sugars 3g
Protein . . . . .15g Fat 13g
Carbohydrate . . . .4g Saturates 3g

 3¼ hours   30 mins

SERVES 4

I N G R E D I E N T S

9–10½ oz/250–300 g shoulder or leg of
   pork, in one piece

1 small green bell pepper, cored and
   seeded

1 small red bell pepper, cored and seeded

4½ oz/125 g canned bamboo shoots, rinsed,
   drained, and sliced

3 tbsp vegetable oil

1 scallion, cut into short sections

1 tsp salt

½ tsp sugar

1 tbsp light soy sauce

1 tsp chili bean sauce or freshly ground chili

1 tsp rice wine or dry sherry

a few drops of sesame oil

1 Immerse the pork in a pot of boiling water to cover. Return to a boil and skim the surface. Reduce the heat, cover and simmer for 15–20 minutes. Turn off the heat and let the pork cool in the water for at least 2–3 hours.

2 Remove the pork and drain well. Trim off any excess fat, then cut into small, thin slices. Cut the bell peppers into pieces about the same size as the pork and the sliced bamboo shoots.

3 Heat the vegetable oil in a preheated wok and add the vegetables together with the scallion. Cook the vegetables for about 1 minute.

4 Add the pork, followed by the salt, sugar, light soy sauce, chili bean sauce, and wine or sherry. Blend well and continue stirring for another minute. Transfer the stir-fry to a warm serving dish, sprinkle with sesame oil and serve.

COOK'S TIP

For ease of handling, buy a boned piece of meat, and roll into a compact shape. Tie securely with string before placing in the boiling water.

Pork with Daikon

Pork and daikon are a perfect combination, especially with the added heat of the sweet chili sauce.

NUTRITIONAL INFORMATION

Calories 280	Sugars 1g	
Protein 25g	Fat 19g	
Carbohydrate 2g	Saturates 4g	

🧊 10 mins   🕐 15 mins

SERVES 4

INGREDIENTS

4 tbsp vegetable oil

1 lb/450 g pork tenderloin

1 eggplant

8 oz/225 g daikon

2 cloves garlic, crushed

3 tbsp soy sauce

2 tbsp sweet chili sauce

boiled rice or noodles, to serve

1 Heat 2 tablespoons of the vegetable oil in a large preheated wok or skillet.

2 Using a sharp knife, thinly slice the pork into even-sized pieces.

3 Add the slices of pork to the wok or skillet and cook for about 5 minutes.

4 Using a sharp knife, trim and dice the eggplant. Peel and slice the daikon.

5 Add the remaining vegetable oil to the wok.

6 Add the diced eggplant to the wok or skillet together with the garlic and cook for 5 minutes.

7 Add the daikon to the wok and cook for about 2 minutes.

8 Stir the soy sauce and sweet chili sauce into the mixture in the wok and cook until heated through.

9 Transfer the pork and daikon to warm serving bowls and serve immediately with boiled rice or noodles.

COOK'S TIP

Daikon are long white vegetables common in Chinese cooking. Usually grated, they have a milder flavor than red radish. They are generally available in most large food stores.

Pork Fry with Vegetables

This is a very simple dish which lends itself to almost any combination of vegetables that you have to hand.

NUTRITIONAL INFORMATION

Calories . . . . .216 Sugars 3g
Protein . . . . .19g Fat 12g
Carbohydrate . . . .5g Saturates 3g

5 mins   15 mins

SERVES 4

INGREDIENTS

12 oz/350 g pork tenderloin

2 tbsp vegetable oil

2 garlic cloves, crushed

½-inch/1-cm piece of fresh root ginger, cut into slivers

1 carrot, cut into thin strips

1 red bell pepper, seeded and diced

1 fennel bulb, sliced

1 oz/25 g canned water chestnuts, drained and halved

¾ cup beansprouts

2 tbsp Chinese rice wine

1¼ cups pork or chicken bouillon

pinch of dark brown sugar

1 tsp cornstarch

2 tsp water

1 Cut the pork into thin slices. Heat the oil in a preheated wok. Add the garlic, ginger, and pork, and cook for 1–2 minutes, until the meat is sealed.

2 Add the carrot, bell pepper, fennel, and water chestnuts to the wok, and cook for about 2–3 minutes.

3 Add the beansprouts and cook for 1 minute. Remove the pork and vegetables from the wok and keep warm.

4 Add the Chinese rice wine, pork or chicken bouillon, and sugar to the wok. Blend the cornstarch to a smooth paste with the water and stir it into the sauce. Bring to a boil, stirring constantly, until thickened and clear.

5 Return the meat and vegetables to the wok and cook for 1–2 minutes, until heated through and coated with the sauce. Serve immediately.

VARIATION

Use dry sherry instead of the Chinese rice wine if you have difficulty obtaining it.

Sweet & Sour Pork

This dish is a popular choice in Western diets, and must be one of the best-known Chinese recipes.

NUTRITIONAL INFORMATION

Calories . . . . .471 Sugars 47g
Protein . . . . .16g Fat 13g
Carbohydrate . . .77g Saturates 2g

10 mins   20 mins

SERVES 4

INGREDIENTS

⅔ cup vegetable oil, for
    deep-frying

8 oz/225 g pork tenderloin, cut into
    ½-inch/1-cm cubes

1 onion, sliced

1 green bell pepper, seeded and sliced

8 oz/225 g pineapple pieces

1 small carrot, cut into thin strips

1 oz/25 g canned bamboo shoots,
    drained, rinsed and halved

rice or noodles, to serve

BATTER

scant ¾ cup all-purpose flour

1 tbsp cornstarch

1½ tsp baking powder

1 tbsp vegetable oil

SAUCE

⅔ cup light brown sugar

2 tbsp cornstarch

½ cup white wine vinegar

2 garlic cloves, crushed

4 tbsp tomato paste

6 tbsp pineapple juice

1 To make the batter, sift the all-purpose flour into a mixing bowl, together with the cornstarch and baking powder. Add the vegetable oil and stir in enough water to make a thick, smooth batter (about ¾ cup).

2 Pour the vegetable oil into a preheated wok and heat until almost smoking.

3 Dip the cubes of pork into the batter, and cook in the hot oil, in batches, until the pork is cooked through. Remove the pork from the wok with a slotted spoon and drain on paper towels. Set aside and keep the pork pieces warm until they are required.

4 Drain all but 1 tablespoon of oil from the wok and return it to the heat. Add the onion, bell pepper, pineapple pieces, carrot, and bamboo shoots, and cook for 1–2 minutes. Remove from the wok with a slotted spoon and set aside.

5 Mix all of the sauce ingredients together and pour into the wok. Bring to a boil, stirring until thickened and clear. Cook for 1 minute, then return the pork and vegetables to the wok. Cook for a further 1–2 minutes, then transfer to a serving plate and serve with rice or noodles.

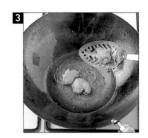

Pork with Plums

Plum sauce is often used in Chinese cooking with duck or rich, fattier meat to counteract the flavor.

NUTRITIONAL INFORMATION

Calories . . . . .281 Sugars 6g
Protein . . . . .25g Fat 14g
Carbohydrate . . .10g Saturates 4g

35 mins   25 mins

SERVES 4

I N G R E D I E N T S

1 lb/450 g pork tenderloin

1 tbsp cornstarch

2 tbsp light soy sauce

2 tbsp Chinese rice wine

4 tsp light brown sugar

pinch of ground cinnamon

5 tsp vegetable oil

2 garlic cloves, crushed

2 scallions, chopped

4 tbsp plum sauce

1 tbsp hoisin sauce

⅔ cup water

dash of chili sauce

T O   G A R N I S H

fried plum quarters

scallions

 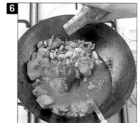 

1 Cut the pork tenderloin into thin slices.

2 Combine the cornstarch, soy sauce, rice wine, sugar, and cinnamon in a small bowl.

3 Place the pork in a shallow dish and pour the cornstarch mixture over it. Toss the meat in the marinade until it is completely coated. Cover and let marinate for at least 30 minutes.

4 Remove the pork from the dish, reserving the marinade.

5 Heat the oil in a preheated wok or large skillet. Add the pork and cook for 3–4 minutes, until a light golden color.

6 Stir in the garlic, scallions, plum sauce, hoisin sauce, water and chili sauce. Bring the sauce to a boil. Reduce the heat, cover, and let simmer for 8–10 minutes, or

until the pork is cooked through and tender.

7 Stir in the reserved marinade and cook, stirring, for about 5 minutes.

8 Transfer the pork stir-fry to a warm serving dish and garnish with fried plum quarters and scallions. Serve immediately.

Deep-Fried Pork Fritters

Small pieces of pork are coated in a light batter and deep-fried in this recipe—they are delicious dipped in a soy and honey sauce.

NUTRITIONAL INFORMATION

Calories 528   Sugars 12g
Protein . . . . .32g   Fat 22g
Carbohydrate . . .52g   Saturates 6g

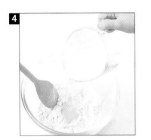

10 mins   15 mins

SERVES 4

INGREDIENTS

1 lb/450 g pork tenderloin

2 tbsp peanut oil

Scant 1½ cups all-purpose flour

2 tsp baking powder

1 egg, beaten

scant 1 cup milk

pinch of chili powder

vegetable oil, for deep-frying

fresh chives, to garnish

SAUCE

2 tbsp dark soy sauce

3 tbsp clear honey

1 tbsp wine vinegar

1 tbsp snipped fresh chives

1 tbsp tomato paste

1 Using a sharp knife, cut the pork into 1-inch/2.5-cm cubes.

2 Heat the peanut oil in a preheated wok. Add the pork to the wok and cook for 2–3 minutes, until sealed.

3 Remove the pork with a slotted spoon and set aside until required.

4 Sift the flour and baking powder into a mixing bowl and make a well in the center. Gradually beat in the egg, milk, and chili powder to make a thick batter.

5 Heat the oil for deep-frying in a wok until almost smoking, then reduce the heat slightly.

6 Toss the pork pieces in the batter to coat thoroughly. Add the pork to the wok and deep-fry until golden brown and

cooked through. Remove with a slotted spoon and drain well on paper towels.

7 Meanwhile, mix together the soy sauce, honey, wine vinegar, chives, and tomato paste and spoon into a small serving bowl.

8 Transfer the pork fritters to serving dishes, garnish with chives and serve with the sauce.

Spicy Ground Pork

A warmly spiced dish, this is ideal for a quick family meal. Just cook fine egg noodles for an accompaniment while the meat sizzles.

NUTRITIONAL INFORMATION

Calories ....278 Sugars 4g
Protein ....28g Fat 1g
Carbohydrate ....7g Saturates 4g

 5 mins   15 mins

SERVES 4

I N G R E D I E N T S

2 garlic cloves

3 shallots

2 tsp finely chopped fresh root ginger

2 tbsp sunflower oil

1 lb 2 oz/500 g lean ground pork

2 tbsp fish sauce

1 tbsp dark soy sauce

1 tbsp red curry paste

4 dried kaffir lime leaves, crumbled

4 plum tomatoes, chopped

3 tbsp fresh cilantro, chopped

salt and pepper

boiled fine egg noodles, to serve

fresh cilantro sprigs, to garnish

1 Peel and finely chop the garlic, shallots, and ginger. Heat the oil in a wok over a medium heat. Add the garlic, shallots, and ginger, and cook for about 2 minutes. Stir in the pork and continue cooking until golden brown.

2 Stir in the fish sauce, soy sauce, curry paste, and lime leaves, and cook for a further 1–2 minutes over a high heat.

3 Add the tomatoes and cook for a further 5–6 minutes, stirring occasionally.

4 Stir in the chopped cilantro and season to taste with salt and pepper. Serve hot, spooned on to boiled fine egg noodles, garnished with cilantro sprigs.

COOK'S TIP

Dried kaffir lime leaves are a useful store-cupboard ingredient as they can be crumbled easily straight into quick dishes such as this. If you prefer to use fresh kaffir lime leaves, shred them finely and add to the dish.

Stir-Fried Pork & Corn

A speedy dish, typical of Thai street food. If fresh corn kernels are not available, use drained, canned corn kernels instead.

NUTRITIONAL INFORMATION

Calories .... .336   Sugars .... .49g
Protein .... .30g   Fat .... .16g
Carbohydrate ...18g   Saturates 4g

2 mins   8–10 mins

SERVES 4

I N G R E D I E N T S

2 tbsp vegetable oil

1 lb 2 oz/500 g lean boneless pork, cut in thin strips

1 garlic clove, chopped

2 cups fresh corn kernels

7 oz/200 g green beans, cut into short lengths

2 scallions, chopped

1 small red chili, chopped

1 tsp sugar

1 tbsp light soy sauce

3 tbsp chopped fresh cilantro

egg noodles or boiled rice, to serve

1 Heat the oil in a large skillet or wok and cook the pork quickly over a high heat until lightly browned.

2 Stir in the garlic, corn kernels, beans, scallions, and chili, and continue cooking over a high heat for 2–3 minutes, until the vegetables are heated through and almost tender.

3 Stir in the sugar and soy sauce cook for a further 30 seconds, over a high heat.

4 Sprinkle with the cilantro and serve immediately either with egg noodles or rice.

Lamb with Satay Sauce

This recipe demonstrates the classic lamb satay—lamb marinated in chili and coconut and threaded on to wooden skewers.

NUTRITIONAL INFORMATION

Calories 501   Sugars 6g
Protein . . . . .34g   Fat 37g
Carbohydrate . . . .9g   Saturates 10g

 35 mins   25 mins

SERVES 4

INGREDIENTS

1 lb/450 g lamb loin fillet

1 tbsp mild curry paste

⅔ cup coconut milk

2 cloves garlic, crushed

½ tsp chili powder

½ tsp cumin

SATAY SAUCE

1 tbsp corn oil

1 onion, diced

6 tbsp crunchy peanut butter

1 tsp tomato paste

1 tsp fresh lime juice

generous ⅓ cup cold water

1 Using a sharp knife, thinly slice the lamb and place in a large dish.

2 Mix together the curry paste, coconut milk, garlic, chili powder, and cumin in a bowl. Pour over the lamb, toss well, cover, and marinate for 30 minutes.

3 To make the satay sauce, heat the oil in a large wok and cook the onion for 5 minutes, then reduce the heat and cook for 5 minutes.

4 Stir in the peanut butter, tomato paste, lime juice, and water.

5 Thread the lamb on to wooden skewers, reserving the marinade.

6 Broil the lamb skewers under a hot broiler for 6–8 minutes, turning once.

7 Add the reserved marinade to the wok, bring to a boil and cook for 5 minutes. Serve the lamb skewers with the satay sauce.

COOK'S TIP

Soak the wooden skewers in cold water for 30 minutes before broiling to prevent them from burning.

Lamb with Black Bean Sauce

Red onions add great color to recipes and are perfect in this dish, combining with the colors of the bell peppers.

NUTRITIONAL INFORMATION

Calories 328	Sugars 5g
Protein 26g	Fat 20g
Carbohydrate ...12g	Saturates 6g

10 mins   15 mins

SERVES 4

I N G R E D I E N T S

1 lb/450 g lamb neck fillet or boneless
    leg of lamb

1 egg white, lightly beaten

4 tbsp cornstarch

1 tsp Chinese five-spice powder

3 tbsp sunflower oil

1 red onion

1 red bell pepper, seeded
    and sliced

1 green bell pepper, seeded
    and sliced

1 yellow or orange bell pepper,
    seeded and sliced

5 tbsp black bean sauce

boiled rice or noodles, to serve

1 Using a sharp knife, slice the lamb into very thin strips.

2 Mix together the egg white, cornstarch, and Chinese five-spice powder. Toss the lamb strips in the mixture until evenly coated.

3 Heat the oil in a wok and cook the lamb over a high heat for 5 minutes or until it crispens around the edges.

4 Slice the red onion. Add the onion and bell pepper slices to the wok and cook for 5–6 minutes or until the vegetables just begin to soften.

5 Stir the black bean sauce into the mixture in the wok and heat through.

6 Transfer the lamb and sauce to warm serving plates and serve hot with freshly boiled rice or noodles.

COOK'S TIP

Take care when frying the lamb as the cornstarch mixture may cause it to stick to the wok. Move the lamb around the wok constantly while cooking.

Oyster Sauce Lamb

This really is a speedy dish, lamb leg steaks being perfect for the short cooking time.

NUTRITIONAL INFORMATION

Calories 243   Sugars 0.4g
Protein . . . . .26g   Fat 14
Carbohydrate . . . .3g   Saturates 5g

 5 mins   10 mins

SERVES 4

INGREDIENTS

1 lb/450 g lamb leg steaks

1 tsp ground Szechuan peppercorns

1 tbsp peanut oil

2 cloves garlic, crushed

8 scallions, sliced

2 tbsp dark soy sauce

6 tbsp oyster sauce

6 oz/175 g Napa cabbage

shrimp crackers, to serve
(optional)

1 Using a sharp knife, remove any excess fat from the lamb. Slice the lamb thinly.

2 Sprinkle the ground Szechuan peppercorns over the meat and toss together until well combined.

3 Heat the peanut oil in a preheated wok or large heavy-based skillet.

4 Add the lamb to the wok or skillet and cook for about 5 minutes.

5 Meanwhile, crush the garlic cloves in a pestle and mortar and slice the scallions. Add the garlic and scallions to the wok, together with the dark soy sauce, and cook for 2 minutes.

6 Add the oyster sauce and Napa cabbage and cook for a further 2 minutes, or until the cabbage has wilted and the juices are bubbling.

7 Transfer the stir-fry to warm serving bowls and serve hot with shrimp crackers (if using).

COOK'S TIP

Oyster sauce is made from oysters which are cooked in brine and soy sauce. Sold in bottles, it will keep in the refrigerator for months.

Garlic Lamb with Soy Sauce

The long marinating time allows the garlic to really penetrate the meat, creating a much more flavorful dish.

NUTRITIONAL INFORMATION

Calories ....309 Sugars 0.2g
Protein ....25g Fat 21g
Carbohydrate ....3g Saturates 9g

1¼ hours   15 mins

SERVES 4

I N G R E D I E N T S

1 lb/450 g lamb loin fillet

2 cloves garlic

2 tbsp peanut oil

3 tbsp dry sherry or rice wine

3 tbsp dark soy sauce

1 tsp cornstarch

2 tbsp cold water

2 tbsp butter

1 Using a sharp knife, make small slits in the flesh of the lamb.

2 Carefully peel the cloves of garlic and cut them into slices, using a sharp knife.

3 Push the slices of garlic into the slits in the lamb. Place the garlic-infused lamb in a shallow dish.

4 In a small bowl, mix together 1 tablespoon each of the peanut oil, dry sherry or rice wine, and dark soy sauce. Drizzle this mixture over the lamb, cover with plastic wrap and marinate for at least 1 hour, preferably overnight.

5 Using a sharp knife or meat cleaver, thinly slice the marinated lamb.

6 Heat the remaining oil in a preheated wok or large skillet. Add the marinated lamb and cook for 5 minutes.

7 Add the marinade juices and the remaining sherry and soy sauce to the wok and allow the juices to bubble for 5 minutes.

8 Blend the cornstarch to a smooth paste with the cold water. Add the cornstarch mixture to the wok and cook, stirring occasionally, until the juices start to thicken.

9 Cut the butter into small pieces. Add the butter to the wok or skillet and stir until the butter melts. Transfer the lamb to serving dishes and serve immediately.

COOK'S TIP

Adding the butter at the end of the recipe gives a glossy, rich sauce which is ideal with the lamb.

Lamb with Lime Leaves

Peanut oil is used here for flavor—it is a common oil used for stir-fries.

NUTRITIONAL INFORMATION

Calories 302   Sugars 15g
Protein ....24g   Fat 16g
Carbohydrate ...17g   Saturates 6g

5 mins   35 mins

SERVES 4

INGREDIENTS

2 red chilies

2 tbsp peanut oil

2 cloves garlic, crushed

4 shallots, chopped

2 stems lemongrass, sliced

6 lime leaves

1 tbsp tamarind paste

2 tbsp palm sugar

1 lb/450 g lean lamb (leg or loin fillet)

2½ cups coconut milk

6 oz/175 g cherry tomatoes, halved

1 tbsp chopped fresh cilantro

fragrant rice, to serve

1 Using a sharp knife, seed and very finely chop the red chilies.

2 Heat the oil in a large preheated wok or skillet.

3 Add the garlic, shallots, lemongrass, lime leaves, tamarind paste, palm sugar, and chilies to the wok and cook for about 2 minutes.

4 Using a sharp knife, cut the lamb into thin strips or cubes. Add the lamb to the wok or skillet and cook for about 5 minutes, tossing well so that the lamb is evenly coated in the spice mixture.

5 Pour the coconut milk into the wok and bring to a boil. Reduce the heat and let simmer for 20 minutes.

6 Add the tomatoes and cilantro to the wok and let simmer for 5 minutes. Transfer to serving plates and serve hot with fragrant rice.

COOK'S TIP

When buying fresh cilantro, look for bright green, unwilted leaves. To store it, wash and dry the leaves, leaving them on the stem. Wrap the leaves in damp paper towels and keep them in a plastic bag in the refrigerator.

Stir-Fried Lamb with Orange

Oranges and lamb are a great combination because the citrus flavor offsets the fattier, fuller flavor of the lamb.

NUTRITIONAL INFORMATION

Calories . . . . . . .209 Sugars 4g
Protein . . . . .25g Fat 10g
Carbohydrate . . . .5g Saturates 5g

 5 mins   30 mins

SERVES 4

I N G R E D I E N T S

1 lb/450 g ground lamb

2 cloves garlic, crushed

1 tsp cumin seeds

1 tsp ground coriander

1 red onion, sliced

finely grated zest and juice of
  1 orange

2 tbsp soy sauce

1 orange, peeled and segmented

salt and pepper

snipped fresh chives, to garnish

1 Heat a wok or large, heavy-based skillet, without adding any oil.

2 Add the ground lamb to the wok. Dry-cook the ground lamb for 5 minutes, or until the meat is evenly browned. Drain away any excess fat from the wok.

3 Add the garlic, cumin seeds, coriander, and red onion to the wok and cook for a further 5 minutes.

4 Stir in the finely grated orange zest and juice and the soy sauce, mixing until thoroughly combined. Cover, reduce the heat, and let simmer, stirring occasionally, for 15 minutes.

5 Remove the lid, increase the heat and add the orange segments. Stir to mix.

6 Season with salt and pepper to taste and heat through for a further 2–3 minutes.

7 Transfer the stir-fry to warm serving plates and garnish with snipped fresh chives. Serve immediately.

COOK'S TIP

If you wish to serve wine with your meal, try light, dry white wines and lighter Burgundy-style red wines as they blend well with Asian food.

Lamb's Liver with Peppers

This is a richly flavored dish which is great served with plain rice or noodles to soak up the delicious juices.

NUTRITIONAL INFORMATION

Calories . . . . .369 Sugars 5g
Protein . . . . .25g Fat 18g
Carbohydrate . . .27g Saturates 4g

 15 hrs   10 mins

SERVES 4

INGREDIENTS

1 lb/450 g lamb's liver

2 tbsp cornstarch

2 tbsp peanut oil

1 onion, sliced

2 cloves garlic, crushed

2 green bell peppers, seeded and sliced

2 tbsp tomato paste

3 tbsp dry sherry

1 tbsp cornstarch

2 tbsp soy sauce

1 Using a sharp knife, trim any excess fat from the lamb's liver. Slice the lamb's liver into thin strips.

2 Place the cornstarch in a large bowl.

3 Add the strips of lamb's liver to the cornstarch and toss well until coated evenly all over.

4 Heat the peanut oil in a large preheated wok.

5 Add the lamb's liver, onion, garlic and green bell pepper to the wok and cook

for 6–7 minutes, or until the lamb's liver is just cooked through and the vegetables are tender.

6 Mix together the tomato paste, sherry, cornstarch and soy sauce. Stir the mixture into the wok and cook for a further 2 minutes or until the juices have thickened. Transfer to warm serving bowls and serve immediately.

VARIATION

Use rice wine instead of the sherry for a really authentic Asian flavor. Chinese rice wine is made from glutinous rice and is also known as "yellow wine" because of its golden color. The best variety, from south-east China, is called Shao Hsing or Shaoxing.

Lamb Meatballs

These small meatballs are made with ground lamb and flavored with chili, garlic, parsley, and Chinese curry powder.

NUTRITIONAL INFORMATION

Calories .... .320   Sugars 1g
Protein .... .28g   Fat .... .20g
Carbohydrate ... .8g   Saturates 6g

   5 mins   20 mins

SERVES 4

INGREDIENTS

1 lb/450 g ground lamb

3 garlic cloves, crushed

2 scallions, finely chopped

½ tsp chili powder

1 tsp Chinese curry powder

1 tbsp chopped fresh parsley

½ cup fresh white breadcrumbs

1 egg, beaten

3 tbsp vegetable oil

4½ oz/125 g Napa cabbage, shredded

1 leek, sliced

1 tbsp cornstarch

2 tbsp water

1¼ cups lamb bouillon

1 tbsp dark soy sauce

shredded leek, to garnish

1 Mix the lamb, garlic, scallions, chili powder, Chinese curry powder, parsley, and breadcrumbs together in a bowl. Work the egg into the mixture, bringing it together to form a firm mixture. Roll into 16 small, even-sized balls.

2 Heat the oil in a preheated wok. Add the Napa cabbage and leek and cook for 1 minute. Remove from the wok with a slotted spoon and set aside.

3 Add the meatballs to the wok and cook in batches, turning gently, for 3–4 minutes, or until golden brown all over.

4 Mix the cornstarch and water together to form a smooth paste and set aside. Pour the lamb bouillon and soy sauce into the wok and cook for 2–3 minutes. Stir in the cornstarch paste. Bring to a boil and cook, stirring constantly, until the sauce is thickened and clear.

5 Return the Napa cabbage and leek to the wok and cook for 1 minute, until heated through. Arrange the Napa cabbage and leek on a warm serving dish, top with the meatballs, garnish with shredded leek and serve immediately.

VARIATION

Use ground pork or beef instead of the lamb as an alternative.

Lamb with Mushroom Sauce

Use a lean cut of lamb such as tenderloin, for this recipe for both flavor and tenderness.

NUTRITIONAL INFORMATION

Calories 219	Sugars 1g
Protein 21g	Fat 14g
Carbohydrate 4g	Saturates 4g

🍋 5 mins   🕐 10 mins

SERVES 4

INGREDIENTS

12 oz/350 g lean boneless lamb

2 tbsp vegetable oil

3 garlic cloves, crushed

1 leek, sliced

6 oz/175 g large mushrooms, sliced

½ tsp sesame oil

fresh red chilies, to garnish

SAUCE

1 tsp cornstarch

4 tbsp light soy sauce

3 tbsp Chinese rice wine or dry sherry

3 tbsp water

½ tsp chili sauce

1 Using a sharp knife or meat cleaver, cut the lamb into thin strips.

2 Heat the vegetable oil in a preheated wok or large skillet.

3 Add the lamb strips, garlic, and leek, and cook for about 2–3 minutes.

4 To make the sauce, mix together the cornstarch, soy sauce, Chinese rice wine or dry sherry, water, and chili sauce and set aside.

5 Add the sliced mushrooms to the wok and cook for 1 minute.

6 Stir in the prepared sauce and cook for 2–3 minutes, or until the lamb is cooked through and tender.

7 Sprinkle the sesame oil over the top and transfer the lamb and mushrooms to a warm serving dish. Garnish with red chilies and serve immediately.

VARIATION

The lamb can be replaced with lean steak or pork tenderloin in this classic recipe from Beijing. You could also use 2–3 scallions, 1 shallot, or 1 small onion, instead of the leek, if you prefer.

Red Lamb Curry

This richly spiced curry uses the typically red-hot chili flavor of red curry paste, made with dried red chilies, to give it a warm, russet-red color.

NUTRITIONAL INFORMATION

Calories	363	Sugars	........11g
Protein	........29g	Fat	..........19g
Carbohydrate	...21g	Saturates	.......6g

5 mins

35–40 mins

SERVES 4

INGREDIENTS

1 lb 2 oz/500 g boneless lean leg of lamb

2 tbsp vegetable oil

1 large onion, sliced

2 garlic cloves, crushed

2 tbsp red curry paste

⅔ cup coconut milk

1 tbsp light brown sugar

1 large red bell pepper, seeded and thickly sliced

½ cup lamb or beef bouillon

1 tbsp fish sauce

2 tbsp lime juice

8 oz/227 g canned water chestnuts, drained

2 tbsp chopped fresh cilantro

2 tbsp chopped fresh basil

salt and pepper

boiled jasmine rice, to serve

fresh basil leaves, to garnish

1 Trim the meat and cut it into 1¼-inch/3-cm cubes. Heat the oil in a large skillet or wok over a high heat and cook the onion and garlic for 2–3 minutes to soften. Add the meat and cook the mixture quickly until lightly browned.

2 Stir in the red curry paste and cook for a few seconds, then add the coconut milk and sugar and bring to a boil. Reduce the heat and simmer for 15 minutes, stirring occasionally.

3 Stir in the red bell pepper, bouillon, fish sauce, and lime juice, cover and continue simmering for a further 15 minutes, or until the meat is tender.

4 Add the water chestnuts, cilantro, and basil, adjust the seasoning to taste.

Serve with jasmine rice garnished with fresh basil leaves.

COOK'S TIP

This curry can also be made with other lean red meats. Try replacing the lamb with trimmed duck breasts or pieces of lean braising beef.

Lamb with Garlic Sauce

This dish contains Szechuan pepper which is quite hot and may be replaced with black pepper, if preferred.

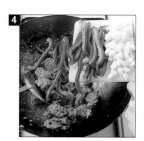

NUTRITIONAL INFORMATION

Calories 320	Sugars 2g
Protein 25g	Fat 21g
Carbohydrate 4g	Saturates 6g

 35 mins   10 mins

SERVES 4

I N G R E D I E N T S

1 lb/450 g lamb fillet or loin

2 tbsp dark soy sauce

2 tsp sesame oil

2 tbsp Chinese rice wine or dry sherry

½ tsp Szechuan pepper

4 tbsp vegetable oil

4 garlic cloves, crushed

2 oz/60 g canned water chestnuts, drained and quartered

1 green bell pepper, seeded and sliced

1 tbsp wine vinegar

1 tbsp sesame oil

rice or noodles, to serve

1 Cut the lamb into 1-inch /2.5-cm pieces and place in a shallow dish.

2 Mix together 1 tablespoon of the soy sauce, the sesame oil, Chinese rice wine or sherry, and Szechuan pepper. Pour the mixture over the lamb, turning to coat, and marinate for 30 minutes.

3 Heat the vegetable oil in a preheated wok. Remove the lamb from the marinade and add to the wok, together with the garlic. Cook for 2–3 minutes.

4 Add the water chestnuts and bell pepper and cook for 1 minute.

5 Add the remaining soy sauce and the wine vinegar, mixing together well.

6 Add the sesame oil and cook, stirring constantly, for 1–2 minutes, or until the lamb is cooked through.

7 Transfer the lamb and garlic sauce to a warm serving dish and serve immediately with rice or noodles.

COOK'S TIP

Chinese chives, also known as garlic chives, would make an appropriate garnish for this dish.

Sesame oil is used as a flavoring, rather than for frying, as it burns readily, hence it is added at the end of cooking.

Hot Lamb

This is quite a spicy dish, using 2 chilies in the sauce. Halve the number of chilies to reduce the heat, or seed the chilies before using, if desired.

NUTRITIONAL INFORMATION

Calories . . . . . . .323 Sugars 4g
Protein . . . . .26g Fat 22g
Carbohydrate . . . .5g Saturates 7g

🍲 25 mins   🕐 15 mins

SERVES 4

I N G R E D I E N T S

1 lb/450 g lean, boneless lamb

2 tbsp hoisin sauce

1 tbsp dark soy sauce

1 garlic clove, crushed

2 tsp grated fresh root ginger

2 tbsp vegetable oil

2 onions, sliced

1 fennel bulb, sliced

4 tbsp water

S A U C E

1 large fresh red chili, cut into thin strips

1 fresh green chili, cut into thin strips

2 tbsp rice wine vinegar

2 tsp light brown sugar

2 tbsp peanut oil

1 tsp sesame oil

 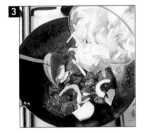 

1 Cut the lamb into 1-inch/2.5-cm cubes and place in a glass dish.

2 Mix together the hoisin sauce, soy sauce, garlic, and ginger and pour over the lamb, turning to coat well. Marinate for 20 minutes.

3 Heat the oil in a preheated wok and cook the lamb for 1–2 minutes. Add the onions and fennel and cook for a further 2 minutes, or until they are just beginning to brown. Stir in the water, cover, and cook for 2–3 minutes.

4 To make the sauce, place all the ingredients in a pan and cook over a low heat for 3–4 minutes, stirring.

5 Transfer the lamb and onions to a serving dish, toss lightly in the sauce and serve immediately.

VARIATION

Try using beef, pork, or duck instead of the lamb, and vary the vegetables, using leeks or celery instead of the onion and fennel.

Sesame Lamb Stir-Fry

This is a very simple, but delicious dish, in which lean pieces of lamb are cooked in sugar and soy sauce and then sprinkled with sesame seeds.

NUTRITIONAL INFORMATION

Calories	276	Sugars	.........4g
Protein	........25g	Fat	..........18g
Carbohydrate	....5g	Saturates	.......6g

 5 mins 10 mins

SERVES 4

I N G R E D I E N T S

1 lb/450 g boneless lean lamb

2 tbsp peanut oil

2 leeks, sliced

1 carrot, cut into matchsticks

2 garlic cloves, crushed

⅓ cup lamb or vegetable bouillon

2 tsp light brown sugar

1 tbsp dark soy sauce

4½ tsp sesame seeds

1 Using a sharp knife, cut the lamb into thin strips.

2 Heat the peanut oil in a preheated wok or large skillet until it is really hot.

3 Add the lamb and cook for 2–3 minutes. Remove the lamb from the wok with a slotted spoon and set aside until required.

4 Add the leeks, carrot, and garlic to the wok or skillet and cook in the remaining oil for 1–2 minutes.

5 Remove the vegetables from the wok with a slotted spoon and set aside.

6 Drain any remaining oil from the wok. Place the lamb or vegetable bouillon,

light brown sugar and dark soy sauce in the wok and add the lamb. Cook, stirring constantly to coat the lamb, for 2–3 minutes.

7 Sprinkle the sesame seeds over the top, turning the lamb to coat.

8 Spoon the leek, carrot, and garlic mixture on to a warm serving dish and top with the lamb. Serve immediately.

COOK'S TIP

Be careful not to burn the sugar in the wok when heating and coating the meat, otherwise the flavor of the dish will be spoiled.

Beef & Bell Peppers

A delicately flavored stir-fry infused with lemongrass and ginger.
Colorful bell peppers help to complete the dish.

NUTRITIONAL INFORMATION

Calories	230	Sugars	.........4g
Protein	........26g	Fat	..........12g
Carbohydrate	....6g	Saturates	.......3g

 5 mins   8 mins

SERVES 4

INGREDIENTS

1 lb 2 oz/500 g beef fillet

2 tbsp vegetable oil

1 garlic clove, finely chopped

1 lemongrass stem, finely shredded

2 tsp finely chopped, fresh root ginger

1 red bell pepper, seeded and thickly sliced

1 green bell pepper, seeded and thickly sliced

1 onion, thickly sliced

2 tbsp lime juice

boiled noodles or rice, to serve

1 Cut the beef into long, thin strips, cutting across the grain for ease of slicing.

2 Heat the oil in a large wok or large skillet over a high heat. Add the garlic and cook for 1 minute.

3 Add the beef and cook for a further 2–3 minutes until lightly colored. Stir in the lemongrass and ginger and remove the wok from the heat.

4 Remove the beef from the wok or pan and keep to one side. Next add the bell peppers and onion to the wok and cook over a high heat for 2–3 minutes until the onions are just turning golden brown and slightly softened.

5 Return the beef to the pan, stir in the lime juice and season to taste with salt and pepper. Serve with noodles or rice.

COOK'S TIP

When preparing lemongrass,
take care to remove
the outer layers, which can be
tough and fibrous. Use only the
tender center part, which has the
finest flavor.

Stir-Fried Beef & Vegetables

Beef is perfect for stir-fries as it is so tender and lends itself to quick cooking.

NUTRITIONAL INFORMATION

Calories	521	Sugars	.........7g
Protein	........31g	Fat	..........35g
Carbohydrate	...18g	Saturates	.......8g

10 mins   20 mins

SERVES 4

INGREDIENTS

2 tbsp sunflower oil

12 oz/350 g beef fillet, sliced

1 red onion, sliced

6 oz/175 g zucchini

2 carrots, thinly sliced

1 red bell pepper, seeded and sliced

1 small head Napa cabbage, shredded

1½ cups beansprouts

8 oz/225 g canned bamboo shoots, drained

1½ cups cashew nuts, toasted

SAUCE

3 tbsp medium sherry

3 tbsp light soy sauce

1 tsp ground ginger

1 clove garlic, crushed

1 tsp cornstarch

1 tbsp tomato paste

1 Heat the sunflower oil in a large preheated wok. Add the sliced beef and red onion to the wok and cook for about 4–5 minutes or until the onion begins to soften and the meat is just browning.

2 Trim the zucchini and slice diagonally.

3 Add the carrots, bell pepper, and zucchini to the wok and cook the mixture for 5 minutes.

4 Toss in the Napa cabbage, beansprouts, and bamboo shoots and heat through for 2–3 minutes, or until the leaves are just beginning to wilt.

5 Scatter the cashews nuts over the stir-fry and toss well to mix.

6 To make the sauce, mix together the sherry, soy sauce, ground ginger, garlic, cornstarch, and tomato paste until well combined.

7 Pour the sauce over the stir-fry and toss to mix. Allow the sauce to bubble for 2–3 minutes or until the juices thicken.

8 Transfer to warm serving dishes and serve at once.

Chili Beef Stir-Fry Salad

This dish has a Mexican feel to it, combining all of the classic flavors.

NUTRITIONAL INFORMATION

Calories	243	Sugars	.........2g
Protein	........21g	Fat	..........18g
Carbohydrate	....7g	Saturates	.......4g

5 mins   10 mins

SERVES 4

INGREDIENTS

1 lb/450 g lean rump steak

2 cloves garlic, crushed

1 tsp chili powder

½ tsp salt

1 tsp ground coriander

1 ripe avocado

2 tbsp sunflower oil

15 oz/425 g canned red kidney beans

6 oz/175 g cherry tomatoes, halved

1 large packet tortilla chips

shredded Iceberg lettuce

chopped fresh cilantro, to serve

1 Using a sharp knife, slice the beef into thin strips.

2 Place the garlic, chili powder, salt, and ground cilantro in a large bowl and mix until well combined.

3 Add the strips of beef to the marinade and toss well to coat all over.

4 Using a sharp knife, peel the avocado. Slice the avocado lengthwise and then crosswise to form small dice.

5 Heat the oil in a large preheated wok. Add the beef and cook for 5 minutes, tossing frequently.

6 Add the kidney beans, tomatoes, and avocado, and heat through for 2 minutes.

7 Arrange a bed of tortilla chips and Iceberg lettuce around the edge of a large serving plate and spoon the beef mixture into the center. Alternatively, serve the tortilla chips and Iceberg lettuce separately.

8 Garnish with chopped fresh cilantro and serve immediately.

COOK'S TIP

Serve this dish immediately as avocado tends to discolor quickly. Once you have cut the avocado into dice, sprinkle it with a little lemon juice to prevent discoloration.

Beef with Bamboo Shoots

Tender beef, marinated in a soy and tomato sauce, is cooked with crisp bamboo shoots and snow peas in this simple recipe.

NUTRITIONAL INFORMATION

Calories	275	Sugars	........3g
Protein	........21g	Fat	..........19g
Carbohydrate	....6g	Saturates	.......6g

 1¼ hours   🕐 10 mins

SERVES 4

I N G R E D I E N T S

12 oz/350 g rump steak

3 tbsp dark soy sauce

1 tbsp tomato ketchup

2 cloves garlic, crushed

1 tbsp fresh lemon juice

1 tsp ground coriander

2 tbsp vegetable oil

6 oz/175 g snow peas

7 oz/200 g canned bamboo shoots, drained

1 tsp sesame oil

COOK'S TIP

Let the meat marinate for at least 1 hour in order for the flavors to penetrate and increase the tenderness of the meat. If possible, marinate for a little longer for a fuller flavor to develop.

1 Thinly slice the meat and place in a non-metallic dish together with the dark soy sauce, tomato ketchup, garlic, lemon juice, and ground coriander. Mix well so that all of the meat is coated in the marinade, cover, and let stand for at least 1 hour.

2 Heat the vegetable oil in a preheated wok. Add the meat to the wok and cook for 2–4 minutes (depending on how

well cooked you like your meat) or until cooked through.

3 Add the snow peas and bamboo shoots to the mixture in the wok and cook over a high heat, tossing frequently, for a further 5 minutes.

4 Drizzle with the sesame oil and toss well to combine. Transfer to serving dishes and serve hot.

Caramelized Beef

Palm sugar or brown sugar is used in this recipe to give the beef a slightly caramelized flavor.

NUTRITIONAL INFORMATION

Calories 335	Sugars 8g	
Protein 23g	Fat 21g	
Carbohydrate ...14g	Saturates 7g	

 1¼ hours   10 mins

SERVES 4

INGREDIENTS

1 lb/450 g beef fillet

2 tbsp soy sauce

1 tsp chili oil

1 tbsp tamarind paste

2 tbsp palm sugar or raw brown sugar

2 cloves garlic, crushed

2 tbsp sunflower oil

8 oz/225 g pearl onions

2 tbsp chopped fresh cilantro

1 Using a sharp knife, thinly slice the beef.

2 Place the slices of beef in a large, shallow, non-metallic dish.

3 Mix together the soy sauce, chili oil, tamarind paste, palm sugar, and garlic.

4 Spoon the palm sugar mixture over the beef. Toss well to coat the beef in the mixture, cover with plastic wrap and let marinate for at least 1 hour.

5 Heat the sunflower oil in a preheated wok or large skillet.

6 Peel the onions and cut them in half. Add the onions to the wok and cook for 2–3 minutes, or until just browning.

7 Add the beef and marinade juices to the wok and cook over a high heat for about 5 minutes.

8 Scatter with chopped fresh cilantro and serve at once.

COOK'S TIP

Use the chili oil carefully as it is very hot and could easily spoil the dish if too much is added.

Beef & Black Bean Sauce

It is not necessary to use the expensive cuts of beef steak for this recipe: the meat will be tender as it is cut into small thin slices and marinated.

NUTRITIONAL INFORMATION

Calories	392	Sugars	.........2g
Protein	........13g	Fat	..........36g
Carbohydrate	....3g	Saturates	.......7g

3¼ hours   10 mins

SERVES 4

INGREDIENTS

9–10½ oz/250–300 g beef steak (such as rump)

1 small onion

1 small green bell pepper, cored and seeded

about 1¼ cups vegetable oil

1 scallion, cut into short sections

a few small slices of fresh root ginger

1-2 small green or red chilies, seeded and sliced

2 tbsp crushed black bean sauce

MARINADE

½ tsp baking soda or baking powder

½ tsp sugar

1 tbsp light soy sauce

2 tsp rice wine or dry sherry

2 tsp cornstarch

2 tsp sesame oil

1 Using a sharp knife or meat cleaver, cut the beef into small, thin strips.

2 To make the marinade, mix together all the ingredients in a shallow dish. Add the beef strips, turn to coat and marinate for at least 2–3 hours.

3 Cut the onion and green bell pepper into small cubes.

4 Heat the vegetable oil in a preheated wok or large skillet. Add the beef strips and cook for about 1 minute, or until the color changes. Remove the beef strips with a slotted spoon and drain on paper towels. Keep warm and set aside until required.

5 Pour off the excess oil, leaving about 1 tablespoon in the wok. Add the scallion, ginger, chilies, onion, and green bell pepper and cook for about 1 minute.

6 Add the black bean sauce and stir until smooth. Return the beef strips to the wok, blend well and cook for another minute. Transfer the stir-fry to a warm serving dish and serve hot.

Soy & Sesame Beef

Soy sauce and sesame seeds are classic ingredients in Chinese cooking.
Use a dark soy sauce for fuller flavor and richness.

NUTRITIONAL INFORMATION

Calories 324	Sugars 2g	
Protein 25g	Fat 22g	
Carbohydrate 3g	Saturates 6g	

🥟 5 mins   🕐 10 mins

SERVES 4

I N G R E D I E N T S

2 tbsp sesame seeds

1 lb/450 g beef fillet

2 tbsp vegetable oil

1 green bell pepper, seeded and thinly
    sliced

4 cloves garlic, crushed

2 tbsp dry sherry

4 tbsp soy sauce

6 scallions, sliced

noodles, to serve

1 Heat a large wok or heavy-based
skillet until it is very hot.

2 Add the sesame seeds to the wok or
skillet and dry-cook, stirring, for 1–2
minutes or until they just begin to brown.
Remove the sesame seeds from the wok
and set aside until required.

3 Using a sharp knife or meat cleaver,
thinly slice the beef.

4 Heat the vegetable oil in the wok or
skillet. Add the beef and cook for 2–3
minutes or until sealed on all sides.

5 Add the sliced bell pepper and
crushed garlic to the wok and
continue cooking for 2 minutes.

6 Add the dry sherry and soy sauce to
the wok together with the scallions.
Allow the mixture in the wok to bubble,
stirring occasionally, for about 1 minute,
but do not let the mixture burn.

7 Transfer the garlic beef stir-fry to
warm serving bowls and scatter with
the dry-cooked sesame seeds. Serve hot
with boiled noodles.

COOK'S TIP

You can spread the
sesame seeds out on a
cookie sheet and toast them under a
preheated broiler until browned all
over, if you prefer.

Beef & Broccoli Stir-Fry

This is a great combination of ingredients in terms of color and flavor, and it is so simple to prepare.

NUTRITIONAL INFORMATION

Calories	232	Sugars	.........1g
Protein	........12g	Fat	..........19g
Carbohydrate	....4g	Saturates	.......6g

 4¼ hours   15 mins

SERVES 4

INGREDIENTS

8 oz/225 g lean steak, trimmed

2 garlic cloves, crushed

dash of chili oil

1 tsp grated, fresh root ginger

½ tsp Chinese five-spice powder

2 tbsp dark soy sauce

2 tbsp vegetable oil

5½ oz/150 g broccoli florets

1 tbsp light soy sauce

⅔ cup beef bouillon

2 tsp cornstarch

4 tsp water

carrot strips, to garnish

1 Using a sharp knife, cut the steak into thin strips and place in a shallow glass dish.

2 Mix together the garlic, chili oil, grated ginger, Chinese five-spice powder, and dark soy sauce in a small bowl and pour over the beef, tossing to coat the strips evenly.

3 Cover the bowl and let the meat marinate in the refrigerator for several hours to allow the flavors to develop fully.

4 Heat 1 tablespoon of the vegetable oil in a preheated wok or large skillet. Add the broccoli and cook over a medium heat for 4–5 minutes. Remove from the wok with a slotted spoon and set aside until required.

5 Heat the remaining oil in the wok. Add the steak together with the marinade, and cook for 2-3 minutes, until the steak is browned and sealed.

6 Return the broccoli to the wok and stir in the light soy sauce and bouillon.

7 Blend the cornstarch with the water to form a smooth paste and stir into the wok. Bring to a boil, stirring, until thickened and clear. Cook for 1 minute. Transfer the stir-fry to a warm serving dish, arrange the carrot strips in a lattice on top and serve immediately.

Oyster Sauce Beef

Like other stir-fry dishes, the vegetables used in this recipe can be varied as you wish.

NUTRITIONAL INFORMATION

Calories 462   Sugars 2g
Protein . . . . .16g   Fat 42g
Carbohydrate . . . .4g   Saturates 8g

40 mins   10 mins

SERVES 4

INGREDIENTS

10½ oz/300 g beef steak

1 tsp sugar

1 tbsp light soy sauce

1 tsp rice wine or dry sherry

1 tsp cornstarch

½ small carrot

2 oz/60 g snow peas

2 oz/60 g canned bamboo shoots, drained

2 oz/60 g canned straw mushrooms

about 1¼ cups vegetable oil

1 scallion, cut into short sections

2–3 small slices fresh root ginger

½ tsp salt

2 tbsp oyster sauce

2–3 tbsp vegetable bouillon or water

1 Cut the beef into small, thin slices. Place in a shallow dish with the sugar, soy sauce, wine, and cornstarch and let marinate for 25–30 minutes.

2 Slice the carrot, snow peas, bamboo shoots, and straw mushrooms into roughly the same size pieces as each other.

3 Heat the oil in a wok and add the beef slices. Cook for 1 minute, then remove and keep warm.

4 Pour off the oil, leaving about 1 tablespoon in the wok. Add the sliced vegetables with the scallion and ginger and cook for about 2 minutes. Add the salt, beef, and oyster sauce, with bouillon or water. Blend well until heated through and serve.

VARIATION

You can use whatever vegetables are available for this dish, but it is important to get a good contrast of color—don't use all red or all green, for example.

Spicy Beef

In this recipe, beef is marinated in a five-spice and chili marinade for a spicy flavor.

NUTRITIONAL INFORMATION

Calories 246   Sugars 2g
Protein . . . . .21g   Fat 13g
Carbohydrate . . .10g   Saturates 3g

  1¼ hours   10 mins

SERVES 4

INGREDIENTS

8 oz/225 g beef

2 garlic cloves, crushed

1 tsp powdered star anise

1 tbsp dark soy sauce

scallion tassels, to garnish

SAUCE

2 tbsp vegetable oil

1 bunch scallions, halved lengthwise

1 tbsp dark soy sauce

1 tbsp dry sherry

¼ tsp chili sauce

⅔ cup water

2 tsp cornstarch

4 tsp water

1 Cut the steak into thin strips and place in a shallow dish.

2 Mix together the garlic, star anise, and dark soy sauce in a bowl.

3 Pour the sauce mixture over the steak strips, turning them to coat thoroughly. Cover and marinate in the refrigerator for at least 1 hour.

4 To make the sauce, heat the oil in a preheated wok or large skillet. Reduce the heat and cook the scallions for 1–2 minutes.

5 Remove the scallions from the wok with a slotted spoon, drain on paper towels and set aside until required.

6 Add the beef to the wok, together with the marinade, and cook for 3–4 minutes. Return the scallions to the wok and add the soy sauce, sherry, chili sauce, and two-thirds of the water.

7 Blend the cornstarch with the remaining water and stir into the wok. Bring to a boil, stirring until the sauce thickens and clears.

8 Transfer to a warm serving dish, garnish and serve immediately.

Beef & Beans

The green of the beans complements the dark color of the beef, served in a rich sauce.

NUTRITIONAL INFORMATION

Calories 381   Sugars 3g
Protein . . . . .25g   Fat 27g
Carbohydrate . . .10g   Saturates 8g

35 mins   15 mins

SERVES 4

I N G R E D I E N T S

1 lb/450 g beef fillet steak or rump steak,
cut into 1-inch/2.5-cm pieces

M A R I N A D E

2 tsp cornstarch

2 tbsp dark soy sauce

2 tsp peanut oil

S A U C E

2 tbsp vegetable oil

3 garlic cloves, crushed

1 small onion, cut into 8 pieces

8 oz/225 g thin green beans, halved

¼ cup unsalted cashews

1 oz/25 g canned bamboo shoots, drained

2 tsp dark soy sauce

2 tsp Chinese rice wine or dry sherry

½ cup beef bouillon

2 tsp cornstarch

4 tsp water

salt and pepper

1 To make the marinade, mix together thoroughly the cornstarch, soy sauce, and peanut oil.

2 Place the steak in a shallow glass bowl. Pour the marinade over the steak, turn to coat thoroughly, cover and marinate in the refrigerator for at least 30 minutes—the longer the better.

3 To make the sauce, heat the oil in a preheated wok. Add the garlic, onion, beans, cashews, and bamboo shoots, and cook for 2–3 minutes.

4 Remove the steak from the marinade, drain, add to the wok, and cook for 3–4 minutes.

5 Mix the soy sauce, Chinese rice wine or sherry, and beef bouillon together. Blend the cornstarch with the water and add to the soy sauce mixture, mixing everything well to combine.

6 Stir the mixture into the wok and bring the sauce to a boil, stirring until thickened and clear. Reduce the heat and let simmer for 2–3 minutes. Season to taste and serve immediately.

Beef & Peanut Salad

This recipe looks stunning if you arrange the ingredients rather than toss them together.

  10 mins   10 mins

SERVES 4

INGREDIENTS

½ head Napa cabbage

1 large carrot

4 oz/115 g radishes

3½ oz/100 g baby corn cobs

1 tbsp peanut oil

1 red chili, seeded and finely chopped

1 clove garlic, finely chopped

12 oz/350 g lean beef (such as fillet, sirloin or rump), trimmed and shredded finely

1 tbsp dark soy sauce

¼ cup fresh peanuts, optional

sliced red chili, to garnish

DRESSING

1 tbsp smooth peanut butter

1 tsp superfine sugar

2 tbsp light soy sauce

1 tbsp sherry vinegar

salt and pepper

VARIATION

If preferred, use chicken, turkey, lean pork, or even strips of venison instead of beef in this recipe. Cut off all visible fat before you begin.

1 Finely shred the Napa cabbage and arrange attractively on a platter.

2 Peel the carrot and cut into very thin strips. Wash, trim, and quarter the radishes, and halve the baby corn lengthwise. Arrange these ingredients around the edge of the dish and set aside.

3 Heat the peanut oil in a non-stick wok or large skillet until really hot.

4 Add the red chili, garlic, and beef to the wok or skillet and cook for 5 minutes.

5 Add the dark soy sauce and cook for a further 1–2 minutes until tender and cooked through.

6 Meanwhile, make the dressing. Place all of the ingredients in a small bowl and blend them together until smooth.

7 Place the hot cooked beef in the center of the salad ingredients. Spoon over the dressing and sprinkle with a few peanuts, if using. Garnish with slices of red chili and serve immediately.

Beef with Beansprouts

A quick-and-easy stir-fry for any day of the week, this simple beef recipe is a good one-pan main dish.

NUTRITIONAL INFORMATION

Calories	544	Sugars	........8g
Protein	........39g	Fat	..........21g
Carbohydrate	...55g	Saturates	.......5g

5 mins   15 mins

SERVES 4

I N G R E D I E N T S

1 bunch scallions

2 tbsp sunflower oil

1 garlic clove, crushed

1 tsp finely chopped fresh root ginger

1 lb 2 oz/500 g tender beef, cut into thin strips

1 large red bell pepper, seeded and sliced

1 small red chili, seeded and chopped

3⅓ cups fresh beansprouts

1 small lemongrass stem, finely chopped

2 tbsp smooth peanut butter

4 tbsp coconut milk

1 tbsp rice vinegar

1 tbsp soy sauce

1 tsp soft light brown sugar

9 oz/250 g medium egg noodles

salt and pepper

1 Trim and thinly slice the scallions, setting aside some slices to use as a garnish.

2 Heat the oil in a skillet or wok over a high heat. Add the scallions, garlic, and ginger and then cook for 2–3 minutes to soften. Add the beef and continue cooking for 4–5 minutes until everything is browned evenly.

3 Add the bell pepper and cook for a further 3–4 minutes. Add the chili and beansprouts and cook for 2 minutes. Mix together the lemongrass, peanut butter, coconut milk, vinegar, soy sauce, and sugar, then pour this mixture into the wok and stir.

4 Meanwhile, cook the egg noodles in boiling, lightly salted water for 4 minutes, or according to the package directions. Drain and stir into the skillet or wok, tossing to mix evenly.

5 Adjust seasoning with salt and pepper to taste. Sprinkle with the reserved scallions and serve hot.

Fish & Seafood

Throughout the Far Eastern countries, fish and seafood play a major role in the diet of the native people; this is because these foods are both plentiful and very healthy. They are also very versatile: there are many different ways

of cooking fish and seafood in a wok— they may be steamed, deep-fried, or cooked with a range of delicious spices and sauces.

Japan is famed for its *sushimi*, or raw fish, but this is just one of the wide range of fish dishes served. Fish and seafood are offered at every meal in Japan, many of them cooked in a wok.

When buying fish and seafood for the recipes in this chapter, freshness is imperative to flavor, so be sure to buy and use the fish that you have chosen as soon as possible, preferably on the same day.

Stir-Fried Cod with Mango

Fish and fruit are a classic combination, and in this recipe a tropical flavor is added which gives a great scented taste to the dish.

NUTRITIONAL INFORMATION

Calories 200   Sugars 12g
Protein ....21g   Fat 7g
Carbohydrate ...14g   Saturates 1g

10 mins   15 mins

SERVES 4

INGREDIENTS

2 carrots

2 tbsp vegetable oil

1 red onion, sliced

1 red bell pepper, seeded
  and sliced

1 green bell pepper, seeded and sliced

1 lb/450 g skinless cod fillet

1 ripe mango

1 tsp cornstarch

1 tbsp soy sauce

generous ⅓ cup tropical fruit juice

1 tbsp lime juice

1 tbsp chopped fresh cilantro, to garnish

1 Using a sharp knife, slice the carrots into thin sticks.

2 Heat the oil in a preheated wok and cook the onion, carrots, and bell peppers for 5 minutes.

3 Using a sharp knife, cut the cod into small cubes. Peel the mango, then carefully remove the flesh from the center pit. Cut the flesh into thin slices.

4 Add the cod and mango to the wok and cook for a further 4–5 minutes, or until the fish is cooked through. Be careful not to break the fish up.

5 Mix together the cornstarch, soy sauce, fruit juice, and lime juice. Pour the mixture into the wok and stir until the mixture bubbles and the juices thicken. Scatter with cilantro and serve immediately on warm serving plates.

VARIATION

You can use papaya as an alternative to the mango, if you prefer.

Braised Fish Fillets

Any white fish, such as lemon sole or flounder, is ideal for this delicious dish.

NUTRITIONAL INFORMATION

Calories 107	Sugars 2g	
Protein 17g	Fat 2g	
Carbohydrate 6g	Saturates 0.3g	

  35 mins   10 mins

SERVES 4

I N G R E D I E N T S

3-4 small Chinese dried mushrooms

10½–12 oz/300–350 g fish fillets

1 tsp salt

½ egg white, lightly beaten

1 tsp cornstarch

2½ cups vegetable oil

1 tsp finely chopped fresh root ginger

2 scallions, finely chopped

1 garlic clove, finely chopped

½ small green bell pepper, seeded and cut into small cubes

½ small carrot, thinly sliced

½ cup canned bamboo shoots, rinsed and sliced

½ tsp sugar

1 tbsp light soy sauce

1 tsp rice wine or dry sherry

1 tbsp chili bean sauce

2–3 tbsp vegetable bouillon or water

a few drops of sesame oil

1 Soak the dried mushrooms in a bowl of warm water for 30 minutes. Drain thoroughly on paper towels, reserving the soaking water for bouillon or soup. Squeeze the mushrooms to extract all of the moisture, cut off and discard any hard stems, and slice thinly.

2 Cut the fish into bite-sized pieces, then place in a shallow dish and mix with a pinch of salt, the egg white, and cornstarch, turning the fish to coat well.

3 Heat the oil in a preheated wok. Add the fish pieces to the wok and deep-fry for about 1 minute. Remove the fish pieces with a slotted spoon and drain on paper towels.

4 Pour off the excess oil, leaving about 1 tablespoon in the wok. Add the ginger, scallions, and garlic to flavor the oil for a few seconds, then add the bell pepper, carrot, and bamboo shoots, and cook for about 1 minute.

5 Add the sugar, soy sauce, wine, chili bean sauce, bouillon or water, and the remaining salt, and bring to a boil. Add the fish pieces, stirring to coat with the sauce, and braise for 1 minute. Sprinkle with sesame oil and serve.

Fish with Coconut & Basil

Fish curries are sensational and this is no exception. Red curry and coconut are fantastic flavors with the fried fish.

NUTRITIONAL INFORMATION

Calories ....209 Sugars 10g
Protein ....21g Fat 8g
Carbohydrate ...15g Saturates 1g

 5 mins   15 mins

SERVES 4

INGREDIENTS

2 tbsp vegetable oil

1 lb/450 g skinless cod fillet

3 tbsp seasoned flour

1 clove garlic, crushed

2 tbsp red curry paste

1 tbsp fish sauce

1¼ cups coconut milk

6 oz/175 g cherry tomatoes, halved

20 fresh basil leaves

fragrant rice, to serve

1 Heat the vegetable oil in a large preheated wok.

2 Using a sharp knife, cut the fish into large cubes, removing any bones with a pair of clean tweezers.

3 Place the seasoned flour in a bowl. Add the cubes of fish and mix until well coated.

4 Add the coated fish to the wok and cook over a high heat for 3–4 minutes, or until the fish just begins to brown at the edges.

5 In a small bowl, mix together the garlic, curry paste, fish sauce, and coconut milk. Pour the mixture over the fish and bring to a boil.

6 Add the tomatoes to the mixture in the wok and let them simmer for 5 minutes.

7 Roughly chop or tear the fresh basil leaves. Add the basil to the wok and stir carefully to combine, taking care not to break up the cubes of fish.

8 Transfer to serving plates and serve hot with fragrant rice.

COOK'S TIP

Take care not to overcook the dish once the tomatoes are added, otherwise they will break down and the skins will come away.

Szechuan White Fish

Szechuan pepper is quite hot and should be used sparingly to avoid making the dish unbearably spicy.

NUTRITIONAL INFORMATION

Calories	225	Sugars	.........3g
Protein	........20g	Fat	...........8g
Carbohydrate	...17g	Saturates	.......1g

5 mins   20 mins

SERVES 4

INGREDIENTS

12 oz/350 g white fish fillets

1 small egg, beaten

3 tbsp all-purpose flour

4 tbsp dry white wine

3 tbsp light soy sauce

vegetable oil

1 garlic clove, cut into slivers

1tsp finely chopped fresh root ginger

1 onion, finely chopped

1 celery stalk, chopped

1 fresh red chili, chopped

3 scallions, chopped

1 tsp rice wine vinegar

½ tsp ground Szechuan pepper

¾ cup fish bouillon

1 tsp superfine sugar

1 tsp cornstarch

2 tsp water

for 2–3 minutes, until golden brown. Remove with a slotted spoon, drain on paper towels, set aside, and keep warm.

3 Pour all but 1 tablespoon of oil from the wok and return to the heat. Add the garlic, ginger, onion, celery, chili, and scallions, and cook for 1–2 minutes. Stir in the remaining soy sauce and the vinegar.

4 Add the Szechuan pepper, fish bouillon and superfine sugar to the wok. Mix the cornstarch with the water to form a smooth paste and stir it into the bouillon. Bring to a boil and cook, stirring, for 1 minute, until the sauce thickens and clears.

5 Return the fish cubes to the wok and cook for 1–2 minutes. Serve immediately on warm serving plates.

1 Cut the fish into 1½-inch/4-cm cubes. Beat together the egg, flour, wine, and 1 tablespoon of soy sauce to make a batter. Dip the cubes of fish into the batter to coat well.

2 Heat the oil in a wok, reduce the heat slightly and cook the fish, in batches,

Crispy Fish

This is a very hot dish—not for the faint-hearted! It can be made without the chili flavorings, if preferred.

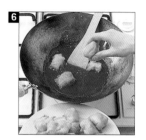

NUTRITIONAL INFORMATION

Calories	281	Sugars	.........3g
Protein	.......25g	Fat	.........12g
Carbohydrate	...15g	Saturates	.......2g

 30 mins   40 mins

SERVES 4

I N G R E D I E N T S

1 lb/450 g white fish fillets

vegetable oil, for deep-frying

B A T T E R

scant ½ cup all-purpose flour

1 egg, separated

1 tbsp peanut oil

4 tbsp milk

S A U C E

1 fresh red chili, chopped

2 garlic cloves, crushed

pinch of chili powder

3 tbsp tomato paste

1 tbsp rice wine vinegar

2 tbsp dark soy sauce

2 tbsp Chinese rice wine

2 tbsp water

pinch of superfine sugar

1 Cut the fish into 1-inch/2.5-cm cubes and set aside.

2 Sift the all-purpose flour into a mixing bowl and make a well in the center. Add the egg yolk and peanut oil to the mixing bowl and gradually stir in the milk, incorporating the flour to form a smooth batter. Let stand for about 20 minutes.

3 Whisk the egg white until it forms peaks and fold into the batter until thoroughly incorporated.

4 Heat the vegetable oil in a preheated wok or large skillet. Dip the fish into the batter and fry, in batches, for 8–10 minutes, until cooked through. Remove the fish from the wok with a slotted spoon, set aside, and keep the fish pieces warm until they are required.

5 Pour off all but 1 tablespoon of oil from the wok and return to the heat. Add the chili, garlic, chili powder, tomato paste, rice wine vinegar, soy sauce, Chinese rice wine, water, and sugar, and cook, stirring, for 3–4 minutes.

6 Return the fish to the wok and stir gently to coat it in the sauce. Cook for 2–3 minutes, until hot. Transfer to a serving dish and serve immediately.

Gingered Monkfish

This dish is a real treat and is perfect for special occasions. Monkfish has a tender flavor which is ideal with asparagus, chili, and ginger.

NUTRITIONAL INFORMATION

Calories . . . . . . .133 Sugars 0g
Protein . . . . .21g Fat 5g
Carbohydrate . . . .1g Saturates 1g

5 mins   10 mins

SERVES 4

I N G R E D I E N T S

1 lb/450 g monkfish

1 tbsp grated fresh root ginger

2 tbsp sweet chili sauce

1 tbsp corn oil

3½ oz/100 g fine asparagus

3 scallions, sliced

1 tsp sesame oil

1 Using a sharp knife, slice the monkfish into thin flat rounds. Set aside until required.

2 Mix together the grated fresh root ginger and the sweet chili sauce in a small bowl until they are thoroughly blended. Brush the ginger and chili sauce mixture over the monkfish pieces, using a pastry brush.

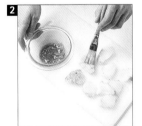

COOK'S TIP

Monkfish is quite expensive, but it is well worth using as it has a wonderful flavor and texture. You could use cubes of chunky cod fillet instead.

3 Heat the corn oil in a large preheated wok or heavy-based skillet.

4 Add the monkfish pieces, asparagus, and chopped scallions to the wok or skillet and cook for about 5 minutes, stirring gently so the fish pieces do not break up.

5 Remove the wok or skillet from the heat, drizzle the sesame oil over the

stir-fry and toss well to combine.

6 Transfer the stir-fried gingered monkfish to warm serving plates and serve immediately.

Trout with Pineapple

Pineapple is widely used in Chinese cooking. The tartness of fresh pineapple complements fish particularly well.

NUTRITIONAL INFORMATION

Calories 243	Sugars 4g	
Protein 30g	Fat 11g	
Carbohydrate 6g	Saturates 2g	

5 mins   15 mins

SERVES 4

I N G R E D I E N T S

4 trout fillets, skinned

2 tbsp vegetable oil

2 garlic cloves, cut into slivers

4 slices fresh pineapple, peeled and diced

1 celery stalk, sliced

1 tbsp light soy sauce

scant ¼ cup fresh or unsweetened
     pineapple juice

⅔ cup fish bouillon

1 tsp cornstarch

2 tsp water

TO GARNISH

shredded celery leaves

fresh red chili slices

1 Cut the trout fillets into strips. Heat 1 tablespoon of the vegetable oil in a preheated wok until almost smoking. Reduce the heat slightly, add the fish, and sauté for 2 minutes. Remove from the wok.

2 Add the remaining oil to the wok, reduce the heat and add the garlic, diced pineapple and celery. Cook for 1–2 minutes.

3 Add the soy sauce, pineapple juice, and fish bouillon to the wok. Bring to a boil and cook, stirring, for 2–3 minutes, or until the sauce has reduced.

4 Blend the cornstarch with the water to form a paste and stir it into the wok. Bring the sauce to a boil and cook, stirring constantly, until the sauce thickens and clears.

5 Return the fish to the wok, and cook, stirring gently, until heated through. Transfer to a warmed serving dish and serve, garnished with shredded celery leaves and red chili slices.

VARIATION

Use canned pineapple instead of fresh pineapple if you wish, choosing slices in unsweetened juice in preference to a syrup.

Stir-Fried Salmon with Leeks

Salmon is marinated in a deliciously rich, sweet sauce, stir-fried and served on a bed of crispy leeks.

NUTRITIONAL INFORMATION

Calories . . . . . . .360 Sugars 9g
Protein . . . . .24g Fat 25
Carbohydrate . . . .11g Saturates 4g

35 mins   15 mins

SERVES 4

I N G R E D I E N T S

1 lb/450 g salmon fillet, skinned

2 tbsp sweet soy sauce

2 tbsp tomato catsup

1 tsp rice wine vinegar

1 tbsp raw brown sugar

1 clove garlic, crushed

4 tbsp corn oil

1 lb/450 g leeks, thinly shredded

finely chopped red chilies,
   to garnish

1 Using a sharp knife, cut the salmon into slices. Place the slices of salmon in a shallow, non-metallic dish.

2 Mix together the soy sauce, tomato catsup, rice wine vinegar, sugar, and garlic.

3 Pour the mixture over the salmon, toss well and marinate for about 30 minutes.

4 Meanwhile, heat 3 tablespoons of the corn oil in a large preheated wok.

5 Add the leeks to the wok and cook over a medium-high heat for about 10 minutes, or until the leeks become crispy and tender.

6 Using a slotted spoon, carefully remove the leeks from the wok and transfer to warmed serving plates.

7 Add the remaining oil to the wok. Add the salmon and the marinade to the wok and cook for 2 minutes.

8 Remove the salmon from the wok and spoon over the leeks, garnish with finely chopped red chilies, and serve immediately on warm serving plates.

VARIATION

You can use a fillet of beef instead of the salmon, if you prefer.

Salmon with Pineapple

Presentation plays a major part in Chinese cooking and this dish demonstrates this perfectly with a wonderful combination of colors.

NUTRITIONAL INFORMATION

Calories . . . . . . .347 Sugars 12g
Protein . . . . .24g Fat 20g
Carbohydrate . . .16g Saturates 3g

 10 mins   15 mins

SERVES 4

INGREDIENTS

2 tbsp sunflower oil

1 red onion, sliced

1 orange bell pepper, seeded and sliced

1 green bell pepper, seeded and sliced

1 cup baby corn cobs, halved

1 lb /450 g salmon fillet, skin removed

1 tbsp paprika

8 oz/225 g canned cubed pineapple, drained

1 cup beansprouts

2 tbsp tomato catsup

2 tbsp soy sauce

2 tbsp medium sherry

1 tsp cornstarch

1 Heat the oil in a large preheated wok. Add the onion, bell peppers, and baby corn cobs to the wok, and cook for 5 minutes.

2 Rinse the salmon fillet under cold running water and pat dry with paper towels.

3 Cut the salmon flesh into thin strips and place in a large bowl. Sprinkle with the paprika and toss well to coat.

4 Add the salmon to the wok together with the pineapple and cook for a further 2–3 minutes or until the fish is tender.

5 Add the beansprouts to the wok and toss well.

6 Mix together the tomato catsup, soy sauce, sherry, and cornstarch. Add to the wok and cook until the juices start to thicken. Transfer to warm serving plates and serve immediately.

VARIATION

You can use trout fillets instead of the salmon as an alternative, if you prefer.

Five-Spice Salmon

Five-spice powder is a blend of star anise, fennel, cinnamon, cloves, and Szechuan peppercorns that is often used in Chinese dishes.

NUTRITIONAL INFORMATION

Calories	267	Sugars	.........3g
Protein	........24g	Fat	..........17g
Carbohydrate	....4g	Saturates	......3g

🍲 🍲

❄ 15 mins   🕐 15 mins

SERVES 4

I N G R E D I E N T S

4 salmon fillets, skinned, 4½ oz/125 g each

2 tsp Chinese five-spice powder

1 large leek

1 large carrot

4 oz/115 g snow peas

1-inch/2.5-cm piece fresh root ginger

2 tbsp ginger wine

2 tbsp light soy sauce

1 tbsp vegetable oil

salt and pepper

T O   G A R N I S H

shredded leek

shredded fresh root ginger

shredded carrot

1 Wash the salmon and pat dry on paper towels. Rub the Chinese five-spice powder into both sides of the fish and season with salt and pepper. Set aside until required.

2 Trim the leek, slice it down the center and rinse under cold water to remove any dirt. Finely shred the leek. Peel the carrot and cut it into very thin strips. Top and tail the snow peas and cut them into shreds. Peel the ginger and slice thinly into strips.

3 Place all of the vegetables into a large bowl and toss in the ginger wine and 1 tablespoon of soy sauce.

4 Preheat the broiler to medium. Place the salmon fillets on the rack and brush with the remaining soy sauce. Cook for 2–3 minutes on each side until cooked through.

5 While the salmon is cooking, heat the oil in a non-stick wok or large skillet and cook the vegetables for 5 minutes until just tender. Take care that you do not overcook the vegetables—they should still have bite. Transfer to serving plates. Drain the salmon on paper towels and serve on a bed of cooked vegetables. Garnish with shredded leek, ginger, and carrot.

COOK'S TIP

Five-spice powder is strong and pungent and should be used sparingly.

Spicy Thai Seafood Stew

The fish in this fragrant, curry-like stew can be varied according to taste or availability, but do stick with those which stay firm when cooked.

NUTRITIONAL INFORMATION

Calories 267	Sugars 7g
Protein 42g	Fat 7g
Carbohydrate 9g	Saturates 1g

5 mins   10 mins

SERVES 4

I N G R E D I E N T S

7 oz/200 g squid, cleaned

1 lb 2 oz/500 g firm white fish fillet, preferably monkfish or halibut

1 tbsp sunflower oil

4 shallots, finely chopped

2 garlic cloves, finely chopped

2 tbsp green curry paste

2 small lemongrass stems, finely chopped

1 tsp shrimp paste

scant 2¼ cups coconut milk

7 oz/200 g raw jumbo shrimp, peeled and de-veined

12 fresh clams in shells, cleaned

8 basil leaves, finely shredded

extra basil leaves, to garnish

boiled rice, to serve

COOK'S TIP

If you prefer, fresh mussels in shells can be used instead of clams—add them in Step 4 and follow the recipe.

  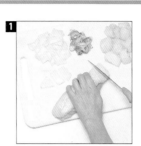  

1 Cut the squid body cavities into thick rings, and the fish into bite-sized chunks.

2 Heat the oil in a large skillet or wok and cook the shallots, garlic, and curry paste for 1–2 minutes. Add the lemongrass and shrimp paste, stir in the coconut milk, and bring to a boil.

3 Reduce the heat until the liquid is simmering gently, then add the white fish, squid and shrimp to the pan, and simmer for 2 minutes.

4 Add the clams and simmer for a further minute until the clams open. Discard any clams that do not open.

5 Scatter the shredded basil leaves over the stew, and serve immediately, garnished with whole basil leaves and spooned over boiled rice.

Tuna & Vegetable Stir-Fry

Fresh tuna is a dark, meaty fish, and is now widely available. It lends itself perfectly to the rich flavors in this recipe.

NUTRITIONAL INFORMATION

Calories	245	Sugars	........11g
Protein	........30g	Fat	...........7g
Carbohydrate	...14g	Saturates	.......1g

10 mins

10 mins

SERVES 4

INGREDIENTS

3 small carrots

1 onion

6 oz/175 g baby corn cobs

2 tbsp corn oil

6 oz/175 g snow peas

1 lb/ 450 g fresh tuna

2 tbsp fish sauce

1 tbsp palm sugar

finely grated zest and juice of 1 orange

2 tbsp sherry

1 tsp cornstarch

rice or noodles, to serve

1 Using a sharp knife, cut the carrots into thin sticks, slice the onion, and halve the baby corn cobs.

2 Heat the corn oil in a large preheated wok or skillet.

3 Add the onion, carrots, snow peas, and baby corn cobs to the wok or skillet and cook for 5 minutes.

4 Using a sharp knife, thinly slice the fresh tuna.

5 Add the tuna slices to the wok or skillet and cook for about 2–3 minutes, or until the tuna turns opaque.

6 Mix together the fish sauce, palm sugar, orange zest and juice, sherry, and cornstarch.

7 Pour the mixture over the tuna and vegetables and cook for 2 minutes, or until the juices thicken. Serve the stir-fry with rice or noodles.

VARIATION

Try using swordfish steaks instead of the tuna. Swordfish steaks are now widely available and are similar in texture to tuna.

Coconut Shrimp

Fan-tail shrimp make any meal a special occasion, especially when cooked in such a delicious crispy coating.

NUTRITIONAL INFORMATION

Calories 236   Sugars 1g
Protein . . . . .27g   Fat 13g
Carbohydrate . . . .3g   Saturates 7g

  5 mins   10 mins

SERVES 4

I N G R E D I E N T S

½ cup shredded coconut

½ cup fresh white breadcrumbs

1 tsp Chinese five-spice powder

½ tsp salt

finely grated zest of 1 lime

1 egg white

1 lb/450 g fan-tail shrimp

sunflower or corn oil

lemon wedges, to garnish

soy or chili sauce, to serve

1 Mix together the shredded coconut, white breadcrumbs, Chinese five-spice powder, salt, and finely grated lime zest in a bowl.

2 Lightly whisk the egg white in a separate bowl.

3 Rinse the shrimp under cold running water, and pat dry with paper towels.

4 Dip the shrimp into the egg white then into the coconut and breadcrumb mixture, so that they are evenly coated.

5 Heat about 2 inches/5 cm of sunflower or corn oil in a large preheated wok.

6 Add the shrimp to the wok and cook for about 5 minutes or until golden and crispy.

7 Remove the shrimp with a slotted spoon and let drain on paper towels.

8 Transfer the coconut shrimp to warm serving dishes and garnish with lemon wedges. Serve immediately with a soy or chili sauce.

COOK'S TIP

Chinese five-spice powder is a mixture of star anise, fennel seeds, cloves, cinnamon bark, and Szechuan pepper. It is very pungent, so should be used sparingly. It will keep indefinitely in an airtight container.

Szechuan Shrimp

Raw shrimp should be used if possible, otherwise add the
ready-cooked shrimp at the beginning of step 3.

NUTRITIONAL INFORMATION

Calories . . . . .315 Sugars 1g
Protein . . . . .16g Fat 27g
Carbohydrate . . . .3g Saturates 3g

5 mins   10 mins

SERVES 4

I N G R E D I E N T S

9–10½ oz/250–300 g raw jumbo shrimp

pinch of salt

½ egg white, lightly beaten

1 tsp cornstarch

2½ cups vegetable oil

fresh cilantro leaves, to garnish

S A U C E

1 tsp finely chopped fresh ginger root

2 scallions, finely chopped

1 garlic clove, finely chopped

3–4 small dried red chilies, seeded and
  chopped

1 tbsp light soy sauce

1 tsp rice wine or dry sherry

1 tbsp tomato paste

1 tbsp oyster sauce

2–3 tbsp vegetable bouillon or water

a few drops of sesame oil

1 Peel the raw shrimp, then mix with
the salt, egg white, and cornstarch
paste until the shrimp are well coated.

2 Heat the oil in a preheated wok or
large skillet until it is smoking, then
deep-fry the shrimp in hot oil for about 1
minute. Remove with a slotted spoon and
drain on paper towels.

3 Pour off the oil, leaving about 1
tablespoon in the wok. Add all the
ingredients for the sauce, in the order
listed, bring to a boil, and stir until smooth
and well blended.

4 Add the shrimp to the sauce and stir
until blended well.

5 Serve the shrimp garnished with fresh
cilantro leaves.

Shrimp & Leek Omelet

This really is a meal in minutes, combining many Chinese ingredients for a truly tasty dish.

NUTRITIONAL INFORMATION

Calories 270   Sugars 1g
Protein . . . . .30g   Fat 15g
Carbohydrate . . . .3g   Saturates 3g

🥪 5 mins   🕐 10 mins

SERVES 4

INGREDIENTS

2 tbsp sunflower oil

4 scallions

12 oz/350 g peeled shrimp

1 cup beansprouts

1 tsp cornstarch

1 tbsp light soy sauce

6 eggs

3 tbsp cold water

1 Heat the sunflower oil in a large preheated wok or skillet.

2 Using a sharp knife, trim the scallions and cut into slices.

3 Add the shrimp, scallions and beansprouts to the wok and cook for 2 minutes.

4 In a small bowl, mix together the cornstarch and soy sauce until all the ingredients are well combined.

5 In a separate bowl, beat the eggs with the water, using a metal fork, and then blend with the cornstarch and soy mixture.

6 Add the egg mixture to the wok and cook for 5–6 minutes, or until the mixture sets.

7 Transfer the omelet to a warm serving plate and cut into quarters to serve.

COOK'S TIP

It is important to use fresh beansprouts for this dish as the canned ones don't have the necessary crunchy texture.

Shrimp with Spicy Tomatoes

Basil and tomatoes are ideal flavorings for shrimp, spiced with cumin seeds and garlic.

NUTRITIONAL INFORMATION

Calories 237	Sugar 9g
Protein 27g	Fat 10g
Carbohydrate 11g	Saturates 1g

 2 mins   20 mins

SERVES 4

I N G R E D I E N T S

2 tbsp corn oil

1 onion

2 cloves garlic, crushed

1 tsp cumin seeds

1 tbsp brown sugar

14 oz/400 g canned chopped tomatoes

1 tbsp sun-dried tomato paste

1 tbsp chopped fresh basil

1 lb/450 g peeled jumbo shrimp

salt and pepper

1 Heat the corn oil in a large preheated wok or heavy-based skillet.

2 Using a sharp knife, finely chop the onion.

3 Add the onion and garlic to the wok and cook for 2–3 minutes, or until softened.

4 Stir in the cumin seeds and cook for 1 minute.

5 Add the sugar, chopped tomatoes, and sun-dried tomato paste to the wok. Bring the mixture to a boil, then reduce the heat and let the sauce simmer for 10 minutes.

6 Add the basil, shrimp, and salt and pepper to taste to the mixture in the wok. Increase the heat and cook for a further 2–3 minutes or until the shrimp are completely cooked through.

COOK'S TIP

Always heat your wok before you add oil or other ingredients. This will prevent anything from sticking to it.

Shrimp with Ginger

Crispy ginger is a wonderful garnish which offsets the spicy shrimp both visually and in flavor.

NUTRITIONAL INFORMATION

Calories 229   Sugars 7g
Protein . . . . .29g   Fat 8g
Carbohydrate . . .10g   Saturates 1g

10 mins   15 mins

SERVES 4

I N G R E D I E N T S

2-inch/5-cm piece fresh root ginger

oil, for frying

1 onion, diced

3 small carrots, diced

1 cup frozen peas

1 cup beansprouts

1 lb/450 g peeled jumbo shrimp

1 tsp Chinese five-spice powder

1 tbsp tomato paste

1 tbsp soy sauce

1 Using a sharp knife, peel the ginger and slice it into very thin sticks.

2 Heat about 1 inch/2.5 cm of oil in a large preheated wok. Add the ginger and cook for 1 minute or until the ginger is crispy. Remove the ginger with a slotted spoon and let drain on paper towels.

3 Drain all of the oil from the wok except for about 2 tablespoons. Add the onion and carrots to the wok and cook for 5 minutes. Add the peas and beansprouts and cook for 2 minutes.

4 Rinse the shrimp under cold running water and pat dry with paper towels.

5 Combine the Chinese five-spice, tomato paste, and soy sauce. Brush the mixture over the shrimp.

6 Add the shrimp to the wok and cook for a further 2 minutes or until the shrimp are completely cooked through. Transfer the shrimp mixture to a warm serving bowl and top with the reserved crispy ginger. Serve immediately.

VARIATION

Use slices of white fish instead of the shrimp as an alternative, if you wish.

Shrimp with Vegetables

In this recipe, a light Chinese omelet is shredded and tossed back into the dish before serving.

NUTRITIONAL INFORMATION

Calories ....258 Sugars 7g
Protein ....21g Fat 15g
Carbohydrate ...10g Saturates 3g

10 mins   15 mins

SERVES 4

I N G R E D I E N T S

8 oz/225 g zucchini

3 tbsp vegetable oil

2 eggs

2 tbsp cold water

3 carrots, grated

1 onion, sliced

1½ cups beansprouts

8 oz/225 g peeled shrimp

2 tbsp soy sauce

pinch of Chinese five-spice powder

¼ cup peanuts, chopped

2 tbsp chopped fresh cilantro

1 Finely grate the zucchini.

2 Heat 1 tablespoon of the vegetable oil in a large preheated wok.

3 Beat the eggs with the water and pour the mixture into the wok and cook for 2–3 minutes or until the egg sets.

4 Remove the omelet from the wok and transfer to a clean board. Fold the omelet, cut it into thin strips and set aside until required.

5 Add the remaining oil to the wok. Add the carrots, onion, and zucchini and cook for 5 minutes.

6 Add the beansprouts and shrimp to the wok and cook for a further 2 minutes, or until the shrimp are heated through.

7 Add the soy sauce, Chinese five-spice powder, and peanuts to the wok, together with the strips of omelet and heat through. Garnish with chopped fresh cilantro and serve.

COOK'S TIP

The water is mixed with the egg in step 3 for a lighter, less rubbery omelet.

Shrimp with Cashews

Cashew nuts are delicious as part of a stir-fry with almost any other ingredient. Use the unsalted variety in cooking.

NUTRITIONAL INFORMATION

Calories ....406 Sugar 3g
Protein ....31g Fat 25g
Carbohydrate ...13g Saturates 4g

5 mins   5 mins

SERVES 4

INGREDIENTS

2 garlic cloves, crushed

1 tbsp cornstarch

pinch of superfine sugar

1 lb/450 g raw jumbo shrimp

4 tbsp vegetable oil

1 leek, sliced

4½ oz/125 g broccoli florets

1 orange bell pepper, seeded and diced

¾ cup unsalted cashew nuts

SAUCE

¾ cup fish bouillon

1 tbsp cornstarch

dash of chili sauce

2 tsp sesame oil

1 tbsp Chinese rice wine

1 Mix together the garlic, cornstarch, and sugar in a bowl.

2 Peel and de-vein the shrimp. Stir the shrimp into the mixture to coat thoroughly.

3 Heat the vegetable oil in a preheated wok and add the shrimp mixture. Cook over a high heat for 20–30 seconds until the shrimp turn pink. Remove the shrimp from the wok with a slotted spoon, drain on paper towels and set aside until required.

4 Add the leek, broccoli, and bell pepper to the wok and cook for 2 minutes.

5 To make the sauce, place the fish bouillon, cornstarch, chili sauce to taste, sesame oil, and Chinese rice wine in a small bowl. Mix until all the ingredients are thoroughly combined.

6 Add the sauce to the wok, together with the cashew nuts. Return the shrimp to the wok and cook for 1 minute to heat through.

7 Transfer the shrimp stir-fry to a warm serving dish and serve immediately.

Shrimp Foo Yung

The classic ingredients of this popular dish are eggs, carrots, and small shrimp. Add extra ingredients such as peas or crabmeat, if desired.

NUTRITIONAL INFORMATION

Calories	240	Sugars	.........1g
Protein	........22g	Fat	..........16g
Carbohydrate	....1g	Saturates	.......3g

5 mins   10 mins

SERVES 4

I N G R E D I E N T S

2 tbsp vegetable oil

1 carrot, grated

5 eggs, beaten

8 oz/225 g raw small shrimp, peeled

1 tbsp light soy sauce

pinch of Chinese five-spice powder

2 scallions, chopped

2 tsp sesame seeds

1 tsp sesame oil

COOK'S TIP

If only cooked shrimp are available, add them just before the end of cooking, but make sure they are fully incorporated into the foo yung. They require only heating through. Overcooking will make them chewy and tasteless.

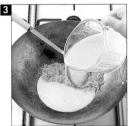  

1 Heat the vegetable oil in a preheated wok or skillet, swirling it around until the oil is really hot.

2 Add the grated carrot and cook for 1–2 minutes.

3 Push the carrot to one side of the wok or skillet and add the beaten eggs. Cook, stirring gently, for 1–2 minutes.

4 Stir the small shrimp, light soy sauce, and Chinese five-spice powder into the mixture in the wok. Cook the mixture for 2–3 minutes, or until the small shrimp change color and the mixture feels almost dry in consistency.

5 Turn the small shrimp foo yung out on to a warm plate and sprinkle the scallions, sesame seeds, and sesame oil on top. Serve immediately.

Cantonese Shrimp

This shrimp dish is very simple and is ideal for supper or lunch when time is short.

NUTRITIONAL INFORMATION

Calories ....460 Sugar 3g
Protein ....53g Fat 24
Carbohydrate ....6g Saturates 5g

🧊 10 mins   🕐 20 mins

SERVES 4

I N G R E D I E N T S

5 tbsp vegetable oil

4 garlic cloves, crushed

1½ lb/675 g raw shrimp, shelled
    and de-veined

4 tsp chopped fresh root ginger

6 oz/175 g lean pork, diced

1 leek, sliced

3 eggs, beaten

rice, to serve

S A U C E

2 tbsp Chinese rice wine or dry sherry

2 tbsp light soy sauce

2 tsp superfine sugar

⅔ cup fish bouillon

4½ tsp cornstarch

3 tbsp water

T O   G A R N I S H

shredded leek

sliced red bell pepper

1 Heat 2 tablespoons of the vegetable
  oil in a preheated wok.

2 Add the garlic to the wok and cook
  for 30 seconds.

3 Add the shrimp to the wok and cook
  for 5 minutes, or until they change

color. Remove the shrimp from the wok or skillet with a slotted spoon, set aside and keep warm.

4 Add the remaining oil to the wok and heat, swirling the oil around the bottom of the wok until it is really hot.

5 Add the ginger, diced pork, and leek to the wok and cook over a medium heat for 4–5 minutes, or until the pork is lightly colored and sealed.

6 To make the sauce, add the rice wine or sherry, soy sauce, superfine sugar, and fish bouillon to the wok and stir to blend.

7 In a small bowl, blend the cornstarch with the water to form a smooth paste and stir it into the wok. Cook, stirring, until the sauce thickens and clears.

8 Return the shrimp to the wok and add the beaten eggs. Cook for 5–6 minutes, gently stirring occasionally, until the eggs set.

9 Transfer to a warm serving dish, garnish with shredded leek and sliced bell pepper and serve with rice.

Scallop Pancakes

Scallops, like most shellfish, require very little cooking, and this original dish is a perfect example of how to use shellfish to its full potential.

NUTRITIONAL INFORMATION

Calories	240	Sugars	.........1g
Protein	........29g	Fat	..........9g
Carbohydrate	....11g	Saturates	.......1g

5 mins ⏱ 30 mins

SERVES 4

I N G R E D I E N T S

3½ oz/100 g fine green beans

1 red chili

1 lb/450 g scallops, without roe

1 egg

3 scallions, sliced

generous ⅓ cup rice flour

1 tbsp fish sauce

oil

salt

sweet chili dip, to serve

1 Using a sharp knife, trim the green beans and slice them very thinly.

2 Using a sharp knife, seed and very finely chop the red chili.

3 Bring a small pan of lightly salted water to a boil. Add the green beans to the pan and cook for 3–4 minutes or until just softened.

4 Roughly chop the scallops and place them in a large bowl. Add the cooked beans to the scallops.

5 Mix the egg with the scallions, rice flour, fish sauce, and chili until well combined. Add to the scallops and mix well.

6 Heat about 1-inch/2.5-cm of oil in a large preheated wok. Add a ladleful of the mixture to the wok and cook for 5 minutes until golden and set.

7 Remove the pancake from the wok and leave to drain on paper towels. Keep warm while cooking the remaining pancake mixture. Serve the pancakes hot with a sweet chili dip.

VARIATION

You could use prawns or shelled clams instead of the scallops, if you prefer.

Seared Scallops

Scallops have a terrific, subtle flavor which is complemented in this dish by the buttery sauce.

NUTRITIONAL INFORMATION

Calories 272   Sugars 0g
Protein . . . . .28g   Fat 17g
Carbohydrate . . . .2g   Saturates 8g

🍴 5 mins   🕐 10 mins

SERVES 4

I N G R E D I E N T S

1 lb/450 g fresh scallops, without roe, or
    the same amount of frozen scallops,
    thawed thoroughly

6 scallions

2 tbsp vegetable oil

1 green chili, seeded and sliced

3 tbsp sweet soy sauce

2 tbsp butter, cubed

1 Rinse the scallops thoroughly under cold running water, drain, and pat the scallops dry with paper towels.

2 Using a sharp knife, slice each scallop in half horizontally.

3 Using a sharp knife, trim and slice the scallions.

4 Heat the vegetable oil in a large preheated wok or heavy-based skillet, swirling the oil around the bottom of the wok or skillet until it is really hot.

5 Add the sliced green chili, scallions, and scallops to the wok, and cook over a high heat for 4–5 minutes, or until the scallops are just cooked through. If using frozen scallops, be sure not to overcook them as they will easily disintegrate.

6 Add the soy sauce and butter to the scallop stir-fry and heat through until the butter melts.

7 Transfer to warm serving bowls and serve hot.

COOK'S TIP

If you buy scallops on the shell, slide a knife underneath the membrane to loosen it and cut off the tough muscle that holds the scallop to the shell. Discard the black stomach sac and intestinal vein.

Scallops in Ginger Sauce

Scallops are both attractive and delicious. Cooked with ginger and orange, this dish is perfect served with plain rice.

NUTRITIONAL INFORMATION

Calories	216	Sugars	....4g
Protein	....30g	Fat	....8g
Carbohydrate	....8g	Saturates	....1g

5 mins   10 mins

SERVES 4

INGREDIENTS

2 tbsp vegetable oil

1 lb/450 g scallops, cleaned and halved

2 tsp finely chopped fresh root ginger

3 garlic cloves, crushed

2 leeks, shredded

¾ cup peas

4½ oz/125 g canned bamboo shoots, drained and rinsed

2 tbsp light soy sauce

2 tbsp unsweetened orange juice

1 tsp superfine sugar

orange zest, to garnish

1 Heat the vegetable oil in a preheated wok or large skillet. Add the scallops and cook for 1–2 minutes. Remove the scallops from the wok with a slotted spoon, keep warm and set aside until required.

2 Add the ginger and garlic to the wok and cook for 30 seconds. Stir in the leeks and peas and cook, stirring, for a further 2 minutes.

3 Add the bamboo shoots and return the scallops to the wok. Stir gently to mix without breaking up the scallops.

4 Stir in the soy sauce, orange juice, and superfine sugar and cook for 1–2 minutes.

5 Transfer the stir-fry to a serving dish, garnish with the orange zest and serve immediately.

COOK'S TIP

The edible parts of a scallop are the round white muscle and the orange and white coral or roe. The frilly skirt surrounding the muscle—the gills and mantle—may be used for making shellfish bouillon. All other parts should be discarded.

Mussels with Lettuce

Mussels require careful preparation but very little cooking. They are available fresh or in vacuum packs when out of season.

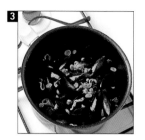

NUTRITIONAL INFORMATION

Calories	205	Sugars	.......0.3g
Protein	........31g	Fat	...........9g
Carbohydrate	....1g	Saturates	.......4g

  15 mins   5 mins

SERVES 4

I N G R E D I E N T S

2 lb 4 oz/1 kg mussels in their shells, scrubbed

2 stems lemongrass

1 Iceberg lettuce

2 tbsp lemon juice

generous ⅓ cup water

2 tbsp butter

finely grated zest of 1 lemon

2 tbsp oyster sauce

1 Place the scrubbed mussels in a large pan.

2 Using a sharp knife, thinly slice the lemongrass and shred the lettuce.

3 Add the lemongrass, lemon juice, and water to the pan of mussels, cover with a tight-fitting lid, and cook for 5 minutes or until the mussels have opened. Discard any mussels that do not open.

4 Carefully remove the cooked mussels from their shells using a fork, and set aside until required.

5 Heat the butter in a large preheated wok or skillet. Add the lettuce and finely grated lemon zest to the wok or frying pan skillet and cook for

2 minutes, or until the lettuce begins to wilt.

6 Add the oyster sauce to the mixture in the wok and heat through, stirring well until the sauce is thoroughly incorporated in the mixture.

7 Transfer the mixture in the wok to a warm serving dish and serve immediately.

COOK'S TIP

When using fresh mussels, be sure to discard any opened mussels before scrubbing and any unopened mussels after cooking.

Mussels in Black Bean Sauce

This dish looks so impressive, the combination of colors making it look almost too good to eat!

NUTRITIONAL INFORMATION

Calories	174	Sugars	.........4g
Protein	........19g	Fat	..........8g
Carbohydrate	....6g	Saturates	.......1g

🦀 🦀 🦀

🍲 5 mins   🕐 10 mins

SERVES 4

I N G R E D I E N T S

12 oz/350 g leeks

12 oz/350 g cooked, shelled green-lipped mussels

1 tsp cumin seeds

2 tbsp vegetable oil

2 cloves garlic, crushed

1 red bell pepper, seeded and sliced

1¾ oz/50 g canned bamboo shoots, drained

6 oz/175 g baby spinach

5¾ oz/160 g jar black bean sauce

1 Using a sharp knife, trim the leeks and shred them.

2 Place the cooked green-lipped mussels in a large bowl, sprinkle with the cumin seeds and toss well to coat all over. Set aside until required.

3 Heat the vegetable oil in a preheated wok, swirling the oil around the bottom of the wok until it is really hot.

4 Add the shredded leeks, garlic, and sliced red bell pepper to the wok and cook for 5 minutes, or until the vegetables are tender.

5 Add the bamboo shoots, baby spinach leaves, and cooked green-lipped mussels to the wok and cook for about 2 minutes.

6 Pour the black bean sauce over the ingredients in the wok, toss well to coat all the ingredients in the sauce and let simmer for a few seconds, stirring occasionally.

7 Transfer the stir-fry to warm serving bowls and serve immediately.

COOK'S TIP

If the green-lipped mussels are not available they can be bought shelled in cans and jars from most large food stores.

Oysters with Bean Curd

Oysters are often eaten raw, but are delicious when quickly cooked as in this recipe, and mixed with salt and citrus flavors.

NUTRITIONAL INFORMATION

Calories 175	Sugars 2g
Protein 18g	Fat 10g
Carbohydrate 3g	Saturates 1g

5 mins   10 mins

SERVES 4

I N G R E D I E N T S

8 oz/225 g leeks

12 oz/350 g firm bean curd

2 tbsp sunflower oil

12 oz/350 g shelled oysters

2 tbsp fresh lemon juice

1 tsp cornstarch

2 tbsp light soy sauce

generous ⅓ cup fish bouillon

2 tbsp chopped fresh cilantro

1 tsp finely grated lemon zest

1 Using a sharp knife, trim and slice the leeks.

2 Cut the bean curd into bite-sized pieces.

3 Heat the sunflower oil in a large preheated wok or skillet. Add the leeks to the wok and cook for about 2 minutes.

4 Add the bean curd and oysters to the wok or skillet and cook for 1–2 minutes.

5 Mix together the lemon juice, cornstarch, light soy sauce, and fish bouillon in a small bowl, stirring until well blended.

6 Pour the cornstarch mixture into the wok and cook, stirring occasionally, until the juices start to thicken.

7 Transfer to serving bowls and scatter the cilantro and lemon zest on top. Serve immediately.

VARIATION

Shelled clams or mussels could be used instead of the oysters, if you prefer.

Crab Claws with Chili

Crab claws are frequently used in Chinese cooking, and look sensational. They are perfect with this delicious chili sauce.

NUTRITIONAL INFORMATION

Calories 154	Sugar 3g
Protein 16g	Fat 7g
Carbohydrate 8g	Saturates 1g

5 mins

10 mins

SERVES 4

I N G R E D I E N T S

1 lb 9 oz/700 g crab claws

1 tbsp corn oil

2 cloves garlic, crushed

1 tbsp grated fresh root ginger

3 red chilies, seeded and finely chopped

2 tbsp sweet chili sauce

3 tbsp tomato catsup

1¼ cups cooled fish bouillon

1 tbsp cornstarch

salt and pepper

1 tbsp snipped fresh chives

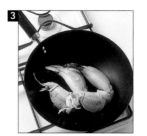

1 Gently crack the crab claws with a nut cracker. This process will allow the flavors of the chili, garlic, and ginger to fully penetrate the crab meat.

2 Heat the corn oil in a large preheated wok.

3 Add the crab claws to the wok and cook for about 5 minutes.

4 Add the garlic, ginger, and chilies to the wok and cook for 1 minute, tossing the crab claws to coat all over.

5 Mix together the sweet chili sauce, tomato catsup, fish bouillon, and cornstarch in a small bowl. Add this mixture to the wok and cook, stirring occasionally, until the sauce starts to thicken and clear.

6 Season the mixture in the wok with salt and pepper to taste.

7 Transfer the crab claws and chili sauce to warm serving dishes, garnish with snipped fresh chives and serve.

COOK'S TIP

If crab claws are not easily available, use a whole crab, cut into eight pieces, instead.

Crab with Napa Cabbage

The delicate flavor of Napa cabbage and crab meat are enhanced by the coconut milk in this recipe.

NUTRITIONAL INFORMATION

Calories 109   Sugars 1g
Protein . . . . .11g   Fat 6g
Carbohydrate . . . .2g   Saturates 1g

5 mins   10 mins

SERVES 4

INGREDIENTS

8 oz/225 g shiitake mushrooms

2 tbsp vegetable oil

2 cloves garlic, crushed

6 scallions, sliced

1 head Napa cabbage, shredded

1 tbsp mild curry paste

6 tbsp coconut milk

7 oz/200 g canned white crab meat, drained

1 tsp chili flakes

1 Using a sharp knife, cut the mushrooms into slices.

2 Heat the vegetable oil in a large preheated wok or heavy-based skillet.

COOK'S TIP

Shiitake mushrooms are now readily available in the fresh vegetable section of most large food stores.

3 Add the mushrooms and garlic to the wok or skillet and cook for 3 minutes or until the mushrooms have softened.

4 Add the scallions and shredded Napa cabbage to the wok and cook until the leaves have wilted.

5 Mix together the mild curry paste and coconut milk in a small bowl.

6 Add the curry paste and coconut milk mixture to the wok, together with the crab meat and chili flakes. Mix together until well combined.

7 Heat the mixture in the wok until the juices start to bubble.

8 Transfer the crab and vegetable stir-fry to warm serving bowls and serve immediately.

Crab in Ginger Sauce

In this recipe, the crabs are served in the shell for ease and visual effect and coated in a glossy ginger sauce.

NUTRITIONAL INFORMATION

Calories 125   Sugars 2g
Protein . . . . .8g   Fat 8g
Carbohydrate . . . .5g   Saturates 1g

🦀 🦀 🦀

10 mins   10 mins

SERVES 4

I N G R E D I E N T S

2 small cooked crabs

2 tbsp vegetable oil

6 tsp grated fresh root ginger

2 garlic cloves, thinly sliced

1 green bell pepper, seeded and cut into
   thin strips

6 scallions, cut into 1-inch/2.5-cm lengths

2 tbsp dry sherry

½ tsp sesame oil

⅔ cup fish bouillon

1 tsp light brown sugar

2 tsp cornstarch

⅔ cup water

1 Rinse the crabs and gently loosen around the shell at the top. Using a sharp knife, cut away the grey tissue and discard. Rinse the crabs again.

2 Twist off the legs and claws from the crabs. Using a pair of crab claw crackers or a cleaver, gently crack the claws to break through the shell to expose the flesh. Remove and discard any loose pieces of shell.

3 Separate the body and discard the inedible lungs and sac. Cut down the center of each crab to separate the body into two pieces and then cut each of these in half again.

4 Heat the oil in a preheated wok. Add the ginger and garlic and cook for 1 minute. Add the crab pieces and cook for a further minute.

5 Stir in the bell pepper, scallions, sherry, sesame oil, bouillon, and sugar. Bring to a boil, reduce the heat, cover, and simmer for 3–4 minutes.

6 Blend the cornstarch with the water and stir into the wok. Bring to a boil, stirring, until the sauce is thickened and clear. Transfer to a warm serving dish and serve immediately.

VARIATION

If preferred, remove the crabmeat from the shells prior to stir-frying and add to the wok with the bell pepper.

Crispy Squid

Squid tubes are classically used in Chinese cooking and are most attractive when presented as in the following recipe.

NUTRITIONAL INFORMATION

Calories . . . . . . .156 Sugars 0g
Protein . . . . .17g Fat 6g
Carbohydrate . . . .7g Saturates 8g

   10 mins 🕐 10 mins

SERVES 4

INGREDIENTS

1 lb/450 g squid, cleaned

4 tbsp cornstarch

1 tsp salt

1 tsp freshly ground black pepper

1 tsp chili flakes

peanut oil

dipping sauce, to serve

1 Using a sharp knife, remove the tentacles from the squid and trim. Slice the bodies down one side and open out to give a flat piece.

2 Score the flat pieces with a criss-cross pattern then cut each piece into 4.

3 Mix together the cornstarch, salt, pepper, and chili flakes.

4 Place the salt and pepper mixture in a large polythene bag. Add the squid pieces and shake the bag thoroughly to coat the squid in the flour mixture.

5 Heat about 2 inches/5 cm of peanut oil in a large preheated wok.

6 Add the squid pieces to the wok and cook, in batches, for about 2 minutes, or until the squid pieces start to curl up.

Do not overcook or the squid will become tough and inedible.

7 Remove the squid pieces with a slotted spoon, transfer to paper towels and let drain thoroughly.

8 Transfer the fried squid pieces to serving plates and serve immediately with a dipping sauce.

COOK'S TIP

Squid tubes may be purchased frozen if they are not available fresh. They are usually ready-cleaned and are easy to use. Ensure that they are completely defrosted before cooking.

Squid with Black Bean Sauce

Squid really is wonderful if quickly cooked as in this recipe, and contrary to popular belief it is not tough and rubbery unless it is overcooked.

NUTRITIONAL INFORMATION

Calories ....180 Sugars 2g
Protein ....19g Fat 7g
Carbohydrate ...10g Saturates 1g

5 mins   20 mins

SERVES 4

INGREDIENTS

1 lb/450 g squid rings

2 tbsp all-purpose flour

½ tsp salt

1 green bell pepper

2 tbsp peanut oil

1 red onion, sliced

5¾ oz/160 g jar black bean sauce

1 Rinse the squid rings under cold running water and pat dry thoroughly with paper towels.

2 Place the all-purpose flour and salt in a bowl and mix together. Add the squid rings and toss until they are evenly coated.

3 Using a sharp knife, seed the bell pepper. Slice the bell pepper into thin strips.

4 Heat the peanut oil in a large preheated wok or heavy-based skillet, swirling the oil around the bottom of the wok until it is really hot.

5 Add the bell pepper slices and red onion to the wok or skillet and cook for about 2 minutes, or until the vegetables are just beginning to soften.

6 Add the squid rings to the wok or skillet and cook for a further 5

minutes, or until the squid is cooked through. Be careful not to overcook the squid.

7 Add the black bean sauce to the wok and heat through until the juices are bubbling. Transfer the squid stir-fry to warm serving bowls and serve immediately.

COOK'S TIP

Serve this recipe with fried rice or noodles tossed in soy sauce, if you wish.

Squid with Oyster Sauce

Squid is a delicious fish, which, if prepared and cooked correctly, is a quick cooking, attractive, and tasty ingredient.

NUTRITIONAL INFORMATION

Calories ....320 Sugars 1g
Protein ....18g Fat 26g
Carbohydrate ....2g Saturates 3g

 5 mins   15 mins

SERVES 4

INGREDIENTS

1 lb/450 g squid

⅔ cup vegetable oil

1 tsp grated fresh root ginger

2 oz/60 g snow peas

5 tbsp hot fish bouillon

red bell pepper triangles, to garnish

SAUCE

1 tbsp oyster sauce

1 tbsp light soy sauce

pinch of superfine sugar

1 garlic clove, crushed

1 To prepare the squid, cut down the center of the body lengthwise. Flatten the squid out, inside uppermost, and score a lattice design deep into the flesh, using a sharp knife.

2 To make the sauce, combine the oyster sauce, soy sauce, sugar, and garlic in a small bowl. Stir to dissolve the sugar and set aside until required.

3 Heat the oil in a preheated wok until almost smoking. Lower the heat slightly, add the squid and cook until they curl up. Remove with a slotted spoon and drain thoroughly on paper towels.

4 Pour off all but 2 tablespoons of the oil and return the wok to the heat. Add the ginger and snow peas and cook for 1 minute.

5 Return the squid to the wok and pour in the sauce and hot fish bouillon. Let simmer for 3 minutes until thickened. Transfer to a warm serving dish, garnish with bell pepper triangles and serve immediately.

COOK'S TIP

Take care not to overcook the squid, otherwise it will be rubbery and unappetizing.

Seafood Stir-Fry

This combination of assorted seafood and tender vegetables flavored with ginger makes an ideal light meal served with thread noodles.

NUTRITIONAL INFORMATION

Calories	226	Sugars	.........5g
Protein	........35g	Fat	..........7g
Carbohydrate	....6g	Saturates	......1g

5 mins   15 mins

SERVES 4

I N G R E D I E N T S

3½ oz/100 g small, thin asparagus spears, trimmed

1 tbsp sunflower oil

1-inch/2.5-cm piece fresh root ginger, cut into thin strips

1 leek, shredded

2 carrots, cut into very thin strips

3½ oz/100 g baby corn cobs, quartered lengthwise

2 tbsp light soy sauce

1 tbsp oyster sauce

1 tsp clear honey

1 lb/450 g cooked, assorted shellfish, thawed if frozen

freshly cooked egg noodles, to serve

TO GARNISH

4 cooked jumbo shrimp

small bunch snipped fresh chives

1 Bring a small pan of water to a boil and blanch the asparagus for 1–2 minutes.

2 Drain the asparagus, set aside and keep warm.

3 Heat the oil in a wok or large skillet and cook the ginger, leek, carrot, and corn for about 3 minutes. Do not allow the vegetables to brown.

4 Add the soy sauce, oyster sauce, and honey to the wok or skillet.

5 Stir in the cooked shellfish and continue to cook for 2–3 minutes until the vegetables are just tender and the shellfish are thoroughly heated through. Add the blanched asparagus and cook for about 2 minutes.

6 To serve, pile the cooked noodles on to 4 warm serving plates and spoon the seafood and vegetable stir-fry over them.

7 Garnish with the cooked shrimp and snipped fresh chives and serve immediately on warm serving plates.

Vegetables

Vegetables play an important role in wok and stir-fry cooking in the Far East and are used extensively in all meals. It is perfectly possible to enjoy a meal from a selection of the following recipes contained in this chapter without meat or fish. Baby corn cobs, Napa cabbage and green beans, young spinach leaves, and bok choy can all bring a unique flavor and freshness to a stir-fried dish.

Native Far Eastern people enjoy their vegetables crisp, so cooking times in this chapter reflect this factor in order to bring out the flavors and textures of the ingredients used.

When selecting vegetables for cooking, great importance is attached to the freshness of the ingredients used. Always buy firm, crisp vegetables, and cook them as soon as possible. Another point to remember is to wash the vegetables just before cutting and to cook them as soon as they have been cut so that the vitamin content is not lost.

Napa Cabbage in Honey

Napa cabbage is rather similar to lettuce in that the leaves are delicate with a sweet flavor.

NUTRITIONAL INFORMATION

Calories	121	Sugars 6g
Protein	. . . . .5g	Fat 7g
Carbohydrate	. . .10g	Saturates 1g

5 mins   10 mins

SERVES 4

INGREDIENTS

1 lb/450 g Napa cabbage

1 tbsp peanut oil

1 tsp grated fresh root ginger

2 garlic cloves, crushed

1 fresh red chili, sliced

1 tbsp Chinese rice wine or dry sherry

4½ tsp light soy sauce

1 tbsp clear honey

½ cup orange juice

1 tbsp sesame oil

2 tsp sesame seeds

orange zest, to garnish

COOK'S TIP

Single-flower honey has a better, more individual flavor than blended honey. Acacia honey is typically Chinese, but you could also try clover, lemon blossom, lime flower, or orange blossom honey.

 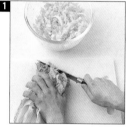 

1 Separate the Napa cabbage and shred the leaves finely, using a sharp knife.

2 Heat the peanut oil in a preheated wok. Add the ginger, garlic, and chili to the wok and cook the mixture for about 30 seconds.

3 Add the Napa cabbage, Chinese rice wine or sherry, soy sauce, honey, and orange juice to the wok. Reduce the heat and let simmer for 5 minutes.

4 Add the sesame oil to the wok, sprinkle the sesame seeds on top and mix to combine.

5 Transfer to a warm serving dish, garnish with the orange zest and serve immediately.

Green Stir-Fry

The basis of this recipe is bok choy, also known as Chinese greens.
If unavailable, use Swiss chard or Savoy cabbage instead.

NUTRITIONAL INFORMATION

Calories 107	Sugars 6g
Protein 4g	Fat 8g
Carbohydrate 6g	Saturates 1g

5 mins   10 mins

SERVES 4

I N G R E D I E N T S

2 tbsp peanut oil

2 garlic cloves, crushed

½ tsp ground star anise

1 tsp salt

12 oz/350 g bok choy, shredded

8 oz/225 g baby spinach

1 oz/25 g snow peas

1 celery stalk, sliced

1 green bell pepper, seeded and sliced

scant ¼ cup vegetable bouillon

1 tsp sesame oil

1 Heat the peanut oil in a preheated wok or large skillet, swirling the oil around the bottom of the wok until it is really hot.

2 Add the crushed garlic to the wok or skillet and cook for about 30 seconds.

3 Stir in the ground star anise, salt, shredded bok choy, spinach, snow peas, celery, and green bell pepper and cook for 3–4 minutes.

4 Add the vegetable bouillon, cover the wok and cook for 3–4 minutes.

5 Remove the lid from the wok and stir in the sesame oil. Mix thoroughly to combine all the ingredients.

6 Transfer the green vegetable stir-fry to a warm serving dish and serve.

COOK'S TIP

Star anise is an important ingredient in Chinese cuisine. The attractive star-shaped pods are often used whole to add a decorative garnish to dishes. The flavor is similar to licorice, but with spicy undertones, and is quite strong.

Crispy Cabbage & Almonds

This dish is better known as crispy seaweed. It does not actually contain seaweed, but consists of bok choy or collard greens.

NUTRITIONAL INFORMATION

Calories 431   Sugars 17g
Protein . . . . .9g   Fat 37g
Carbohydrate . . .17g   Saturates 4g

🍲 10 mins   🕙 10 mins

SERVES 4

I N G R E D I E N T S

2 lb 12 oz/1.25 kg bok choy or
  collard greens

3 cups vegetable oil

¾ cup blanched almonds

1 tsp salt

1 tbsp light brown sugar

pinch of ground cinnamon

1 Separate the leaves from the bok choy or collard greens and rinse them well. Drain thoroughly and pat dry with paper towels.

2 Shred the collard greens into thin strips, using a sharp knife.

3 Heat the vegetable oil in a preheated wok or large, heavy-based skillet until the oil is almost smoking.

4 Reduce the heat and add the bok choy or collard greens. Cook for 2–3 minutes, or until the greens begin to float in the oil and are crisp.

5 Remove the greens from the oil with a slotted spoon and leave to drain thoroughly on paper towels.

6 Add the blanched almonds to the oil in the wok and cook for 30 seconds. Remove the almonds from the oil with a slotted spoon and drain thoroughly on paper towels.

7 Mix together the salt, light brown sugar, and ground cinnamon and sprinkle on to the greens.

8 Toss the almonds into the greens.

9 Transfer the greens and almonds to a warm serving dish and serve immediately.

COOK'S TIP

Ensure that the greens are completely dry before adding them to the oil, otherwise it will spit. The greens will not become crisp if they are wet when placed in the oil.

Creamy Green Vegetables

This dish is very quick to make. A dash of cream is added to the sauce, but this may be omitted, if preferred.

NUTRITIONAL INFORMATION

Calories 111   Sugars 2g
Protein ....5g   Fat 8g
Carbohydrate ....7g   Saturates 2g

5 mins   20 mins

SERVES 4

I N G R E D I E N T S

1 lb/450 g Napa cabbage, shredded

2 tbsp peanut oil

2 leeks, shredded

4 garlic cloves, crushed

1¼ cups vegetable bouillon

1 tbsp light soy sauce

2 tsp cornstarch

4 tsp water

2 tbsp light cream or unsweetened yogurt

1 tbsp chopped cilantro

1 Blanch the Napa cabbage in boiling water for 30 seconds. Drain, rinse under cold running water, then drain thoroughly again.

2 Heat the oil in a preheated wok and add the cabbage, leeks, and garlic. Cook for 2–3 minutes.

3 Add the bouillon and soy sauce to the wok, reduce the heat to low, cover and simmer for 10 minutes.

4 Remove the vegetables from the wok with a slotted spoon and set aside. Bring the bouillon to a boil and boil vigorously until reduced by about half.

5 Blend the cornstarch with the water and stir into the wok. Bring to a boil, and cook, stirring constantly, until thickened and clear.

6 Reduce the heat and stir in the vegetables and cream or yogurt. Cook over a low heat for 1 minute.

7 Transfer to a serving dish, sprinkle over the chopped cilantro and serve.

COOK'S TIP

Do not boil the sauce once the cream or yogurt has been added, as it will separate.

Stir-Fried Chili Cucumber

Warm cucumbers are absolutely delicious, especially when combined with the heat of chili and the flavor of ginger.

NUTRITIONAL INFORMATION

Calories 67	Sugars 4g
Protein 1g	Fat 5g
Carbohydrate 5g	Saturates 1g

30 mins · 5 mins

SERVES 4

I N G R E D I E N T S

2 medium cucumbers

2 tsp salt

1 tbsp vegetable oil

2 garlic cloves, crushed

1 tsp grated fresh root ginger

2 fresh red chilies, chopped

2 scallions, chopped

1 tsp yellow bean sauce

1 tbsp clear honey

½ cup water

1 tsp sesame oil

1 Peel the cucumbers and cut in half lengthwise. Scrape the seeds from the center with a teaspoon or melon baller and discard.

2 Cut the cucumber into strips and place on a plate. Sprinkle the salt over the cucumber strips and set aside for 20 minutes. Rinse well under cold running water and pat dry with paper towels.

3 Heat the vegetable oil in a preheated wok or large skillet until it is almost smoking. Lower the heat slightly and add the garlic, ginger, chilies, and scallions, and cook for 30 seconds.

4 Add the cucumbers to the wok, together with the yellow bean sauce and honey and cook for 30 seconds.

5 Add the water and cook over a high heat until most of the water has evaporated.

6 Sprinkle the sesame oil over the stir-fry. Transfer to a warm serving dish and serve immediately.

COOK'S TIP

The cucumber is sprinkled with salt and left to stand in order to draw out the excess water, thus preventing a soggy meal!

Garlic Spinach

This has to be one of the simplest recipes, yet it is so tasty. Spinach is fried with garlic and lemongrass and tossed in soy sauce and sugar.

NUTRITIONAL INFORMATION

Calories	118	Sugars	. . . . .6g
Protein	. . . . .7g	Fat	. . . . .7g
Carbohydrate	. . . .7g	Saturates	. . . . . . .1g

  5 mins   🕐 10 mins

SERVES 4

I N G R E D I E N T S

2 garlic cloves

1 tsp lemongrass

2 lb/900 g fresh spinach

2 tbsp peanut oil

salt

1 tbsp dark soy sauce

2 tsp brown sugar

1 Peel the garlic cloves and crush them with a pestle and mortar. Set aside until required.

2 Using a sharp knife, finely chop the lemongrass. Set aside until required.

3 Carefully remove the stems from the spinach. Rinse the spinach leaves and drain them thoroughly, patting them dry with paper towels.

4 Heat the peanut oil in a preheated wok or large skillet until it is almost smoking.

5 Reduce the heat slightly, add the garlic and lemongrass, and cook for 30 seconds.

6 Add the spinach leaves and a pinch of salt to the wok or skillet and cook for 2–3 minutes, or until the spinach leaves

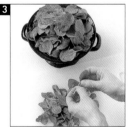  

have just wilted.

7 Stir the dark soy sauce and brown sugar into the mixture in the wok or skillet and cook for a further 3–4 minutes.

8 Transfer the garlic spinach to a warm serving dish and serve as an accompaniment to a main dish.

COOK'S TIP

Lemongrass is available fresh, dried, and canned or bottled. Dried lemongrass must be soaked for 2 hours before using. The stems are hard and are usually used whole and removed from the dish before serving. The roots can be crushed or finely chopped.

Green Bean Stir-Fry

These beans are simply cooked in a spicy, hot sauce for a tasty and very easy recipe.

NUTRITIONAL INFORMATION

Calories 86   Sugars 4g
Protein . . . . .2g   Fat 6g
Carbohydrates . . . .6g   Saturates 1g

5 mins   5 mins

SERVES 4

INGREDIENTS

1 lb/450 g thin green beans

2 fresh red chilies

2 tbsp peanut oil

½ tsp ground star anise

1 garlic clove, crushed

2 tbsp light soy sauce

2 tsp clear honey

½ tsp sesame oil

1 Using a sharp knife, cut the green beans in half.

2 Slice the fresh chilies, removing the seeds first if you prefer a milder dish.

3 Heat the oil in a preheated wok or large skillet until it is almost smoking.

4 Lower the heat slightly, add the halved green beans to the wok and cook for 1 minute.

5 Add the sliced red chilies, star anise, and garlic to the wok and cook for a further 30 seconds.

6 Mix together the soy sauce, honey, and sesame oil in a small bowl.

7 Stir the sauce mixture into the wok. Cook for 2 minutes, tossing the beans to ensure that they are thoroughly coated in the sauce.

8 Transfer the mixture in the wok or pan to a warm serving dish and serve immediately.

VARIATION

This recipe is surprisingly delicious made with Brussels sprouts instead of green beans. Trim the sprouts, then shred them finely. Cook the sprouts in hot oil for 2 minutes, then proceed with the recipe from step 4.

Gingered Broccoli

Ginger and broccoli are a perfect combination of flavors and make an exceptionally tasty side dish.

NUTRITIONAL INFORMATION

Calories	118	Sugars	3g
Protein	8g	Fat	7g
Carbohydrate	6g	Saturates	1g

5 mins   15 mins

SERVES 4

INGREDIENTS

2-inch/5-cm piece fresh root ginger

2 tbsp peanut oil

1 garlic clove, crushed

1½ lb/675 g broccoli florets

1 leek, sliced

2¾ oz/75 g canned water chestnuts, halved

½ tsp superfine sugar

½ cup vegetable bouillon

1 tsp dark soy sauce

1 tsp cornstarch

2 tsp water

1 Using a sharp knife, finely chop the ginger. (Alternatively, cut the ginger into larger strips, to be discarded later, for a slightly milder ginger flavor.)

2 Heat the peanut oil in a preheated wok. Add the garlic and ginger and cook for 30 seconds.

3 Add the broccoli, leek, and water chestnuts and cook for a further 3–4 minutes.

4 Add the superfine sugar, vegetable bouillon, and dark soy sauce to the wok, reduce the heat and simmer for 4–5 minutes, or until the broccoli is almost cooked.

5 Blend the cornstarch with the water to form a smooth paste and stir it into the wok. Bring to a boil and cook, stirring constantly, for 1 minute or until thickened.

6 If using larger strips of ginger, remove from the wok and discard.

7 Transfer the vegetables to a serving dish and serve immediately.

VARIATION

Use spinach instead of the broccoli, if you prefer. Trim the woody ends and cut the remainder into 2-inch/5-cm lengths, keeping the stalks and leaves separate. Add the stalks with the leek in step 3 and add the leaves 2 minutes later. Reduce the cooking time in step 4 to 3–4 minutes.

Green Lentil Pan-Fry

The green lentils used in this recipe require soaking but are worth it for the flavor. If time is short, use red lentils that do not require soaking.

NUTRITIONAL INFORMATION

Calories	0	Sugars	.........0g
Protein	.........0g	Fat	...........0g
Carbohydrates	....0g	Saturates	.......0g

 30 mins   🕐 45 mins

SERVES 4

INGREDIENTS

3¾ cups green lentils

4 tbsp butter or vegetarian margarine

2 garlic cloves, crushed

2 tbsp olive oil

1 tbsp cider vinegar

1 red onion, cut into 8 pieces

1¾ oz/50 g baby corn cobs, halved lengthwise

1 yellow bell pepper, cut into strips

1 red bell pepper, cut into strips

1¾ oz/50 g green beans, halved

½ cup vegetable bouillon

2 tbsp honey

salt and pepper

crusty bread, to serve

1 Soak the lentils in a large pan of cold water for 25 minutes. Bring to the boil, reduce the heat and simmer for 20 minutes. Drain thoroughly.

2 Add 1 tablespoon of the butter or margarine, 1 garlic clove, 1 table-spoon of oil, and the vinegar to the lentils and mix well.

3 Melt the remaining butter, garlic, and oil in a skillet and cook the onion, corn cobs, bell peppers, and beans for 3–4 minutes.

4 Add the vegetable bouillon and bring to a boil for about 10 minutes or until the liquid has evaporated.

5 Add the honey and season with salt and pepper to taste. Stir in the lentil mixture and cook for 1 minute to heat through. Spoon on to warmed serving plates and serve with crusty bread.

VARIATION

This pan-fry is very versatile—you can use a mixture of your favourite vegetables, if you prefer. Try zucchini, carrots, or snow peas.

Bamboo with Bell Peppers

This dish has a wonderfully strong ginger flavor which is integral to Chinese cooking. The mixed bell peppers give the dish a burst of color.

NUTRITIONAL INFORMATION

Calories ....101 Sugars 5g
Protein ....3g Fat 6g
Carbohydrate ....9g Saturates 1g

 5 mins   🕐 15 mins

SERVES 4

INGREDIENTS

2 tbsp peanut oil

8 oz/225 g canned bamboo shoots, drained and rinsed

2 tsp finely chopped fresh root ginger

1 small red bell pepper, seeded and thinly sliced

1 small green bell pepper, seeded and thinly sliced

1 small yellow bell pepper, seeded and thinly sliced

1 leek, sliced

½ cup vegetable bouillon

1 tbsp light soy sauce

2 tsp light brown sugar

2 tsp Chinese rice wine or dry sherry

1 tsp cornstarch

2 tsp water

1 tsp sesame oil

1 Heat the peanut oil in a preheated wok or large skillet, swirling the oil around the bottom of the wok or pan until it is really hot.

2 Add the bamboo shoots, ginger, bell peppers, and leek to the wok and cook for 2–3 minutes.

3 Stir in the vegetable bouillon, soy sauce, light brown sugar, and Chinese rice wine or sherry and bring to a boil, stirring.

4 Reduce the heat and simmer for 4–5 minutes, or until the vegetables begin to soften.

5 Blend the cornstarch with the water to form a smooth paste.

6 Stir the cornstarch paste into the wok. Bring to a boil and cook, stirring constantly, until the sauce thickens and clears.

7 Sprinkle the sesame oil over the vegetables and cook for 1 minute. Transfer to a warm serving dish and serve immediately.

COOK'S TIP

Add a chopped fresh red chili or a few drops of chili sauce for a spicier dish.

Bamboo with Spinach

In this recipe, spinach is fried with spices and then braised in a soy-flavored sauce with bamboo shoots for a rich, delicious dish.

NUTRITIONAL INFORMATION

Calories . . . . .105 Sugars 1g
Protein . . . . .3g Fat 9g
Carbohydrate . . . .3g Saturates 2g

5 mins   10 mins

SERVES 4

I N G R E D I E N T S

3 tbsp peanut oil

8 oz/225 g spinach, chopped

6 oz/175 g canned bamboo shoots, drained and rinsed

1 garlic clove, crushed

2 fresh red chilies, sliced

pinch of ground cinnamon

1¼ cups vegetable bouillon

pinch of sugar

pinch of salt

1 tbsp light soy sauce

COOK'S TIP

Fresh bamboo shoots are rarely available in the West and, in any case, are extremely time-consuming to prepare. Canned bamboo shoots are quite satisfactory, as they are used to provide a crunchy texture, rather than for their flavor, which is fairly insipid.

1 Heat the peanut oil in a preheated wok or large skillet, swirling the oil around the bottom of the wok until it is really hot.

2 Add the spinach and bamboo shoots to the wok and cook for 1 minute.

3 Add the garlic, chilies, and cinnamon to the mixture in the wok and cook for a further 30 seconds.

4 Stir in the bouillon, sugar, salt, and light soy sauce, cover, and cook over a medium heat for 5 minutes, or until the vegetables are cooked through and the sauce has reduced. If there is too much cooking liquid, blend a little cornstarch with double the quantity of cold water and stir into the sauce.

5 Transfer the bamboo shoots and spinach to a serving dish and serve.

Asian Vegetables

Serve this colorful mixture with a pile of golden, crispy noodles as a vegetarian main course, or on its own to accompany meat dishes.

NUTRITIONAL INFORMATION

Calories 0	Sugars 0g	
Protein 0g	Fat 0g	
Carbohydrate 0g	Saturates 0g	

2 mins   8 mins

SERVES 4

I N G R E D I E N T S

1 eggplant

salt

2 tbsp vegetable oil

3 garlic cloves, crushed

4 scallions, chopped

1 small red bell pepper, seeded and thinly sliced

4 baby corn cobs, halved lengthwise

3 oz/80 g snow peas

2 cups coarsely shredded Chinese mustard greens

15 oz/425 g canned Chinese straw mushrooms, drained

1¼ cups beansprouts

2 tbsp rice wine

2 tbsp yellow bean sauce

2 tbsp dark soy sauce

1 tsp chili sauce

1 tsp sugar

½ cup chicken or vegetable bouillon

1 tsp cornstarch

2 tsp water

1 Trim the eggplant and cut into thin 2-inch/50-cm long sticks. Place in a strainer, sprinkle with salt and let drain for 30 minutes. Rinse in cold water and dry with paper towels.

2 Heat the oil in a skillet or wok and cook the garlic, scallions, and bell pepper over a high heat for 1 minute. Stir in the eggplant pieces and cook for a further minute, or until softened.

3 Stir in the baby corn cobs and snow peas and cook for about 1 minute. Add the mustard greens, mushrooms, and beansprouts and cook for 30 seconds.

4 Mix together the rice wine, yellow bean sauce, soy sauce, chili sauce, and sugar, and add to the pan with the bouillon. Bring to a boil, stirring.

5 Slowly blend the cornstarch with the water to form a smooth paste. Stir quickly into the pan or wok and cook for a further minute. Serve immediately.

Vegetable Dim Sum

Dim sum are small Chinese parcels which may be filled with any variety of fillings, steamed or fried and served with a dipping sauce.

NUTRITIONAL INFORMATION

Calories ....295 Sugars 1g
Protein ....5g Fat 22g
Carbohydrate ...20g Saturates 6g

15 mins   15 mins

SERVES 4

INGREDIENTS

2 scallions, chopped

1 oz/25 g green beans, chopped

½ small carrot, finely chopped

1 red chili, chopped

¼ cup beansprouts, chopped

1 oz/25 g white mushrooms, chopped

¼ cup unsalted cashew nuts, chopped

1 small egg, beaten

2 tbsp cornstarch

1 tsp light soy sauce

1 tsp hoisin sauce

1 tsp sesame oil

32 wonton wrappers

oil, for deep-frying

1 tbsp sesame seeds

1 Mix all of the vegetables together in a bowl. Add the nuts, egg, cornstarch, soy sauce, hoisin sauce, and sesame oil to the bowl. Mix well.

2 Lay the wonton wrappers out on a chopping board and spoon small quantities of the mixture into the center of each. Gather the wrapper around the filling at the top, to make little parcels, leaving the top open.

3 Heat the oil for deep-frying in a wok to 350°F/180°C or until a cube of bread browns in 30 seconds. Cook the wontons, in batches, for 1–2 minutes or until golden brown. Drain on paper towels and keep warm while cooking the remaining wontons.

4 Sprinkle the sesame seeds over the wontons. Serve the vegetable dim sum with a soy or plum dipping sauce.

COOK'S TIP

If preferred, arrange the wontons on a heatproof plate and then steam in a steamer for 5–7 minutes for a healthier cooking method.

Chinese Vegetables

The Chinese are known for their colorful, crisp vegetables, quickly stir-fried. In this recipe, they are tossed in a tasty soy and hoisin sauce.

NUTRITIONAL INFORMATION

Calories 137	Sugars 7g
Protein 8g	Fat 7g
Carbohydrate ...10g	Saturates 11g

5 mins

10 mins

SERVES 4

INGREDIENTS

2 tbsp peanut oil

12 oz/350 g broccoli florets

1 tbsp chopped fresh root ginger

2 onions, each cut into 4 pieces

3 celery stalks, sliced

6 oz/175 g baby spinach

4½ oz/125 g snow peas

6 scallions, quartered

2 garlic cloves, crushed

2 tbsp light soy sauce

2 tsp superfine sugar

2 tbsp dry sherry

1 tbsp hoisin sauce

⅔ cup vegetable bouillon

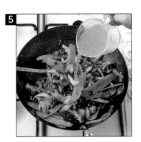

1 Heat the peanut oil in a preheated wok until it is almost smoking.

2 Add the broccoli florets, chopped root ginger, onions, and celery to the wok and cook for 1 minute.

3 Add the spinach, snow peas, scallions, and garlic and cook for 3–4 minutes.

4 Mix together the soy sauce, superfine sugar, sherry, hoisin sauce, and vegetable bouillon.

5 Pour the bouillon mixture into the wok, mixing well to coat the vegetables.

6 Cover the wok and cook over a medium heat for 2–3 minutes, or until the vegetables are cooked through, but still crisp.

7 Transfer the Chinese fried vegetables to a warm serving dish and serve immediately.

COOK'S TIP

You could use this mixture to fill Chinese pancakes. They are available from Chinese food stores and can be reheated in a steamer in 2–3 minutes.

Spicy Mushrooms

A mixture of mushrooms, common in Western cooking, have been used in this recipe for a richly flavored dish.

NUTRITIONAL INFORMATION

Calories	103	Sugars	. . . . .4g
Protein	. . . . .3g	Fat	. . . . .8g
Carbohydrate	. . . .5g	Saturates	. . . . . . .2g

5 mins   10 mins

SERVES 4

INGREDIENTS

2 tbsp peanut oil

2 garlic cloves, crushed

3 scallions, chopped

10½ oz/300 g white mushrooms

2 large open-cap mushrooms, sliced

4½ oz/125 g oyster mushrooms

1 tsp chili sauce

1 tbsp dark soy sauce

1 tbsp hoisin sauce

1 tbsp wine vinegar

½ tsp ground Szechuan pepper

1 tbsp dark brown sugar

1 tsp sesame oil

chopped fresh parsley, to garnish

1 Heat the peanut oil in a preheated wok or large skillet until almost smoking.

2 Reduce the heat slightly, add the garlic and scallions to the wok or skillet and cook for 30 seconds.

3 Add all the mushrooms to the wok, together with the chili sauce, dark soy sauce, hoisin sauce, wine vinegar, ground Szechuan pepper, and dark brown sugar, and cook for 4–5 minutes, or until the mushrooms are cooked through. Stir constantly to prevent the mixture sticking to the bottom of the wok.

4 Sprinkle the sesame oil on top of the mixture in the wok. Transfer to a warm serving dish, garnish with parsley and serve immediately.

COOK'S TIP

If Chinese dried mushrooms are available, add a small quantity to this dish for texture. Wood ears are widely used and are available dried from Chinese food stores. They should be rinsed, soaked in warm water for 20 minutes and rinsed again before use.

Bean Curd & Vegetables

Bean curd is available in different forms from both Chinese and Western food stores. Firm bean curd is used in this recipe.

NUTRITIONAL INFORMATION

Calories 367   Sugars 5g
Protein . . . . .13g   Fat 30g
Carbohydrate . . . .11g   Saturates 4g

5 mins   15 mins

SERVES 4

I N G R E D I E N T S

1 lb/450 g firm bean curd

⅔ cup vegetable oil

1 leek, sliced

4 baby corn cobs, halved lengthwise

2 oz/60 g snow peas

1 red bell pepper, seeded and diced

2 oz/60 g canned bamboo shoots, drained and rinsed

rice or noodles, to serve

S A U C E

1 tbsp Chinese rice wine or dry sherry

4 tbsp oyster sauce

3 tsp light soy sauce

2 tsp superfine sugar

pinch of salt

scant ¼ cup vegetable bouillon

1 tsp cornstarch

2 tsp water

1 Rinse the bean curd in cold water and pat dry with paper towels. Cut the bean curd into 1-inch/2.5-cm cubes.

2 Heat the oil in a preheated wok until almost smoking. Reduce the heat, add the bean curd and cook until golden brown. Remove from the wok with a slotted spoon and drain on paper towels.

3 Pour all but 2 tablespoons of the oil from the wok and return to the heat. Add the leek, corn cobs, snow peas, bell pepper, and bamboo shoots and cook for 2–3 minutes.

4 Add the Chinese rice wine or sherry, oyster sauce, soy sauce, sugar, salt, and bouillon to the wok and bring to a boil. Blend the cornstarch with the water to form a smooth paste and stir it into the sauce. Bring the sauce to a boil and cook, stirring constantly, until thickened and clear.

5 Stir the bean curd into the mixture in the wok and cook for about 1 minute until hot. Serve with rice or noodles.

Vegetarian & Vegan

As vegetables are so plentiful and diverse in the Far East, they play a major role in the diet. Other ingredients, such as bean curd and quorn, are also added to the vegetarian diet, which is both a healthy and an economical choice.

Bean curd is produced from the soya bean, which is grown in abundance in these countries. The cake variety of bean curd is frequently used in stir-frying for texture and it is perfect for absorbing all of the flavors of the dish. It is also an ideal ingredient for the vegan cook.

The wok is perfect for cooking vegetables as it cooks them very quickly, which helps to retain their nutrients and crispness. This produces a range of colorful and flavorsome recipes, which display the wonderful versatility of all the different kinds of vegetables.

Spiced Eggplant

This is a spicy and sweet dish, flavored with mango chutney and heated up with chilies for a really wonderful combination of flavors.

NUTRITIONAL INFORMATION

Calories ....208 Sugars 17g
Protein ....1g Fat 15g
Carbohydrate ...17g Saturates 2g

5 mins   25 mins

SERVES 4

I N G R E D I E N T S

3 tbsp peanut oil

2 onions, sliced

2 cloves garlic, chopped

2 eggplants, diced

2 red chilies, seeded and very finely
  chopped

2 tbsp raw brown sugar

6 scallions, sliced

3 tbsp mango chutney

oil, for deep-frying

2 cloves garlic, sliced, to garnish

1 Heat the peanut oil in a large preheated wok or heavy-based skillet, swirling the oil around the bottom of the wok until it is really hot.

2 Add the onions and chopped garlic to the wok, stirring well.

3 Add the diced eggplant and chilies to the wok and cook for 5 minutes.

4 Add the raw brown sugar, scallions, and mango chutney to the wok, stirring well.

5 Reduce the heat, cover, and let simmer, stirring from time to time, for 15 minutes or until the eggplant is tender.

6 Transfer the stir-fry to serving bowls and keep warm.

7 Heat the oil for deep-frying in the wok and quickly cook the slices of garlic, until they brown slightly. Garnish the stir-fry with the deep-fried garlic and serve immediately.

COOK'S TIP

The "hotness" of chilies varies enormously so always use with caution, but as a general guide the smaller they are the hotter they will be. The seeds are the hottest part and so are usually discarded.

Spicy Eggplants

Try to obtain the smaller Chinese eggplants for this dish, as they have a slightly sweeter taste.

NUTRITIONAL INFORMATION

Calories ....120 Sugars 7g
Protein ....2g Fat 9g
Carbohydrate ....9g Saturates 1g

35 mins   20 mins

SERVES 4

INGREDIENTS

1 lb/450 g eggplants, rinsed

2 tsp salt

3 tbsp vegetable oil

2 garlic cloves, crushed

2tsp chopped fresh root ginger

1 onion, halved and sliced

1 fresh red chili, sliced

2 tbsp dark soy sauce

1 tbsp hoisin sauce

½ tsp chili sauce

1 tbsp dark brown sugar

1 tbsp wine vinegar

1 tsp ground Szechuan pepper

1¼ cups vegetable bouillon

1 Cut the eggplants into cubes if you are using the larger variety, or cut the smaller type in half. Place in a strainer and sprinkle with the salt. Let stand for 30 minutes. Rinse under cold running water and pat dry with paper towels.

2 Heat the oil in a preheated wok and add the garlic, ginger, onion, and fresh chili. Cook for 30 seconds and add the eggplants. Continue to cook for 1–2 minutes.

3 Add the soy sauce, hoisin sauce, chili sauce, sugar, wine vinegar, Szechuan pepper, and vegetable bouillon to the wok, reduce the heat and let simmer, uncovered, for 10 minutes, or until the eggplants are cooked.

4 Increase the heat and boil to reduce the sauce until thickened enough to coat the eggplants. Serve immediately.

COOK'S TIP

Sprinkling the eggplants with salt and letting them stand removes the bitter juices, which would otherwise taint the flavor of the dish.

Carrot & Orange Stir-Fry

Carrots and oranges have long been combined in Asian cooking, the orange juice bringing out the sweetness of the carrots.

NUTRITIONAL INFORMATION

Calories 341	Sugars 26g	
Protein 10g	Fat 21g	
Carbohydrate . . .28g	Saturates 4g	

10 mins   10 mins

SERVES 4

I N G R E D I E N T S

2 tbsp sunflower oil

2¼ cups grated carrots

8 oz/225 g leeks, shredded

2 oranges, peeled and segmented

2 tbsp tomato catsup

1 tbsp raw brown sugar

2 tbsp light soy sauce

½ cup chopped peanuts

VARIATION

You could use pineapple instead of orange, if you prefer. If using canned pineapple, make sure that it is in natural juice not syrup as syrup will spoil the fresh taste of this dish.

1 Heat the sunflower oil in a large preheated wok.

2 Add the grated carrot and leeks to the wok and cook for 2–3 minutes, or until the vegetables have just softened.

3 Add the orange segments to the wok and heat through gently, ensuring that you do not break up the orange segments as you stir the mixture.

4 Mix the tomato catsup, brown sugar, and soy sauce together in a small bowl.

5 Add the tomato and sugar mixture to the wok and cook for a further 2 minutes.

6 Transfer the stir-fry to warm serving bowls and scatter with the chopped peanuts. Serve immediately.

Deep-Fried Chili Corn Balls

These small corn balls have a wonderful hot and sweet flavor, offset by the pungent cilantro.

NUTRITIONAL INFORMATION

Calories 248   Sugars 6g
Protein . . . . .6g   Fat 12
Carbohydrate . . .30g   Saturates 5g

15 mins   30 mins

SERVES 4

I N G R E D I E N T S

6 scallions, sliced

3 tbsp chopped fresh cilantro

8 oz/225 g canned corn kernels

1 tsp mild chili powder

1 tbsp sweet chili sauce

¼ cup shredded coconut

1 egg

⅓ cup cornmeal

oil, for deep-frying

extra sweet chili sauce, to serve

1   In a large bowl, mix together the scallions, cilantro, corn, chili powder, chili sauce, coconut, egg, and cornmeal until well blended.

2   Cover the bowl with plastic wrap and let stand for about 10 minutes.

3   Heat the oil for deep-frying in a large preheated wok or skillet to 350°F /180°C or until a cube of bread browns in 30 seconds.

4   Carefully drop spoonfuls of the chili and cornmeal mixture into the hot oil. Deep-fry the chili corn balls, in batches, for 4–5 minutes or until crispy and a deep golden brown color.

5   Remove the chili corn balls with a slotted spoon, transfer to paper towels and let drain thoroughly.

6   Transfer the chili corn balls to serving plates and serve with an extra sweet chili sauce for dipping.

COOK'S TIP

For safe deep-frying in a round-bottomed wok, place it on a wok rack so that it rests securely. Only half-fill the wok with oil. Never leave the wok unattended over a high heat.

Butternut Squash Stir-Fry

Butternut squash is as its name suggests, deliciously buttery and nutty in flavor. If the squash is not in season, use sweet potatoes instead.

NUTRITIONAL INFORMATION

Calories 301   Sugars 4g
Protein . . . . .9g   Fat 22g
Carbohydrate . . .19g   Saturates 4g

 5 mins   25 mins

SERVES 4

INGREDIENTS

2 lb 4 oz/1 kg butternut squash, peeled

3 tbsp peanut oil

1 onion, sliced

2 cloves garlic, crushed

1 tsp coriander seeds

1 tsp cumin seeds

2 tbsp chopped fresh cilantro

generous ⅓ cup coconut milk

½ cup water

⅔ cup salted cashew nuts

TO GARNISH

freshly grated lime zest

fresh cilantro

lime wedges

1 Using a sharp knife, slice the butternut squash into small, bite-sized cubes.

2 Heat the peanut oil in a large preheated wok.

3 Add the butternut squash, onion, and garlic to the wok and cook for 5 minutes.

4 Stir in the coriander seeds, cumin seeds, and fresh cilantro and cook for 1 minute.

5 Add the coconut milk and water to the wok and bring to a boil. Cover the wok and let simmer for 10–15 minutes, or until the squash is tender.

6 Add the cashew nuts and stir to combine.

7 Transfer to warm serving dishes and garnish with freshly grated lime zest, fresh cilantro, and lime wedges. Serve hot.

COOK'S TIP

If you do not have coconut milk, grate some creamed coconut into the dish with the water in step 5.

Leeks with Yellow Bean Sauce

This is a simple side dish which is ideal with other main meal vegetarian dishes.

NUTRITIONAL INFORMATION

Calories 131   Sugars 3g
Protein . . . . .6g   Fat 9g
Carbohydrate . . . .7g   Saturates 2g

5 mins   10 mins

SERVES 4

INGREDIENTS

1 lb/450 g leeks

6 oz/175 g baby corn cobs

6 scallions

3 tbsp peanut oil

8 oz/225 g Napa cabbage, shredded

4 tbsp yellow bean sauce

1 Using a sharp knife, slice the leeks, halve the baby corn cobs, and thinly slice the scallions.

2 Heat the peanut oil in a large preheated wok or skillet until smoking.

3 Add the leeks, shredded Napa cabbage, and baby corn cobs to the wok or skillet.

4 Cook the vegetables over a high heat for about 5 minutes or until the edges of the vegetables are slightly brown.

5 Add the scallions to the wok or skillet, stirring to combine.

6 Add the yellow bean sauce to the wok or skillet.

7 Cook the mixture in the wok for a further 2 minutes, or until heated through and the vegetables are thoroughly coated in the sauce.

8 Transfer the vegetables and sauce to warm serving dishes and serve immediately.

COOK'S TIP

Yellow bean sauce adds an authentic Chinese flavor to stir-fries. It is made from crushed salted soya beans mixed with flour and spices to make a thick paste. It is mild in flavor and is excellent with a range of vegetables.

Bok Choy with Cashew Nuts

Plum sauce is readily available in jars and has a terrific, sweet flavor which complements the vegetables.

NUTRITIONAL INFORMATION

Calories	.241	Sugars	.7g
Protein	.7g	Fat	.19g
Carbohydrate	.11g	Saturates	.4g

 5 mins   15 mins

SERVES 4

INGREDIENTS

2 red onions

6 oz/175 g red cabbage

2 tbsp peanut oil

8 oz/225 g bok choy

2 tbsp plum sauce

⅔ cup roasted cashew nuts

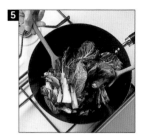

1 Using a sharp knife, cut the red onions into thin wedges and thinly shred the red cabbage.

2 Heat the peanut oil in a large preheated wok or heavy-based skillet until it is really hot.

3 Add the onion wedges to the wok or skillet and cook for about 5 minutes or until they are just beginning to brown.

4 Add the red cabbage to the wok and cook for a further 2–3 minutes.

5 Add the bok choy leaves to the wok or skillet and cook for about 5 minutes, or until the leaves have just wilted.

6 Drizzle the plum sauce over the vegetables, toss together until well combined and heat until the liquid is bubbling.

7 Scatter with the roasted cashew nuts and transfer to warm serving bowls.

VARIATION

Use unsalted peanuts instead of the cashew nuts, if you prefer.

Green & Black Bean Stir-Fry

A terrific side dish, the variety of greens in this recipe make it as attractive as it is tasty.

NUTRITIONAL INFORMATION

Calories	88	Sugars	.........2g
Protein	.........2g	Fat	...........7g
Carbohydrate	....4g	Saturates	.......4g

 5 mins   10 mins

SERVES 4

I N G R E D I E N T S

8 oz/225 g fine green beans, sliced

4 shallots, sliced

3½ oz/100 g shiitake mushrooms, thinly sliced

1 clove garlic, crushed

1 Iceberg lettuce, shredded

1 tsp chili oil

2 tbsp butter

4 tbsp black bean sauce

1 Using a sharp knife, slice the fine green beans, shallots, and shiitake mushrooms. Crush the garlic with a pestle and mortar and shred the Iceberg lettuce.

2 Heat the chili oil and butter in a large preheated wok or skillet.

3 Add the green beans, shallots, garlic, and mushrooms to the wok and cook for 2–3 minutes.

4 Add the shredded lettuce to the wok or skillet and cook until the leaves have wilted.

5 Stir the black bean sauce into the mixture in the wok and heat through, tossing gently to mix, until the sauce is bubbling.

6 Transfer the green and black bean stir-fry to a warm serving dish and serve immediately.

COOK'S TIP

If possible, use Chinese green beans which are tender and can be eaten whole. They are available from Chinese stores.

Deep-Fried Zucchini

These zucchini fritters are irresistible and could be served as an appetizer or snack with a chili dip.

NUTRITIONAL INFORMATION

Calories 117   Sugars 2g
Protein . . . . .3g   Fat 6g
Carbohydrate . . .14g   Saturates 1g

 5 mins   ⏱ 20 mins

SERVES 4

I N G R E D I E N T S

1 lb/450 g zucchini

1 egg white

⅓ cup cornstarch

1 tsp salt

1 tsp Chinese five-spice powder

oil, for deep-frying

chili dip, to serve

1 Using a sharp knife, slice the zucchini into rings or chunky sticks.

2 Place the egg white in a small mixing bowl. Lightly whip the egg white until foamy, using a fork.

3 Mix the cornstarch, salt, and Chinese five-spice powder together and sprinkle on to a large plate.

4 Heat the oil for deep-frying in a large preheated wok or heavy-based skillet.

5 Dip each piece of zucchini into the beaten egg white then coat in the cornstarch and five-spice mixture.

6 Deep-fry the zucchini, in batches, for about 5 minutes or until pale golden and crispy. Repeat with the remaining zucchini.

7 Remove the zucchini with a slotted spoon and let them drain on paper towels while deep-frying the remainder.

8 Transfer the zucchini to warmed serving plates and serve immediately with a chili dip.

VARIATION

Alter the seasoning by using chili powder or curry powder instead of the Chinese five-spice powder, if you prefer.

Asparagus Parcels

These small parcels are ideal as part of a main meal and irresistible as a quick snack with extra plum sauce for dipping.

NUTRITIONAL INFORMATION

Calories 194   Sugars 2g
Protein . . . . .3g   Fat 16g
Carbohydrate . . . .11g   Saturates 4g

5 mins   25 mins

SERVES 4

I N G R E D I E N T S

3½ oz/100 g fine tip asparagus

1 red bell pepper, seeded and thinly sliced

½ cup beansprouts

2 tbsp plum sauce

1 egg yolk

8 sheets phyllo pastry

oil, for deep-frying

1 Place the asparagus, bell pepper, and beansprouts in a large mixing bowl.

2 Add the plum sauce to the vegetables and mix until well-combined.

3 Beat the egg yolk and set aside until required.

4 Lay the sheets of phyllo pastry out on to a clean counter.

5 Place a little of the asparagus and red bell pepper filling at the top end of each phyllo pastry sheet. Brush the edges of the phyllo pastry with a little of the beaten egg yolk.

6 Roll up the phyllo pastry, tucking in the ends and enclosing the filling like a spring roll. Repeat with the remaining phyllo sheets.

7 Heat the oil for deep-frying in a large preheated wok. Carefully cook the parcels, 2 at a time, in the hot oil for 4–5 minutes or until crispy.

8 Remove the parcels with a slotted spoon and let them drain on paper towels.

9 Transfer the parcels to warm serving plates and serve immediately.

COOK'S TIP

Be sure to use fine-tipped asparagus as it is more tender than the larger stems.

Honey-Cooked Spinach

This stir-fry is the perfect accompaniment to bean curd dishes, and it is so quick and simple to make.

NUTRITIONAL INFORMATION

Calories 146	Sugars 9g
Protein 4g	Fat 9g
Carbohydrate ...10g	Saturates 2g

5 mins   15 mins

SERVES 4

I N G R E D I E N T S

4 scallions

3 tbsp peanut oil

12 oz/350 g shiitake mushrooms, sliced

2 cloves garlic, crushed

12 oz/350 g baby leaf spinach

2 tbsp dry sherry

2 tbsp clear honey

1 Using a sharp knife, slice the scallions.

2 Heat the peanut oil in a large preheated wok or heavy-based skillet.

3 Add the shiitake mushrooms to the wok and cook for about 5 minutes, or until the mushrooms have softened.

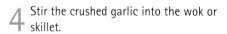

4 Stir the crushed garlic into the wok or skillet.

5 Add the baby leaf spinach to the wok or pan and cook for a further 2–3 minutes, or until the spinach leaves have just wilted.

6 Mix together the dry sherry and clear honey in a small bowl until well

combined. Drizzle the sherry and honey mixture over the spinach and heat through, stirring to coat the spinach leaves thoroughly in the mixture.

7 Transfer the stir-fry to warm serving dishes, scatter with the chopped scallions and serve immediately.

COOK'S TIP

Single-flower honey has a better, more individual flavor than blended honey. Acacia honey is typically Chinese, but you could also try clover, lemon blossom, lime flower, or orange blossom honey.

Sweet & Sour Cauliflower

Although sweet and sour flavorings are mainly associated with pork, they are ideal for flavoring vegetables as in this tasty recipe.

NUTRITIONAL INFORMATION

Calories 154   Sugars 16g
Protein ....6g   Fat 7g
Carbohydrate ...17g   Saturates 1g

5 mins   20 mins

SERVES 4

INGREDIENTS

1 lb/450 g cauliflower florets

2 tbsp sunflower oil

1 onion, sliced

8 oz/225 g carrots, sliced

3½ oz/100 g snow peas

1 ripe mango, sliced

1 cup beansprouts

3 tbsp chopped fresh cilantro

3 tbsp fresh lime juice

1 tbsp clear honey

6 tbsp coconut milk

1 Bring a large pan of water to a boil. Add the cauliflower to the pan and cook for 2 minutes. Drain the cauliflower thoroughly.

2 Heat the sunflower oil in a large preheated wok.

3 Add the onion and carrots to the wok and cook for about 5 minutes.

4 Add the drained cauliflower and snow peas to the wok and cook for 2–3 minutes.

5 Add the mango and bean sprouts to the wok and cook for about 2 minutes.

6 Mix together the cilantro, lime juice, honey, and coconut milk in a bowl.

7 Add the cilantro and coconut mixture to the wok and cook for about 2 minutes or until the juices are bubbling.

8 Transfer the sweet and sour cauliflower stir-fry to serving dishes and serve immediately.

VARIATION

Use broccoli instead of the cauliflower as an alternative, if you prefer.

Broccoli & Black Bean Sauce

Broccoli works well with the black bean sauce in this recipe, while the almonds add extra crunch and flavor.

NUTRITIONAL INFORMATION

Calories 139	Sugars 3g
Protein 7g	Fat 10g
Carbohydrate 5g	Saturates 1g

 5 mins   15 mins

SERVES 4

INGREDIENTS

1 lb/450 g broccoli florets

2 tbsp sunflower oil

1 onion, sliced

2 cloves garlic, thinly sliced

¼ cup flaked, slivered almonds

1 head Napa cabbage, shredded

4 tbsp black bean sauce

1 Bring a large pan of water to the boil.

2 Add the broccoli florets to the pan and cook for 1 minute. Drain the broccoli thoroughly.

3 Meanwhile, heat the sunflower oil in a large preheated wok.

4 Add the onion and garlic slices to the wok and cook until just beginning to brown.

5 Add the drained broccoli florets and the slivered almonds to the mixture in the wok and cook for a further 2–3 minutes.

6 Add the shredded Napa cabbage to the wok and cook for a further 2 minutes, stirring the leaves briskly around the wok.

7 Stir the black bean sauce into the vegetables in the wok, tossing to coat the vegetables thoroughly in the sauce and cook until the juices are just beginning to bubble.

8 Transfer the vegetables to warm serving bowls and serve immediately.

VARIATION

Use unsalted cashew nuts instead of the almonds, if preferred.

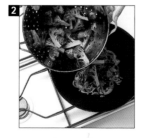

Cabbage & Walnut Stir-Fry

This is a really quick, one-pan dish using white and red cabbage for color and flavor.

NUTRITIONAL INFORMATION

Calories 422   Sugars 9g
Protein . . . . .13g   Fat 37g
Carbohydrate . . .10g   Saturates 5g

10 mins   10 mins

SERVES 4

I N G R E D I E N T S

12 oz/350 g white cabbage

12 oz/350 g red cabbage

4 tbsp peanut oil

1 tbsp walnut oil

2 garlic cloves, crushed

8 scallions, trimmed

8 oz/225 g firm bean curd, cubed

2 tbsp lemon juice

3½ oz/100 g walnut halves

2 tsp Dijon mustard

2 tsp poppy seeds

salt and pepper

1 Using a sharp knife, shred the white and red cabbages thinly and set aside until required.

2 Heat the peanut and walnut oils in a preheated wok. Add the garlic, cabbage, scallions, and bean curd and cook for 5 minutes, stirring.

3 Add the lemon juice, walnuts, and mustard, season with salt and pepper, and cook for a further 5 minutes or until the cabbage is tender.

4 Transfer the stir-fry to a warm serving bowl, sprinkle with poppy seeds and serve immediately.

VARIATION

Sesame seeds could be used instead of the poppy seeds and drizzle 1 teaspoon of sesame oil over the dish just before serving, if you wish.

Stir-Fried Japanese Noodles

This quick dish is an ideal lunchtime meal, packed with mixed mushrooms in a sweet sauce.

NUTRITIONAL INFORMATION

Calories ....379 Sugars 8g
Protein ....12g Fat 13g
Carbohydrate ...53g Saturates 3g

15 mins   15 mins

SERVES 4

INGREDIENTS

8 oz/225 g Japanese egg noodles

2 tbsp sunflower oil

1 red onion, sliced

1 clove garlic, crushed

1 lb/450 g mixed mushrooms (shiitake, oyster, brown cap)

12 oz/350 g bok choy

2 tbsp sweet sherry

6 tbsp oyster sauce

4 scallions, sliced

1 tbsp toasted sesame seeds

1 Place the Japanese egg noodles in a large bowl. Pour over enough boiling water to cover and let the noodles soak for 10 minutes.

2 Heat the sunflower oil in a large preheated wok.

3 Add the red onion and garlic to the wok and cook for 2–3 minutes, or until softened.

4 Add the mushrooms to the wok and cook for about 5 minutes, or until the mushrooms have softened.

5 Drain the egg noodles thoroughly.

6 Add the the bok choy, noodles, sweet sherry, and oyster sauce to the wok. Toss all of the ingredients together and cook for 2–3 minutes or until the liquid is just bubbling.

7 Transfer the mushroom noodles to warm serving bowls and scatter with sliced scallions and toasted sesame seeds. Serve immediately.

COOK'S TIP

The variety of mushrooms in large food stores has improved and a good mixture should be easily obtainable. If not, use the more common white and flat mushrooms.

Bean Curd with Bell Peppers

Bean curd is perfect for marinating as it readily absorbs flavors for a great tasting main dish.

NUTRITIONAL INFORMATION

Calories	267	Sugars	.........2g
Protein	.........9g	Fat	..........23g
Carbohydrate	....5g	Saturates	.......3g

25 mins   15 mins

SERVES 4

I N G R E D I E N T S

12 oz/350 g firm bean curd

2 cloves garlic, crushed

4 tbsp soy sauce

1 tbsp sweet chili sauce

6 tbsp sunflower oil

1 onion, sliced

1 green bell pepper, seeded and diced

1 tbsp sesame oil

1 Using a sharp knife, cut the bean curd into bite-sized pieces. Place the bean curd in a shallow, non-metallic dish.

2 Mix together the garlic, soy sauce, and sweet chili sauce and drizzle over the bean curd. Toss well to coat and leave to marinate for about 20 minutes.

3 Meanwhile, heat the sunflower oil in a large preheated wok.

4 Add the onion to the wok and cook over a high heat until brown and crispy. Remove the onion with a slotted spoon and leave to drain on paper towels.

5 Add the bean curd to the hot oil and cook for about 5 minutes.

6 Remove all but 1 tablespoon of the sunflower oil from the wok. Add the bell pepper to the wok and cook for 2–3 minutes, or until softened.

7 Return the bean curd and onions to the wok and heat through, stirring occasionally.

8 Drizzle with sesame oil. Transfer to serving plates and serve immediately.

COOK'S TIP

If you are in a real hurry, buy ready-marinated bean curd from your food store.

Quorn & Vegetable Stir-Fry

Quorn, like bean curd, absorbs all of the flavors in a dish, making it ideal for this recipe which is packed with classic Chinese flavorings.

NUTRITIONAL INFORMATION

Calories 167   Sugars 8g
Protein ....12g   Fat 9g
Carbohydrate ...10g   Saturates 1g

30 mins   10 mins

SERVES 4

INGREDIENTS

1 tbsp grated fresh root ginger

1 tsp ground ginger

1 tbsp tomato paste

2 tbsp sunflower oil

1 clove garlic, crushed

2 tbsp soy sauce

12 oz/350 g Quorn or soya cubes

3 small carrots, sliced

3½ oz/100 g green beans, sliced

4 stalks celery, sliced

1 red bell pepper, seeded and sliced

boiled rice, to serve

COOK'S TIP

Fresh root ginger will keep for several weeks in a cool, dry place. Root ginger can also be kept frozen—break off lumps as needed.

1 Place the grated fresh root ginger, ground ginger, tomato paste, 1 tablespoon of the sunflower oil, garlic, soy sauce, and Quorn or soya cubes in a large bowl. Mix well to combine, stirring carefully so that you don't break up the Quorn or soya cubes. Cover and let it marinate for 20 minutes.

2 Heat the remaining sunflower oil in a large preheated wok.

3 Add the marinated Quorn mixture to the wok and cook for about 2 minutes.

4 Add the carrots, green beans, celery, and red bell pepper to the wok and cook for a further 5 minutes.

5 Transfer the stir-fry to warm serving dishes and serve immediately with freshly cooked boiled rice.

Bean Curd Casserole

Bean curd is ideal for absorbing all the other flavors in this dish. If marinated bean curd is used, it will add a flavor of its own.

NUTRITIONAL INFORMATION

Calories ....228 Sugars 3g
Protein ....16g Fat 15g
Carbohydrate ....7g Saturates 2g

   5 mins   15 mins

SERVES 4

I N G R E D I E N T S

1 lb/450 g firm bean curd

2 tbsp peanut oil

8 scallions, cut into batons

2 celery stalks, sliced

4½ oz/125 g broccoli florets

4½ oz/125 g zucchini, sliced

2 garlic cloves, thinly sliced

1 lb/450 g baby spinach

rice, to serve

S A U C E

scant 2 cups vegetable bouillon

2 tbsp light soy sauce

3 tbsp hoisin sauce

½ tsp chili powder

1 tbsp sesame oil

VARIATION

This recipe has a green vegetable theme, but you can alter the color and flavor by adding your favourite vegetables. Add 75 g/2¾ oz fresh or canned and drained straw mushrooms with the vegetables in step 2.

1 Cut the bean curd into 1-inch/2.5-cm cubes and set aside until required.

2 Heat the peanut oil in a preheated wok or large skillet.

3 Add the scallions, celery, broccoli, zucchini, garlic, spinach, and bean curd to the wok or skillet and cook for 3–4 minutes.

4 To make the sauce, mix together the vegetable bouillon, soy sauce, hoisin sauce, chili powder, and sesame oil in a flameproof casserole and bring to a boil.

5 Add the stir-fried vegetables and bean curd to the pan, reduce the heat, cover, and simmer for 10 minutes.

6 Transfer the bean curd and vegetables to a warm serving dish and serve with rice.

Sweet & Sour Bean Curd

Sweet-and-sour sauce was one of the first Chinese sauces introduced to Western diets, and remains one of the most popular.

NUTRITIONAL INFORMATION

Calories	205	Sugars	........12g
Protein	........11g	Fat	...........11g
Carbohydrate	...17g	Saturates	.......1g

5 mins   10 mins

SERVES 4

INGREDIENTS

2 celery stalks

1 carrot

1 green bell pepper, seeded

2¾ oz/75 g snow peas

2 tbsp vegetable oil

2 garlic cloves, crushed

8 baby corn cobs

4½ oz/125 g beansprouts

1 lb/450 g firm bean curd, cubed

rice or noodles, to serve

SAUCE

2 tbsp light brown sugar

2 tbsp wine vinegar

1 cup vegetable bouillon

1 tsp tomato paste

1 tbsp cornstarch

1 Using a sharp knife, thinly slice the celery, cut the carrot into thin strips, dice the bell pepper, and cut the snow peas in half diagonally.

2 Heat the vegetable oil in a preheated wok until it is almost smoking. Reduce the heat slightly, add the crushed garlic, celery, carrot, bell pepper, snow peas and corn cobs and cook for 3–4 minutes.

3 Add the beansprouts and bean curd to the wok and cook for 2 minutes, stirring well.

4 To make the sauce, combine the sugar, wine vinegar, bouillon, tomato paste and cornstarch, stirring well to mix. Stir into the wok, bring to a boil and cook, stirring, until the sauce thickens and clears. Continue to cook for 1 minute. Serve with rice or noodles.

COOK'S TIP

Be careful not to break up the bean curd cubes when stirring.

Bean Curd with Mushrooms

Chinese mushrooms are available from Chinese food stores
and health food shops and add a unique flavor to Asian dishes.

NUTRITIONAL INFORMATION

Calories 218	Sugars 1g
Protein 12g	Fat 14g
Carbohydrate . . .13g	Saturates 2g

🍲 🍲 🍲

15 mins ⏱ 15 mins

SERVES 4

I N G R E D I E N T S

1 oz/25 g dried Chinese mushrooms

1 lb/450 g firm bean curd

4 tbsp cornstarch

oil, for deep-frying

2 cloves garlic, finely chopped

2tsp fresh grated root ginger

1 cup frozen or fresh peas

1 Place the Chinese mushrooms in a
large bowl. Pour in enough boiling
water to cover and let stand for about 10
minutes.

2 Meanwhile, cut the bean curd into
bite-sized cubes, using a sharp knife.

3 Place the cornstarch in a large bowl.

4 Add the bean curd to the bowl and
toss in the cornstarch until evenly
coated.

5 Heat the oil for deep-frying in a large
preheated wok.

6 Add the cubes of bean curd to the
wok and deep-fry, in batches, for 2–3
minutes or until golden and crispy.
Remove the bean curd with a slotted
spoon and drain on paper towels.

7 Drain off all but 2 tablespoons of oil
from the wok. Add the garlic, ginger,
and Chinese mushrooms to the wok and
cook for 2–3 minutes.

8 Return the cooked bean curd to the
wok and add the peas. Heat through
for 1 minute then serve hot.

COOK'S TIP

Chinese dried mushrooms add
flavor and a distinctive aroma.
Sold dried in packets, they can be
expensive, but only a few are needed
per dish and they store indefinitely.
If they are unavailable, use
open-cap mushrooms instead.

Sherry & Soy Vegetables

This is a simple, yet tasty side dish which is just as delicious as a snack or main course.

NUTRITIONAL INFORMATION

Calories 374	Sugars 10g
Protein 14g	Fat 25g
Carbohydrate ...20g	Saturates 5g

10 mins   15 mins

SERVES 4

I N G R E D I E N T S

2 tbsp sunflower oil

1 red onion, sliced

2 carrots, thinly sliced

6 oz/175 g zucchini, sliced diagonally

1 red bell pepper, seeded and sliced

1 small head Napa cabbage, shredded

1½ cups beansprouts

8 oz/225 g canned bamboo shoots, drained

1 cup cup cashew nuts, toasted

S A U C E

3 tbsp medium sherry

3 tbsp light soy sauce

1 tsp ground ginger

1 clove garlic, crushed

1 tsp cornstarch

1 tbsp tomato paste

 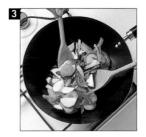 

1 Heat the sunflower oil in a large preheated wok.

2 Add the red onion and cook for 2–3 minutes or until softened.

3 Add the carrots, zucchini, and bell pepper slices to the wok and cook for a further 5 minutes.

4 Add the Napa cabbage, beansprouts, and bamboo shoots and heat through for 2–3 minutes, or until the leaves begin to wilt. Stir in the cashews.

5 Combine the sherry, soy sauce, ginger, garlic, cornstarch, and tomato paste. Pour over the vegetables and toss well. Let simmer for 2–3 minutes or until the juices start to thicken. Serve immediately.

VARIATION

Use any mixture of fresh vegetables that you have to hand in this very versatile dish.

Chinese Vegetable Rice

This tasty rice can either be served as a meal or as an accompaniment to other vegetable recipes.

NUTRITIONAL INFORMATION

Calories 228   Sugars 5g
Protein . . . . .5g   Fat 7g
Carbohydrate . . .37g   Saturates 1g

 5 mins    25 mins

SERVES 4

I N G R E D I E N T S

1¾ cups long-grain white rice

1 tsp turmeric

2 tbsp sunflower oil

8 oz/225 g zucchini, sliced

1 red bell pepper, seeded and sliced

1 green bell pepper, seeded and sliced

1 green chili, seeded and finely chopped

1 medium carrot, coarsely grated

1½ cups beansprouts

6 scallions, sliced, plus extra to garnish (optional)

2 tbsp soy sauce

salt

1 Place the rice and turmeric in a pan of lightly salted water and bring to a boil. Reduce the heat and let simmer until the rice is just tender. Drain the rice thoroughly and press out any excess water with paper towels. Set aside until required.

2 Heat the sunflower oil in a large preheated wok.

3 Add the zucchini to the wok and cook for about 2 minutes.

4 Add the bell peppers and chili to the wok and cook for 2–3 minutes.

5 Add the cooked rice to the mixture in the wok, a little at a time, tossing well after each addition.

6 Add the carrots, beansprouts, and scallions to the wok and cook for a further 2 minutes.

7 Drizzle with soy sauce and serve at once, garnished with extra scallions, if desired.

COOK'S TIP

For real luxury, add a few saffron strands infused in boiling water instead of the turmeric.

Vegetables with Hoisin

This spicy vegetable stir-fry has rice added to it and it can be served as a meal in itself.

NUTRITIONAL INFORMATION

Calories 120   Sugars 6g
Protein ....4g   Fat 6g
Carbohydrate ...12g   Saturates 1g

20 mins   10 mins

SERVES 4

I N G R E D I E N T S

1 red onion

1 carrot

1 yellow bell pepper

2 tbsp sunflower oil

1 cup cooked brown rice

6 oz/175 g snow peas

1¾ cups beansprouts

4 tbsp hoisin sauce

1 tbsp snipped fresh chives

1 Using a sharp knife, thinly slice the red onion.

2 Thinly slice the carrot.

3 Seed and dice the yellow bell pepper.

4 Heat the sunflower oil in a large preheated wok or heavy-based skillet.

5 Add the red onion slices, carrot, and yellow bell pepper to the wok and cook for about 3 minutes.

6 Add the cooked brown rice, snow peas, and bean sprouts to the mixture in the wok and cook for a further 2 minutes. Stir briskly to ensure that the

ingredients are well mixed and the rice grains are separated.

7 Stir the hoisin sauce into the vegetables and mix until well combined and completely heated through.

8 Transfer the vegetable stir-fry to warm serving dishes and scatter with the snipped fresh chives. Serve immediately.

COOK'S TIP

Hoisin sauce is a dark brown, reddish sauce made from soy beans, garlic, chili, and various other spices, and is commonly used in Chinese cooking. It may also be used as a dipping sauce.

Vegetable Stir-Fry

A range of delicious flavors are captured in this simple recipe which is ideal if you are in a hurry.

NUTRITIONAL INFORMATION

Calories	138	Sugars	.........5g
Protein	.........3g	Fat	..........12g
Carbohydrate	....5g	Saturates	.......2g

5 mins　　　25 mins

SERVES 4

INGREDIENTS

3 tbsp vegetable oil

8 pearl onions, halved

1 eggplant, cubed

8 oz/225 g zucchini, sliced

8 oz/225 g open-cap mushrooms, halved

2 cloves garlic, crushed

14 oz/400 g canned chopped tomatoes

2 tbsp sundried tomato paste

2 tbsp soy sauce

1 tsp sesame oil

1 tbsp Chinese rice wine or dry sherry

freshly ground black pepper

fresh basil leaves, to garnish

1 Heat the vegetable oil in a large preheated wok or skillet.

2 Add the pearl onions and eggplant to the wok or skillet and cook for 5 minutes, or until the vegetables are golden and just beginning to soften.

3 Add the sliced zucchini, mushrooms, garlic, chopped tomatoes, and sundried tomato paste to the wok and cook for about 5 minutes. Reduce the heat and simmer for 10 minutes, or until the

vegetables are tender, but not soft.

4 Add the soy sauce, sesame oil, and rice wine or sherry to the wok, bring back to a boil and cook for 1 minute.

5 Season the vegetable stir-fry with freshly ground black pepper and scatter with fresh basil leaves. Serve immediately on warm serving plates.

COOK'S TIP

Basil has a very strong flavor which is perfect with vegetables and Chinese flavorings. Instead of using basil simply as a garnish in this dish, try adding a handful of fresh basil leaves to the stir-fry in step 4.

Bell Peppers with Chestnuts

This is a crisp and colorful recipe, topped with crisp, shredded leeks for both flavor and color.

NUTRITIONAL INFORMATION

Calories ....192 Sugars 5g
Protein ....3g Fat 14g
Carbohydrate ...13g Saturates 13g

5 mins   15 mins

SERVES 4

INGREDIENTS

8 oz/225 g leeks

oil, for deep-frying

3 tbsp peanut oil

1 yellow bell pepper, seeded and diced

1 green bell pepper, seeded and diced

1 red bell pepper, seeded and diced

7 oz/200 g canned water chestnuts, drained and sliced

2 cloves garlic, crushed

3 tbsp light soy sauce

1 To make the garnish, finely slice the leeks into thin strips, using a sharp knife.

2 Heat the oil for deep-frying in a wok or large, heavy-based skillet.

3 Add the sliced leeks to the wok or skillet and cook for 2–3 minutes, or until crispy. Set aside until required.

4 Heat the 3 tablespoons of peanut oil in the wok or skillet.

5 Add the yellow, green, and red bell peppers to the wok and cook over a high heat for about 5 minutes, or until they are just beginning to brown at the edges and to soften.

6 Add the sliced water chestnuts, garlic, and light soy sauce to the wok and cook all of the vegetables for a further 2–3 minutes.

7 Spoon the bell pepper stir-fry on to warm serving plates, garnish with the crispy leeks and serve.

COOK'S TIP

Add 1 tablespoon of hoisin sauce with the soy sauce in step 6 for extra flavor and spice.

Vegetable Stir-Fry with Eggs

Known as Gado Gado in China, this is a true classic which never fades from popularity. A delicious warm salad with a peanut sauce.

NUTRITIONAL INFORMATION

Calories . . . . . . .269 Sugars 12g
Protein . . . . .12g Fat 19g
Carbohydrate . . .14g Saturates 3g

10 mins   15 mins

SERVES 4

I N G R E D I E N T S

2 eggs

3 small carrots

12 oz/350 g white cabbage

2 tbsp vegetable oil

1 red bell pepper, seeded and thinly sliced

1½ cups beansprouts

1 tbsp tomato catsup

2 tbsp soy sauce

½ cup salted peanuts, chopped

2 Peel and coarsely grate the carrots.

3 Remove any outer leaves from the white cabbage and cut out the stem, then shred the leaves very finely, either with a sharp knife or by using the fine slicing blade on a food processor.

4 Heat the vegetable oil in a large preheated wok or large skillet.

5 Add the carrots, white cabbage, and bell pepper to the wok and cook for 3 minutes.

6 Add the bean sprouts to the wok and cook for 2 minutes.

7 Combine the tomato catsup and soy sauce in a small bowl and add to the wok or skillet.

8 Add the chopped peanuts to the wok and cook for 1 minute.

9 Transfer the stir-fry to warm serving plates and garnish with the hard-cooked egg quarters. Serve immediately.

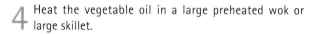

1 Bring a small pan of water to a boil. Add the eggs to the pan and cook for about 7 minutes. Remove the eggs from the pan and let cool under cold running water for 1 minute. Peel the shell from the eggs and then cut the eggs into quarters.

COOK'S TIP

The eggs are cooled in cold water immediately after cooking in order to prevent the egg yolk blackening around the edges.

Vegetable Chop Suey

Make sure that the vegetables are all cut into pieces of a similar size in this recipe, so that they cook within the same amount of time.

NUTRITIONAL INFORMATION

Calories 155	Sugars 6g
Protein 4g	Fat 12g
Carbohydrate 9g	Saturates 2g

🕒 5 mins 🕐 5 mins

SERVES 4

INGREDIENTS

1 yellow bell pepper, seeded

1 red bell pepper, seeded

1 carrot

1 zucchini

1 fennel bulb

1 onion

2 oz/60 g snow peas

2 tbsp peanut oil

3 garlic cloves, crushed

1 tsp grated fresh root ginger

1¼ cups beansprouts

2 tsp light brown sugar

2 tbsp light soy sauce

½ cup vegetable bouillon

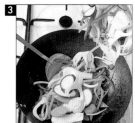

1 Cut the bell peppers, carrot, zucchini, and fennel into thin slices. Cut the onion into quarters and then cut each quarter in half. Slice the snow peas diagonally to create the maximum surface area.

2 Heat the oil in a preheated wok, add the garlic and ginger and cook for 30 seconds. Add the onion and cook for a further 30 seconds.

3 Add the bell peppers, carrot, zucchini, fennel, and snow peas to the wok and cook for 2 minutes.

4 Add the beansprouts to the wok and stir in the sugar, soy sauce, and bouillon. Reduce the heat to low and simmer for 1–2 minutes, until the vegetables are tender and coated in the sauce.

5 Transfer the vegetables and sauce to a serving dish and serve immediately.

VARIATION

Use any combination of colorful vegetables that you have to hand to make this versatile dish.

Vegetable Sesame Stir-Fry

Sesame seeds add a delicious flavor to any recipe and are particularly good with vegetables in this soy and rice wine or sherry sauce.

NUTRITIONAL INFORMATION

Calories	.118	Sugars	.2g
Protein	.3g	Fat	.9g
Carbohydrate	.5g	Saturates	.1g

 5 mins   🕐 10 mins

SERVES 4

I N G R E D I E N T S

2 tbsp vegetable oil

3 garlic cloves, crushed

1 tbsp sesame seeds, plus extra to garnish

2 celery stalks, sliced

2 baby corn cobs, sliced

2 oz/60 g white mushrooms

1 leek, sliced

i zucchini, sliced

1 small red bell pepper, sliced

1 fresh green chili, sliced

2 oz/60 g Napa cabbage, shredded

rice or noodles, to serve

S A U C E

½ tsp Chinese curry powder

2 tbsp light soy sauce

1 tbsp Chinese rice wine or dry sherry

1 tsp sesame oil

1 tsp cornstarch

4 tbsp water

1 Heat the vegetable oil in a preheated wok or heavy-based skillet, swirling the oil around the bottom of the wok until it is almost smoking.

2 Lower the heat slightly, add the garlic and sesame seeds, and cook for 30 seconds.

3 Add the celery, baby corn cobs, mushrooms, leek, zucchini, bell pepper, chili, and Napa cabbage and cook for 4–5 minutes, until the vegetables are beginning to soften.

4 To make the sauce, mix together the Chinese curry powder, light soy sauce, Chinese rice wine, or dry sherry, sesame oil, cornstarch, and water.

5 Stir the sauce mixture into the wok until well combined with the other ingredients.

6 bring to a boil and cook, stirring constantly, until the sauce thickens and clears.

7 Cook for 1 minute, spoon into a warm serving dish and garnish with sesame seeds. Serve the vegetable sesame stir-fry immediately with rice or noodles.

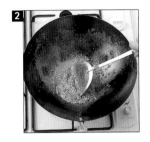

Eight Jewel Vegetables

This recipe, as the title suggests, is a colorful mixture of eight vegetables, cooked in a black bean and soy sauce.

NUTRITIONAL INFORMATION

Calories 110	Sugars 3g
Protein 4g	Fat 8g
Carbohydrate 7g	Saturates 1g

 5 mins 🕐 10 mins

SERVES 4

I N G R E D I E N T S

2 tbsp peanut oil

6 scallions, sliced

3 garlic cloves, crushed

1 green bell pepper, seeded and diced

1 red bell pepper, seeded and diced

1 fresh red chili, sliced

2 tbsp chopped water chestnuts

1 zucchini, chopped

4½ oz/125 g oyster mushrooms

3 tbsp black bean sauce

2 tsp Chinese rice wine or dry sherry

4 tbsp dark soy sauce

1 tsp dark brown sugar

2 tbsp water

1 tsp sesame oil

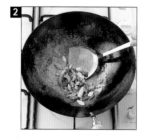  

1 Heat the peanut oil in a preheated wok or large skillet until it is almost smoking.

2 Lower the heat slightly, add the scallions and garlic and cook for about 30 seconds.

3 Add the red and green bell peppers, fresh red chili, water chestnuts, and zucchini to the wok or skillet and cook for 2–3 minutes, or until the vegetables are just beginning to soften.

4 Add the oyster mushrooms, black bean sauce, Chinese rice wine or dry sherry, dark soy sauce, dark brown sugar and water to the wok and cook for a further 4 minutes.

5 Sprinkle the stir-fry with sesame oil and serve immediately.

COOK'S TIP

Eight jewels or treasures form a traditional part of the Chinese New Year celebrations, which start in the last week of the old year. The Kitchen God, an important figure, is sent to give a report to heaven, returning on New Year's Eve in time for the feasting.

Spicy Bean Curd Triangles

Marinated bean curd is ideal in this recipe for added flavor, although the spicy coating is very tasty with plain bean curd.

NUTRITIONAL INFORMATION

Calories ....224 Sugars 17g
Protein ....10g Fat 13g
Carbohydrate ...18g Saturates 2g

1¼ hours   10 mins

SERVES 4

I N G R E D I E N T S

1 tbsp sea salt

4½ tsp Chinese five-spice powder

3 tbsp light brown sugar

2 garlic cloves, crushed

1 tsp grated fresh root ginger

1lb/450 g firm bean curd

vegetable oil, for deep-frying

2 leeks, shredded and halved

shredded leek, to garnish

1 Mix together the salt, Chinese five-spice powder, sugar, garlic, and ginger in a bowl and transfer to a plate.

2 Cut the bean curd cakes in half diagonally to form two triangles. Cut each triangle in half and then in half again to form 16 triangles.

3 Roll the bean curd triangles in the spice mixture, turning to coat thoroughly. Set aside for 1 hour.

4 Heat the vegetable oil for deep-frying in a wok until it is almost smoking.

5 Reduce the heat slightly, add the bean curd triangles and fry for 5 minutes, until golden brown. Remove

the bean curd from the wok with a slotted spoon, set aside and keep warm until required.

6 Add the leeks to the wok and cook for 1 minute. Remove from the wok and drain on paper towels.

7 Arrange the leeks on a warm serving plate and place the fried bean curd on top. Garnish with the fresh shredded leek and serve immediately.

COOK'S TIP

Cook the bean curd in batches and keep each batch warm until all of the bean curd has been cooked and is ready to serve.

Chinese Vegetable Casserole

This mixed vegetable casserole is very versatile and is delicious with any combination of vegetables of your choice.

NUTRITIONAL INFORMATION

Calories . . . . .218 Sugars 4g
Protein . . . . .7g Fat 14g
Carbohydrate . . .12g Saturates 2g

 5 mins   30 mins

SERVES 4

I N G R E D I E N T S

4 tbsp vegetable oil

2 carrots, sliced

1 zucchini, sliced

4 baby corn cobs, halved lengthwise

4½ oz/125 g cauliflower florets

1 leek, sliced

4½ oz/125 g water chestnuts, halved

8 oz/225 g firm bean curd, cubed

1¼ cups vegetable bouillon

1 tsp salt

2 tsp dark brown sugar

2 tsp dark soy sauce

2 tbsp dry sherry

1 tbsp cornstarch

2 tbsp water

1 tbsp chopped fresh cilantro, to garnish

COOK'S TIP

If there is too much liquid remaining, boil vigorously for 1 minute before adding the cornstarch to reduce it slightly.

1 Heat the oil in a preheated wok until it is almost smoking. Lower the heat slightly, add the carrots, zucchini, corn cobs, cauliflower, and leek to the wok and cook for 2–3 minutes.

2 Stir in the water chestnuts, bean curd, bouillon, salt, sugar, soy sauce, and sherry and bring to a boil. Reduce the heat, cover, and simmer for 20 minutes.

3 Blend the cornstarch with the water to form a smooth paste.

4 Stir the cornstarch mixture into the wok. Bring the sauce to a boil and cook, stirring constantly until it thickens and clears.

5 Transfer the casserole to a warm serving dish, sprinkle with chopped cilantro and serve immediately.

Cantonese Garden Vegetables

This dish tastes as fresh as it looks. Try to get hold of baby vegetables as they look and taste so much better in this dish.

NUTRITIONAL INFORMATION

Calories 130   Sugars 8g
Protein ....6g   Fat 8g
Carbohydrate ....8g   Saturates 1g

5 mins   10 mins

SERVES 4

INGREDIENTS

2 tbsp peanut oil

1 tsp Chinese five-spice powder

2¾ oz/75 g baby carrots, halved

2 celery stalks, sliced

2 baby leeks, sliced

1¾ oz/50 g snowpeas

4 baby zucchini, halved lengthwise

8 baby corn cobs

8 oz/225 g firm marinated bean curd, cubed

4 tbsp fresh orange juice

1 tbsp clear honey

cooked rice or noodles, to serve

TO GARNISH

celery leaves

orange zest

VARIATION

Lemon juice would be just as delicious as the orange juice in this recipe, but use 3 tablespoons instead of 4 tablespoons.

1 Heat the peanut oil in a preheated wok or large skillet until it is almost smoking.

2 Add the Chinese five-spice powder, carrots, celery, leeks, snow peas, zucchini, and corn cobs and cook for 3–4 minutes.

3 Add the bean curd to the wok or skillet and cook for a further 2 minutes, stirring gently so the bean curd does not break up.

4 Stir the fresh orange juice and clear honey into the wok or skillet, reduce the heat and cook for 1–2 minutes.

5 Transfer the stir-fry to a serving dish, garnish with celery leaves and orange zest and serve with rice or noodles.

Rice &
Noodles

Rice and noodles are staples in the Far East, as they are cheap, plentiful, nutritious, and delicious. They are extremely versatile ingredients and are therefore always served as part of a meal. Many rice and noodle dishes are

served as accompaniments and others as main dishes combined with meat, vegetables, and fish, all flavored with fragrant spices and seasonings.

Plain rice is served to punctuate a large meal and help settle the stomach between rich, spicy courses. Noodles vary from country to country and are eaten in various forms. Thin egg noodles are made from wheat flour, water, and egg and are probably the most common in the Western diet. Available fresh or dried, they require very little cooking and are perfect for quick and easy meals.

Fried Rice with Spicy Beans

This rice is really colorful and crunchy with the addition of sweetcorn and red kidney beans.

NUTRITIONAL INFORMATION

Calories	374	Sugars	.........6g
Protein	.........9g	Fat	...........9g
Carbohydrate	...64g	Saturates	.......1g

2 mins   25 mins

SERVES 4

INGREDIENTS

3 tbsp sunflower oil

1 onion, finely chopped

scant 1¼ cups long-grain white rice

1 green bell pepper, seeded and diced

1 tsp chili powder

2½ cups boiling water

3½ oz/100 g canned corn kernels

8 oz/225 g canned red kidney beans

2 tbsp chopped fresh cilantro

1 Heat the sunflower oil in a large preheated wok.

2 Add the finely chopped onion to the wok and cook for about 2 minutes or until the onion has softened.

3 Add the long-grain rice, cubed bell pepper, and chili powder to the wok and cook for 1 minute.

4 Pour the boiling water into the wok. Bring back to a boil, then reduce the heat and let the mixture simmer for 15 minutes.

5 Add the corn, kidney beans, and cilantro to the wok and heat through, stirring occasionally.

6 Transfer to a serving bowl and serve hot, scattered with extra cilantro, if wished.

VARIATION

For extra heat, add 1 chopped red chili as well as the chili powder in step 3.

Fragrant Coconut Rice

This fragrant, sweet rice is delicious served with meat, vegetable, or fish dishes as part of a Chinese menu.

NUTRITIONAL INFORMATION

Calories	...... .306	Sugars	.... .2g
Protein	.... .5g	Fat	.... .6g
Carbohydrate	...61g	Saturates	.... .4g

 5 mins (clock) 15 mins

SERVES 4

I N G R E D I E N T S

1⅓ cups long-grain white rice

2½ cups water

½ tsp salt

generous ⅓ cup coconut milk

¼ cup shredded coconut

1 Rinse the rice thoroughly under cold running water until the water runs completely clear.

2 Drain the rice thoroughly in a strainer set over a large bowl. This is to remove some of the starch and to prevent the grains from sticking together.

3 Place the rice in a wok with the water.

4 Add the salt and coconut milk to the wok and bring to a boil.

5 Cover the wok with a lid or a lid made of foil, curved into a domed shape and resting on the sides of the wok. Reduce the heat and let simmer for 10 minutes.

6 Remove the lid from the wok and fluff up the rice with a fork—all of the liquid should be absorbed and the rice grains should be tender. If not, add more water and continue to simmer for a few more minutes until all the liquid has been absorbed.

7 Spoon the rice into a warm serving bowl and scatter with the shredded coconut. Serve immediately.

COOK'S TIP

Coconut milk is not the liquid found inside coconuts— that is called coconut water. Coconut milk is made from the white coconut flesh soaked in water and milk and then squeezed to extract all of the flavor. You can make your own or buy it in cans.

Egg Fried Rice

In this classic Chinese dish, boiled rice is fried with peas, scallions, and egg, and flavored with soy sauce.

NUTRITIONAL INFORMATION

Calories 203	Sugars 1g
Protein 9g	Fat 11g
Carbohydrate . . .19g	Saturates 2g

 🄲 🄲

20 MINS   🕐 10 MINS

SERVES 4

INGREDIENTS

¾ cup long-grain rice

3 eggs, beaten

2 tbsp vegetable oil

2 garlic cloves, crushed

4 scallions, chopped

1 cup cooked peas

1 tbsp light soy sauce

pinch of salt

shredded scallion, to garnish

1 Cook the rice in a pan of boiling water for 10–12 minutes, until almost cooked, but not soft. Drain well, rinse under cold water and drain again.

2 Place the beaten eggs in a pan and cook over a gentle heat, stirring until softly scrambled.

3 Heat the vegetable oil in a preheated wok or large skillet, swirling the oil around the bottom of the wok until it is really hot.

4 Add the crushed garlic, scallions, and peas and sauté, stirring occasionally, for 1–2 minutes. Stir the rice into the wok, mixing to combine.

5 Add the eggs, light soy sauce, and a pinch of salt to the wok or skillet and stir to mix the egg in thoroughly.

6 Transfer the egg fried rice to serving dishes and serve garnished with the shredded scallion.

COOK'S TIP

The rice is rinsed under cold water to wash out the starch and prevent it from sticking together.

Stir-Fried Rice with Egg Strips

Many Thai rice dishes are made from leftover rice that has been cooked for an earlier meal. Any leftover vegetables or meat can also be used.

NUTRITIONAL INFORMATION

Calories 334	Sugars 49g	
Protein 7g	Fat 9g	
Carbohydrate ...60g	Saturates 1g	

5–10 mins   5 mins

SERVES 4

INGREDIENTS

2 tbsp peanut oil

1 egg, beaten with 1 tsp water

1 garlic clove, finely chopped

1 small onion, finely chopped

1 tbsp red curry paste

4 cups cooked long-grain rice

⅓ cup cooked peas

1 tbsp fish sauce

2 tbsp tomato catsup

2 tbsp chopped fresh cilantro

TO GARNISH

red chilies

cucumber slices

1 To make chili flowers for the garnish, hold the stem of each chili with your fingertips and use a small sharp, pointed knife to cut a slit down the length from near the stem end to the tip. Turn the chili about a quarter turn and make another cut. Repeat to make a total of 4 cuts, then scrape out the seeds. Cut each "petal" again in half, or into quarters, to make 8–16 petals. Place the chili in iced water.

2 Heat about 1 teaspoon of the oil in a wok. Pour in the egg mixture, swirling it to coat the pan evenly and make a thin layer. When set and golden, remove the egg from the pan and roll up. Keep to one side.

3 Add the remaining oil to the pan and cook the garlic and onion for 1 minute. Add the curry paste, then stir in the rice and peas.

4 Stir in the fish sauce, catsup, and cilantro. Remove the pan from the heat and pile the rice on to a serving dish.

5 Slice the egg roll into spiral strips, without unrolling, and use to garnish the rice. Add the cucumber slices and chili flowers. Serve hot.

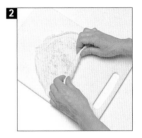

Vegetable Fried Rice

This dish can be served as part of a substantial meal for a number of people or as a vegetarian meal in itself for four.

NUTRITIONAL INFORMATION

Calories	175	Sugars	.........3g
Protein	.........3g	Fat	..........10g
Carbohydrate	...20g	Saturates	.......2g

 10 mins   20 mins

SERVES 4

I N G R E D I E N T S

⅔ cup long-grain white rice

3 tbsp peanut oil

2 garlic cloves, crushed

½ tsp Chinese five-spice powder

2 oz/60 g green beans

1 green bell pepper, seeded and chopped

4 baby corn cobs, sliced

1 oz/25 g canned bamboo shoots, drained and chopped

3 tomatoes, skinned, seeded, and chopped

½ cup cooked peas

1 tsp sesame oil

1 Bring a large pan of water to a boil.

2 Add the long-grain white rice to the pan and cook for about 15 minutes. Drain the rice well, rinse under cold running water and drain thoroughly again.

3 Heat the peanut oil in a preheated wok or large skillet. Add the garlic and Chinese five-spice powder and cook for 30 seconds.

4 Add the green beans, chopped green bell pepper, and sliced corn cobs, and cook the ingredients in the wok for 2 minutes.

5 Stir the bamboo shoots, tomatoes, peas, and rice into the mixture in the wok and cook for 1 further minute.

6 Sprinkle with sesame oil and transfer to serving dishes. Serve immediately.

VARIATION

Use a selection of vegetables of your choice in this recipe, cutting them to a similar size in order to ensure that they cook in the same amount of time.

Green Fried Rice

Spinach is used in this recipe to give the rice a wonderful green coloring. Tossed with the carrot strips, it is a really appealing dish.

NUTRITIONAL INFORMATION

Calories	139	Sugars	.........2g
Protein	.........3g	Fat	...........7g
Carbohydrate	...18g	Saturates	.......1g

5 mins   20 mins

SERVES 4

INGREDIENTS

⅔ cup long-grain rice

2 tbsp vegetable oil

2 garlic cloves, crushed

1 tsp grated fresh root ginger

1 carrot, cut into very thin sticks

1 zucchini, diced

8 oz/225 g baby spinach

2 tsp light soy sauce

2 tsp light brown sugar

1 Cook the rice in a pan of boiling water for about 15 minutes. Drain well, rinse under cold running water, and drain thoroughly again. Set aside until the rice is required.

2 Heat the vegetable oil in a preheated wok or large, heavy-based skillet.

3 Add the crushed garlic and grated fresh root ginger to the wok or skillet and cook for about 30 seconds.

4 Add the carrot sticks and diced zucchini to the mixture in the wok and cook for about 2 minutes, so the vegetables still retain their crunch.

5 Add the baby spinach and cook for 1 minute, until wilted.

6 Add the rice, soy sauce, and sugar to the wok and mix together well.

7 Transfer the green fried rice to serving dishes and serve immediately.

COOK'S TIP

Light soy sauce has more flavor than the sweeter, dark soy sauce, which gives the food a rich, reddish color.

Special Fried Rice

This dish is a popular choice in Chinese restaurants. Ham and shrimp are mixed with vegetables in a soy-flavored rice.

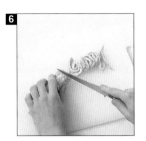

NUTRITIONAL INFORMATION

Calories 301	Sugars 1g
Protein 26g	Fat 13g
Carbohydrate . . .21g	Saturates 3g

 5 mins   30 mins

SERVES 4

I N G R E D I E N T S

⅔ cup long-grain rice

2 tbsp vegetable oil

2 eggs, beaten

2 garlic cloves, crushed

1 tsp grated fresh root ginger

3 scallions, sliced

¾ cup cooked peas

1½ cups beansprouts

1⅓ cups shredded ham

5½ oz/150 g peeled, cooked shrimp

2 tbsp light soy sauce

1 Cook the rice in a pan of boiling water for about 15 minutes. Drain well, rinse under cold water and drain thoroughly again.

2 Heat 1 tablespoon of the vegetable oil in a preheated wok.

3 Add the beaten eggs and a further 1 teaspoon of oil. Tilt the wok so that the egg covers the bottom to make a thin pancake.

4 Cook until lightly browned on the underside, then flip the pancake over and cook on the other side for 1 minute. Remove from the wok and let cool.

5 Heat the remaining oil in the wok and cook the garlic and ginger for 30 seconds. Add the scallions, peas, beansprouts, ham, and shrimp. Cook for 2 minutes.

6 Stir in the soy sauce and rice and cook for a further 2 minutes. Transfer the rice to serving dishes. Roll up the pancake, slice it very thinly and use to garnish the rice. Serve immediately.

COOK'S TIP

As this recipe contains meat and fish, it is ideal served with simpler vegetable dishes.

Crab Congee

This is a typical Chinese breakfast dish although it is probably best served as a lunch or supper dish at a Western table!

NUTRITIONAL INFORMATION

Calories 327	Sugars 0.1g
Protein 18g	Fat 7g
Carbohydrate ...50g	Saturates 2g

5 mins   1¼ hours

SERVES 4

INGREDIENTS

generous 1 cup short-grain rice

6¼ cups fish bouillon

½ tsp salt

3½ oz/100 g Chinese sausage,
   thinly sliced

8 oz/225 g white crab meat

6 scallions, sliced

2 tbsp chopped fresh cilantro

freshly ground black pepper,
   to serve

1 Place the short-grain rice in a large preheated wok or skillet.

2 Add the fish bouillon to the wok or skillet and bring to a boil.

3 Reduce the heat, then simmer gently for 1 hour, stirring the mixture from time to time.

4 Add the salt, sliced Chinese sausage, white crab meat, sliced scallions, and chopped fresh cilantro to the wok and heat through for about 5 minutes.

5 Add a little more water to the wok if the congee "porridge" is too thick, stirring well.

6 Transfer the crab congee to warm serving bowls, sprinkle with freshly ground black pepper and serve immediately.

COOK'S TIP

Always buy the freshest possible crab meat; fresh is best, although frozen or canned will work for this recipe. In the West, crabs are almost always sold ready-cooked. The crab should feel heavy for its size, and when it is shaken, there should be no sound of water inside.

Crab Fried Rice

Canned crabmeat is used in this recipe for convenience, but fresh white crabmeat could be used—quite deliciously—in its place.

NUTRITIONAL INFORMATION

Calories	225	Sugars	.........1g
Protein	........12g	Fat	...........11g
Carbohydrate	...20g	Saturates	.......2g

 5 mins   🕐 25 mins

SERVES 4

INGREDIENTS

⅔ cup long-grain rice

2 tbsp peanut oil

4½ oz/125 g canned white crabmeat, drained

1 leek, sliced

1½ cups beansprouts

2 eggs, beaten

1 tbsp light soy sauce

2 tsp lime juice

1 tsp sesame oil

salt

sliced lime, to garnish

1 Cook the rice in a pan of boiling salted water for 15 minutes. Drain well, rinse under cold running water and drain again thoroughly.

2 Heat the peanut oil in a preheated wok until it is really hot.

3 Add the crabmeat, leek, and beansprouts to the wok and cook for 2–3 minutes. Remove the mixture from the wok with a slotted spoon and set aside until required.

4 Add the eggs to the wok and cook, stirring occasionally, for 2–3 minutes, until they begin to set.

5 Stir the rice and the crabmeat, leek, and beansprout mixture into the eggs in the wok.

6 Add the soy sauce and lime juice to the mixture in the wok. Cook for 1 minute, stirring to combine, and sprinkle with the sesame oil.

7 Transfer the crab fried rice to a serving dish, garnish with the sliced lime and serve immediately.

VARIATION

Cooked lobster may be used instead of the crab for a really special dish.

Rice with Seafood

This soup-like main course rice dish is packed with fresh seafood and is typically Thai in flavor.

NUTRITIONAL INFORMATION

Calories	370	Sugars	.........0g
Protein	........27g	Fat	...........8g
Carbohydrate	...52g	Saturates	.......1g

5–10 mins   20 mins

SERVES 4

INGREDIENTS

12 mussels in their shells, cleaned

8¾ cups fish bouillon

2 tbsp vegetable oil

1 garlic clove, crushed

1 tsp grated fresh root ginger

1 red bird-eye chili, chopped

2 scallions, chopped

scant 1¼ cups long-grain rice

2 small squid, cleaned and sliced

3½ oz/100 g firm white fish fillet, such as halibut or monkfish, cut into chunks

3½ oz/100 g raw shrimp, peeled

2 tbsp fish sauce

3 tbsp shredded fresh cilantro

1 Discard any mussels with damaged shells or open ones that do not close when firmly tapped. Heat 4 tablespoons of the bouillon in a large pan. Add the mussels, cover and shake the pan until the mussels open. Remove from the heat and discard any which do not open.

2 Heat the oil in a large skillet or wok and cook the garlic, ginger, chili, and scallions for 30 seconds. Add the bouillon and bring to a boil.

3 Stir in the rice, then add the squid, fish fillet, and shrimp. Lower the heat and simmer gently for 15 minutes, or until the rice is cooked. Add the fish sauce and mussels.

4 Ladle into wide bowls and sprinkle with cilantro, before serving.

COOK'S TIP

You could use leftover cooked rice for this dish. Just simmer the seafood gently until cooked, then stir in the rice at the end.

Rice with Five-Spice Chicken

This dish has a wonderful color obtained from the turmeric, and a great spicy flavor, making it very appealing all round.

NUTRITIONAL INFORMATION

Calories	.412	Sugars	.1g
Protein	.23g	Fat	.13g
Carbohydrate	.53g	Saturates	.2g

🍗 5 mins   🕐 20 mins

SERVES 4

INGREDIENTS

1 tbsp Chinese five-spice powder

2 tbsp cornstarch

12 oz/350 g boneless, skinless chicken breasts, cubed

3 tbsp peanut oil

1 onion, diced

generous 1 cup long-grain white rice

½ tsp turmeric

2½ cups chicken bouillon

2 tbsp snipped fresh chives

1 Place the Chinese five-spice powder and cornstarch in a large bowl. Add the chicken pieces and toss to coat the chicken pieces all over.

COOK'S TIP

Be careful when using turmeric as it can stain the hands and clothes a distinctive shade of yellow.

2 Heat 2 tablespoons of the peanut oil in a large preheated wok. Add the chicken pieces to the wok and cook for 5 minutes. Using a slotted spoon, remove the chicken and set aside.

3 Add the remaining peanut oil to the wok.

4 Add the onion to the wok and cook for 1 minute.

5 Add the rice, turmeric, and chicken bouillon to the wok and gently bring to a boil.

6 Return the chicken pieces to the wok, reduce the heat and let simmer for 10 minutes, or until the liquid has been absorbed and the rice is tender.

7 Add the snipped fresh chives, stir to mix and serve hot.

Chinese Chicken Rice

This is a really colorful main meal or side dish which tastes just as good as it looks.

NUTRITIONAL INFORMATION

Calories	324	Sugars	.......4g
Protein	......24g	Fat	.........10g
Carbohydrate	...37g	Saturates	......2g

5 mins   25 mins

SERVES 4

INGREDIENTS

1¾ cups long-grain white rice

1 tsp turmeric

2 tbsp sunflower oil

12 oz/350 g skinless, boneless chicken breasts or thighs, sliced

1 red bell pepper, seeded and sliced

1 green bell pepper, seeded and sliced

1 green chili, seeded and finely chopped

1 carrot, coarsely grated

1½ cups beansprouts

6 scallions, sliced, plus extra to garnish

2 tbsp soy sauce

salt

1 Place the rice and turmeric in a large pan of lightly salted water and cook until the grains of rice are just tender, about 10 minutes. Drain the rice thoroughly and press out any excess water with paper towels.

2 Heat the sunflower oil in a large preheated wok or skillet.

3 Add the strips of chicken to the wok or skillet and cook over a high heat until the chicken is just beginning to turn a golden color.

4 Add the sliced bell peppers and green chili to the wok and cook for 2–3 minutes.

5 Add the cooked rice to the wok, a little at a time, tossing well after each addition until well combined and the grains of rice are separated.

6 Add the carrot, beansprouts, and scallions to the wok and cook for a further 2 minutes.

7 Drizzle with the soy sauce and toss to combine.

8 Transfer the Chinese chicken rice to a warm serving dish, garnish with extra scallions, if wished, and serve at once.

Chicken & Rice Casserole

This is a quick-cooking, spicy casserole of rice, chicken, vegetables, and chili in a soy and ginger flavored sauce.

NUTRITIONAL INFORMATION

Calories	502	Sugars	.........2g
Protein	........55g	Fat	...........9g
Carbohydrate	...52g	Saturates	.......3g

35 mins   50 mins

SERVES 4

INGREDIENTS

generous ⅔ cup long-grain rice

1 tbsp dry sherry

2 tbsp light soy sauce

2 tbsp dark soy sauce

2 tsp dark brown sugar

1 tsp salt

1 tsp sesame oil

2 lb/900 g skinless, boneless chicken
  meat, diced

3½ cups chicken bouillon

2 open-cap mushrooms, sliced

2 oz/60 g canned water chestnuts, drained
  and halved

2¾ oz/75 g broccoli florets

1 yellow bell pepper, sliced

4 tsp grated fresh root ginger

whole chives, to garnish

VARIATION

This dish would work
equally well with beef or pork.
Chinese dried mushrooms may be
used instead of the open-cap
mushrooms, if rehydrated before
adding to the dish.

 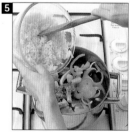

1 Cook the rice in a pan of boiling water for about 15 minutes. Drain well, rinse under cold water and drain again thoroughly.

2 Mix together the sherry, soy sauces, sugar, salt, and sesame oil.

3 Stir the chicken into the soy mixture, turning to coat it well. Let the chicken marinate for about 30 minutes.

4 Bring the bouillon to a boil in a pan or preheated wok. Add the chicken with the marinade, mushrooms, water chestnuts, broccoli, bell pepper, and ginger.

5 Stir in the rice, reduce the heat, cover, and cook for 25–30 minutes, until the chicken and vegetables are cooked through. Transfer to serving plates, garnish with chives and serve.

Chicken Chow Mein

This classic dish requires no introduction as it is already a favorite amongst most Chinese food enthusiasts.

NUTRITIONAL INFORMATION

Calories 460	Sugars 3g	
Protein 31g	Fat 17g	
Carbohydrate . . .49g	Saturates 4g	

🍲 5 mins   🕐 20 mins

SERVES 4

I N G R E D I E N T S

9 oz/250 g medium egg noodles

2 tbsp sunflower oil

9½ oz/275 g cooked chicken breasts, shredded

1 clove garlic, finely chopped

1 red bell pepper, seeded and thinly sliced

3½ oz/100 g shiitake mushrooms, sliced

6 scallions, sliced

1 cup beansprouts

3 tbsp soy sauce

1 tbsp sesame oil

1 Place the egg noodles in a large bowl or dish and break them up slightly. Pour over enough boiling water to cover the noodles and let stand.

2 Heat the sunflower oil in a large preheated wok. Add the shredded chicken, finely chopped garlic, bell pepper slices, mushrooms, scallions, and beansprouts to the wok and cook for about 5 minutes.

3 Drain the noodles thoroughly. Add the noodles to the wok, toss well and cook for a further 5 minutes.

4 Drizzle the soy sauce and sesame oil over the chow mein and toss until well combined.

5 Transfer the chicken chow mein to warm serving bowls and serve immediately.

VARIATION

You can make the chow mein with a selection of vegetables for a vegetarian dish, if you prefer.

  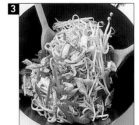

Sweet Chili Pork Fried Rice

This is a variation of egg fried rice which may be served as an accompaniment to a main meal dish.

NUTRITIONAL INFORMATION

Calories 366	Sugars 5g	
Protein 29g	Fat 16g	
Carbohydrate ...28g	Saturates 4g	

 25 mins   🕐 20 mins

SERVES 4

I N G R E D I E N T S

1 lb/450 g pork tenderloin

2 tbsp sunflower oil

2 tbsp sweet chili sauce, plus extra
  to serve

1 onion, sliced

2 carrots, cut into thin sticks

6 oz/175 g zucchini, cut into sticks

1 cup canned bamboo shoots, drained

4¾ cups cooked long-grain rice

1 egg, beaten

1 tbsp chopped fresh parsley

1 Using a sharp knife, cut the pork tenderloin into thin slices.

2 Heat the sunflower oil in a large preheated wok or skillet.

3 Add the pork to the wok and cook for 5 minutes.

4 Add the chili sauce to the wok and allow to bubble, stirring, for 2–3 minutes or until syrupy.

5 Add the onion, carrots, zucchini, and bamboo shoots to the wok and cook for a further 3 minutes.

6 Add the cooked rice and cook for 2–3 minutes, or until the rice is heated through.

7 Drizzle the beaten egg over the top of the fried rice and cook, tossing the ingredients in the wok with two spoons, until the egg sets.

8 Scatter with chopped fresh parsley and serve immediately, with extra sweet chili sauce, if desired.

COOK'S TIP

For a really quick dish, add frozen mixed vegetables to the rice instead of the freshly prepared vegetables.

Fried Rice with Pork

This dish is a meal in itself, containing pieces of pork, fried with rice, peas, tomatoes, and mushrooms.

NUTRITIONAL INFORMATION

Calories 285   Sugars 2g
Protein ....18g   Fat 16g
Carbohydrate ...19g   Saturates 4g

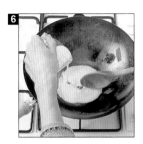

10 mins   30 mins

SERVES 4

I N G R E D I E N T S

¾ cup long-grain rice

3 tbsp peanut oil

1 large onion, cut into 8 pieces

8 oz/225 g pork tenderloin, thinly sliced

2 open-cap mushrooms, sliced

2 garlic cloves, crushed

1 tbsp light soy sauce

1 tsp light brown sugar

2 tomatoes, skinned, seeded and
   chopped

½ cup cooked peas

2 eggs, beaten

1 Cook the rice in a pan of boiling water for about 15 minutes, until tender, but not soft. Drain well, rinse under cold running water and drain again thoroughly.

2 Heat the peanut oil in a preheated wok. Add the sliced onion and pork and cook for 3–4 minutes, until just beginning to color.

3 Add the mushrooms and garlic to the wok and cook for 1 minute.

4 Add the soy sauce and sugar to the mixture in the wok and cook for a further 2 minutes.

5 Stir in the rice, tomatoes, and peas, mixing well. Transfer the mixture to a warmed dish.

6 Stir the eggs into the wok and cook, stirring with a wooden spoon, for 2–3 minutes, until beginning to set.

7 Return the rice mixture to the wok and mix well. Transfer to serving dishes and serve immediately.

COOK'S TIP

You can cook the rice in advance and chill or freeze it until required.

Rice with Seven-Spice Beef

Beef fillet is used in this recipe as it is very suitable for quick cooking and has a wonderful flavor.

NUTRITIONAL INFORMATION

Calories 171	Sugars 8g
Protein 28g	Fat 15g
Carbohydrate . . .60g	Saturates 6g

 5 mins 30 mins

SERVES 4

INGREDIENTS

generous 1 cup long-grain white rice

2½ cups water

12 oz/350 g beef fillet

2 tbsp soy sauce

2 tbsp tomato catsup

1 tbsp seven-spice seasoning

2 tbsp peanut oil

1 onion, diced

3 small carrots, diced

1 cup frozen peas

2 eggs, beaten

2 tbsp cold water

1 Rinse the rice under cold running water, then drain thoroughly. Place the rice in a pan with the water, bring to a boil, cover and let simmer for 12 minutes. Turn the cooked rice out on to a tray and let cool.

2 Using a sharp knife, thinly slice the beef fillet.

3 Mix together the soy sauce, tomato catsup, and seven-spice seasoning. Spoon over the beef and toss well to coat.

4 Heat the oil in a preheated wok. Add the beef and cook for 3–4 minutes.

5 Add the onion, carrots, and peas to the wok and cook for a further 2–3 minutes. Add the cooked rice to the wok and stir to combine.

6 Beat the eggs with 2 tablespoons of cold water. Drizzle the egg mixture over the rice and cook for 3–4 minutes, or until the rice is heated through and the egg has set. Transfer to a warm serving bowl and serve immediately.

VARIATION

You can use pork fillet or chicken instead of the beef, if you prefer.

Stir-Fried Rice with Sausage

This is a very quick rice dish as it uses pre-cooked rice. It is therefore ideal when time is short or for a quick lunch-time dish.

NUTRITIONAL INFORMATION

Calories 383   Sugars 9g
Protein . . . . .19g   Fat 17g
Carbohydrate . . .42g   Saturates 4g

5 mins   20 mins

SERVES 4

INGREDIENTS

12 oz/350 g Chinese sausage

2 tbsp sunflower oil

2 tbsp soy sauce

1 onion, sliced

2 carrots, cut into thin sticks

1¾ cups peas

¾ cup canned pineapple cubes, drained

4¾ cups cooked long-grain rice

1 egg, beaten

1 tbsp chopped fresh parsley

1 Using a sharp knife, thinly slice the Chinese sausage.

2 Heat the sunflower oil in a large preheated wok. Add the sausage to the wok and cook for 5 minutes.

3 Stir in the soy sauce and allow to bubble for about 2–3 minutes, or until syrupy.

4 Add the onion, carrots, peas, and pineapple to the wok and cook for a further 3 minutes.

5 Add the cooked rice to the wok and cook the mixture for about 2–3 minutes, or until the rice is completely heated through.

6 Drizzle the beaten egg over the top of the rice and cook, tossing the ingredients in the wok, until the egg sets.

7 Transfer the stir-fried rice to a large, warm serving bowl and scatter with plenty of chopped fresh parsley. Serve immediately.

COOK'S TIP

Cook extra rice and freeze it in preparation for some of the other rice dishes included in this book, as it saves time and enables you to prepare a meal in minutes. Be sure to cool any leftover cooked rice quickly before freezing to avoid food poisoning.

Chinese Risotto

Risotto is a creamy Italian dish made with risotto rice.
This Chinese version is simply delicious!

NUTRITIONAL INFORMATION

Calories . . . . . . .436 Sugars 7g
Protein . . . . .13g Fat 14g
Carbohydrate . . .70g Saturates 4g

5 mins   25 mins

SERVES 4

INGREDIENTS

2 tbsp peanut oil

1 onion, sliced

2 cloves garlic, crushed

1 tsp Chinese five-spice powder

8 oz/225 g Chinese sausage, sliced

3 small carrots, diced

1 green bell pepper, seeded and diced

1⅓ cups risotto rice

3½ cups vegetable or chicken bouillon

1 tbsp fresh chives

1 Heat the peanut oil in a large preheated wok or heavy-bottomed skillet.

2 Add the onion slices, crushed garlic, and Chinese five-spice powder to the wok or skillet and cook for 1 minute.

3 Add the Chinese sausage, carrots, and green bell pepper to the wok and stir to combine.

4 Stir in the risotto rice and cook for 1 minute.

5 Gradually add the vegetable or chicken bouillon, a little at a time, stirring constantly until the liquid has been completely absorbed and the rice grains are tender.

6 Snip the chives with a pair of clean kitchen scissors and stir into the wok with the last of the bouillon.

7 Transfer the Chinese risotto to warm serving bowls and serve immediately.

COOK'S TIP

Chinese sausage is highly flavored and is made from chopped pork fat, pork meat, and spices. Use a spicy Portuguese sausage if Chinese sausage is unavailable.

Crispy Rice Noodles

This is a version of a favorite Thai dish, "mee krob", one of those exciting dishes which varies from one day to the next.

NUTRITIONAL INFORMATION

Calories 490	Sugars 11g
Protein 24g	Fat 16g
Carbohydrate . . .63g	Saturates 2g

5 mins   15 mins

SERVES 4

I N G R E D I E N T S

vegetable oil for deep-frying, plus an extra 1½ tbsp

7 oz/200 g rice vermicelli noodles

1 onion, finely chopped

4 garlic cloves, finely chopped

1 boneless, skinless chicken breast, finely chopped

2 red bird-eye chilies, seeded and sliced

4 tbsp dried Chinese black mushrooms, soaked, drained, and thinly sliced

3 tbsp dried shrimp

4 scallions, sliced

3 tbsp lime juice

2 tbsp soy sauce

2 tbsp fish sauce

2 tbsp rice vinegar

2 tbsp soft light brown sugar

2 eggs, beaten

3 tbsp chopped fresh cilantro

scallion curls, to garnish

1 Heat the oil in a large skillet or wok until very hot and deep-fry the noodles quickly, occasionally turning them, until puffed up, crisp and pale golden brown. Lift on to paper towels and drain well.

2 Heat 1 tablespoon of oil and cook the onion and garlic for 1 minute. Add the chicken and cook for 3 minutes. Add the chilies, mushrooms, dried shrimp, and scallions.

3 Mix together the lime juice, soy sauce, fish sauce, rice vinegar, and sugar, then stir into the pan and cook for a further minute. Remove the pan from the heat.

4 Heat the remaining oil in a wide pan and pour in the eggs to coat the bottom of the pan evenly, making a thin omelet. Cook until set and golden, then turn it over and cook the other side. Turn out and roll up, then slice into long ribbon strips.

5 Toss together the fried noodles, stir-fried ingredients, cilantro, and omelet strips. Garnish with scallion curls and serve at once.

Spicy Japanese Noodles

These noodles are highly spiced with chili and flavored with sesame seeds for a nutty taste which is a true delight.

NUTRITIONAL INFORMATION

Calories	381	Sugars	........12g
Protein	........11g	Fat	.........13g
Carbohydrate	...59g	Saturates	.......2g

🍳 🍳 🍳

🍲 5 mins   🕐 15 mins

SERVES 4

I N G R E D I E N T S

1 lb 2 oz/450 g fresh Japanese noodles

1 tbsp sesame oil

1 tbsp sesame seeds

1 tbsp sunflower oil

1 red onion, sliced

3½ oz/100 g snow peas

2 carrots, thinly sliced

12 oz/350 g white cabbage, shredded

3 tbsp sweet chili sauce

2 scallions, sliced, to garnish

1 Bring a large pan of water to a boil. Add the Japanese noodles to the pan and cook for 2–3 minutes. Drain the noodles thoroughly.

2 Toss the noodles with the sesame oil and sesame seeds.

3 Heat the sunflower oil in a large preheated wok.

4 Add the onion slices, snow peas, carrot slices, and shredded cabbage to the wok and cook for about 5 minutes.

5 Add the sweet chili sauce to the wok and cook, stirring occasionally, for a further 2 minutes.

6 Add the sesame noodles to the wok, toss well to combine and heat through for a further 2–3 minutes. (You may wish to serve the noodles separately, so transfer them to the serving bowls.)

7 Transfer the Japanese noodles and spicy vegetables to warm serving bowls and garnish with sliced scallions. Serve immediately.

COOK'S TIP

If fresh Japanese noodles are difficult to get hold of, use dried rice noodles or thin egg noodles instead.

Rice Noodles with Beans

These rice noodles and vegetables are tossed in a crunchy peanut and chili sauce for a quick satay-flavored recipe.

NUTRITIONAL INFORMATION

Calories	259	Sugars	.........9g
Protein	........28g	Fat	...........8g
Carbohydrate	...20g	Saturates	.......1g

12 mins   8 mins

SERVES 4

INGREDIENTS

10 oz/275 g flat rice noodles

3 tbsp peanut oil

2 cloves garlic, crushed

2 shallots, sliced

8 oz/225 g green beans, sliced

3¾ oz/100 g cherry tomatoes, halved

1 tsp chili flakes

4 tbsp crunchy peanut butter

⅔ cup coconut milk

1 tbsp tomato paste

sliced scallions, to garnish

1 Place the rice noodles in a large bowl and pour over enough boiling water to cover. Let stand for 10 minutes.

2 Heat the peanut oil in a large preheated wok.

3 Add the garlic and shallots and cook for 1 minute.

4 Drain the flat rice noodles thoroughly.

5 Add the green beans and drained noodles to the wok and cook for 5 minutes.

6 Add the cherry tomatoes to the wok and mix well.

7 Mix together the chili flakes, peanut butter, coconut milk, and tomato paste until well combined.

8 Pour the chili mixture over the noodles, toss well to combine and heat through.

9 Transfer to warm serving dishes and garnish with scallion slices. Serve immediately.

VARIATION

Add slices of chicken or beef to the recipe and cook with the beans and noodles in step 4 for a more substantial main meal.

Hot & Sour Noodles

This simple, fast-food dish is sold from street food stalls in Thailand, with many and varied additions of meat and vegetables.

NUTRITIONAL INFORMATION

Calories	259	Sugars 9g
Protein	........28g	Fat 8g
Carbohydrate	...20g	Saturates 1g

🍲 10 mins   🕐 5 mins

SERVES 4

INGREDIENTS

9 oz/250 g dried medium egg noodles

1 tbsp sesame oil

1 tbsp chili oil

1 garlic clove, crushed

2 scallions, finely chopped

2 oz/55 g white mushrooms, sliced

1 cup dried Chinese black mushrooms, soaked, drained, and sliced

2 tbsp lime juice

3 tbsp light soy sauce

1 tsp sugar

shredded Napa cabbage, to serve

TO GARNISH

2 tbsp shredded cilantro

2 tbsp toasted peanuts, chopped

COOK'S TIP

Thai chili oil is very hot, so if you want a milder flavor, use vegetable oil for the initial cooking instead, then add a final dribble of chili oil just for seasoning.

1 Cook the noodles in a large pan of boiling water for 3–4 minutes, or according to the package directions. Drain well, return to the pan, toss with the sesame oil and set aside.

2 Heat the chili oil in a large skillet or wok and quickly cook the garlic, onions, and white mushrooms to soften them.

3 Add the black mushrooms, lime juice, soy sauce, and sugar and continue cooking until boiling. Add the noodles and toss to mix.

4 Serve spooned over shredded Napa cabbage, garnished with cilantro and peanuts.

Fried Vegetable Noodles

In this recipe, noodles are first boiled and then deep-fried for a crisply textured dish, and tossed with vegetables.

NUTRITIONAL INFORMATION

Calories	229	Sugars	.........4g
Protein	.........5g	Fat	..........15g
Carbohydrate	...20g	Saturates	.......2g

 5 mins   (clock) 25 mins

SERVES 4

I N G R E D I E N T S

12 oz/350 g dried egg noodles

2 tbsp peanut oil

2 garlic cloves, crushed

½ tsp ground star anise

1 carrot, cut into very thin sticks

1 green bell pepper, cut into very thin sticks

1 onion, quartered and sliced

4½ oz/125 g broccoli florets

2¾ oz/75 g canned bamboo shoots

1 celery stalk, sliced

1 tbsp light soy sauce

⅔ cup vegetable bouillon

oil, for deep-frying

1 tsp cornstarch

2 tsp water

1 Cook the noodles in a pan of boiling water for 1–2 minutes. Drain well and rinse under cold running water. Let the noodles drain thoroughly in a strainer until they are required.

2 Heat the peanut oil in a preheated wok until smoking. Reduce the heat, add the crushed garlic and ground star anise and cook for 30 seconds. Add the remaining vegetables and cook for 1–2 minutes.

3 Add the soy sauce and vegetable bouillon to the wok and cook over a low heat for 5 minutes.

4 Heat the oil for deep-frying in a separate wok to 350°F/180°C, or until a cube of bread browns in 30 seconds.

5 Using a fork, twist the drained noodles and form them into rounds. Deep-fry them in batches until crisp, turning once. Let drain on paper towels.

6 Blend the cornstarch with the water to form a paste and stir into the vegetables. Bring to a boil, stirring until the sauce is thickened and clear.

7 Arrange the noodles on a warm serving plate, spoon the vegetables on top and serve immediately.

  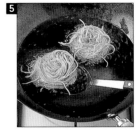

Noodle & Mango Salad

Fruit combines well with the peanut dressing, bell peppers, and chili in this delicious hot salad.

NUTRITIONAL INFORMATION

Calories	368	Sugars	........11g
Protein	........11g	Fat	.........26g
Carbohydrate	...24g	Saturates	.......5g

15 mins · 5 mins

SERVES 4

INGREDIENTS

9 oz/250 g thread egg noodles

2 tbsp peanut oil

4 shallots, sliced

2 cloves garlic, crushed

1 red chili, seeded and sliced

1 red bell pepper, seeded and sliced

1 green bell pepper, seeded and sliced

1 ripe mango, sliced into thin strips

¼ cup salted peanuts, chopped

DRESSING

4 tbsp peanut butter

generous ⅓ cup coconut milk

1 tbsp tomato paste

1 Place the egg noodles in a large dish or bowl. Pour over enough boiling water to cover the noodles and let stand for 10 minutes.

COOK'S TIP

If preferred, gently heat the peanut dressing before pouring over the noodle salad.

2 Heat the peanut oil in a large preheated wok or skillet.

3 Add the shallots, crushed garlic, chili, and bell pepper slices to the wok or skillet and cook for 2–3 minutes.

4 Drain the egg noodles thoroughly in a strainer. Add the drained noodles and mango slices to the wok or skillet and heat through for about 2 minutes.

5 Transfer the noodle and mango salad to warmed serving dishes and scatter with chopped peanuts.

6 To make the dressing, mix together the peanut butter, coconut milk, and tomato paste then spoon over the noodle salad. Serve immediately.

Yellow Bean Noodles

Cellophane or thread noodles are excellent re-heated, unlike other noodles which must be served as soon as they are ready.

NUTRITIONAL INFORMATION

Calories 212   Sugars 0.5g
Protein . . . . .28g   Fat 7g
Carbohydrate . . .10g   Saturates 2g

5 mins   30 mins

SERVES 4

I N G R E D I E N T S

6 oz/175 g cellophane noodles

1 tbsp peanut oil

1 leek, sliced

2 garlic cloves, crushed

1 lb/450 g ground chicken

scant 2 cups chicken bouillon

1 tsp chili sauce

2 tbsp yellow bean sauce

4 tbsp light soy sauce

1 tsp sesame oil

snipped fresh chives, to garnish

1 Place the cellophane noodles in a bowl, pour over boiling water and soak for 15 minutes.

COOK'S TIP

Cellophane noodles are available from many food stores and all Chinese food stores.

2 Drain the noodles thoroughly and cut into short lengths with a pair of kitchen scissors.

3 Heat the oil in a wok or skillet and stir-fry the leek and garlic for 30 seconds.

4 Add the chicken to the wok and cook for 4–5 minutes, until the chicken is completely cooked through.

5 Add the chicken bouillon, chili sauce, yellow bean sauce, and soy sauce to the wok and cook for 3–4 minutes.

6 Add the drained noodles and sesame oil to the wok and cook, tossing to mix well, for 4–5 minutes.

7 Spoon the mixture into warm serving bowls, sprinkle with snipped chives and serve immediately.

Noodles with Cod & Mango

Fish and fruit are tossed with a trio of bell peppers in this spicy dish served with noodles for a quick, healthy meal.

NUTRITIONAL INFORMATION

Calories	274	Sugars 11g
Protein	........25g	Fat 8g
Carbohydrate	...26g	Saturates 1g

 10 mins   🕐 25 mins

SERVES 4

I N G R E D I E N T S

9 oz/250 g egg noodles

1 lb/450 g skinless cod fillet

1 tbsp paprika

2 tbsp sunflower oil

1 red onion, sliced

1 orange bell pepper, seeded and sliced

1 green bell pepper, seeded and sliced

3½ oz/100 g baby corn cobs, halved

1 mango, sliced

1 cup beansprouts

2 tbsp tomato catsup

2 tbsp soy sauce

2 tbsp medium sherry

1 tsp cornstarch

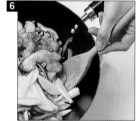

1 Place the egg noodles in a large bowl and cover with boiling water. Let stand for about 10 minutes.

2 Rinse the cod fillet and pat dry with paper towels. Cut the cod flesh into thin strips.

3 Place the cod strips in a large bowl. Add the paprika and toss well to coat the fish.

4 Heat the sunflower oil in a large preheated wok.

5 Add the onion, bell peppers, and baby corn cobs to the wok and cook for about 5 minutes.

6 Add the cod to the wok together with the sliced mango and cook for a further 2–3 minutes or until the fish is tender.

7 Add the beansprouts to the wok and toss well to combine.

8 Mix together the tomato catsup, soy sauce, sherry, and cornstarch. Add the mixture to the wok and cook, stirring occasionally, until the juices thicken.

9 Drain the noodles thoroughly and transfer to warm serving bowls. Transfer the cod and mango stir-fry to separate serving bowls and serve immediately.

Sweet & Sour Noodles

This delicious dish combines sweet and sour flavors with the addition of egg, rice noodles, jumbo shrimp, and vegetables for a real treat.

NUTRITIONAL INFORMATION

Calories	352	Sugars	........14g
Protein	........23g	Fat	..........17g
Carbohydrate	...29g	Saturates	.......3g

 10 mins   10 mins

SERVES 4

I N G R E D I E N T S

3 tbsp fish sauce

2 tbsp distilled white vinegar

2 tbsp palm or superfine sugar

2 tbsp tomato paste

2 tbsp sunflower oil

3 cloves garlic, crushed

12 oz/350 g rice noodles, soaked in boiling water for 5 minutes

8 scallions, sliced

2 carrots, grated

1½ cups beansprouts

2 eggs, beaten

8 oz/225 g peeled king shrimp

½ cup chopped peanuts

1 tsp chili flakes, to garnish

1 Mix together the fish sauce, vinegar, sugar, and tomato paste.

2 Heat the sunflower oil in a large preheated wok.

3 Add the garlic to the wok and cook for 30 seconds.

4 Drain the noodles thoroughly and add them to the wok together with the fish sauce and tomato paste mixture. Mix well to combine.

5 Add the scallions, carrots, and beansprouts to the wok and cook for 2–3 minutes.

6 Move the stir-fry mixture to one side of the wok, add the beaten eggs to the empty part of the wok and cook until the egg sets. Add the noodles, shrimp, and peanuts to the wok and mix well. Transfer to warm serving dishes and garnish with chili flakes. Serve hot.

COOK'S TIP
Chili flakes may be found in the spice section of large food stores.

Chili Shrimp Noodles

This is a simple dish to prepare and is packed with flavor, making it an ideal choice for special occasions.

NUTRITIONAL INFORMATION

Calories ....259 Sugars 9g
Protein ....28g Fat 8g
Carbohydrate ...20g Saturates 1g

10 mins   5 mins

SERVES 4

INGREDIENTS

9 oz/250 g thin glass noodles

2 tbsp sunflower oil

1 onion, sliced

2 red chilies, seeded and very finely chopped

4 lime leaves, thinly shredded

1 tbsp fresh cilantro

2 tbsp palm or superfine sugar

2 tbsp fish sauce

1 lb/450 g raw jumbo shrimp, peeled

1 Place the noodles in a large bowl. Pour over enough boiling water to cover the noodles and let stand for 5 minutes. Drain thoroughly and set aside until required.

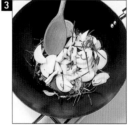  

COOK'S TIP

If you cannot buy raw jumbo shrimp, use cooked shrimp instead and cook them with the noodles for 1 minute only, just to heat through.

2 Heat the sunflower oil in a large preheated wok or skillet until it is really hot.

3 Add the onion, red chilies, and lime leaves to the wok and cook for 1 minute.

4 Add the cilantro, palm or superfine sugar, fish sauce, and shrimp to the wok or skillet and cook for a further

2 minutes or until the shrimp turn pink.

5 Add the drained noodles to the wok, toss to mix well, and cook for 1–2 minutes or until heated through.

6 Transfer the noodles and shrimp to warm serving bowls and serve immediately.

Special Noodles

This dish combines meat, vegetables, shrimp, and noodles in a curried coconut sauce. Serve as a main meal or as an accompaniment.

NUTRITIONAL INFORMATION

Calories . . . . . . .409 Sugars 12g
Protein . . . . .24g Fat 23g
Carbohydrate . . .28g Saturates 8g

5 mins   25 mins

SERVES 4

INGREDIENTS

9 oz/250 g thin rice noodles

4 tbsp peanut oil

2 cloves garlic, crushed

2 red chilies, seeded and very
   finely chopped

1 tsp grated fresh root ginger

2 tbsp Madras curry paste

2 tbsp rice wine vinegar

1 tbsp superfine sugar

8 oz/225 g cooked ham, finely shredded

3½ oz/100 g canned water chestnuts, sliced

100 g/3½ oz mushrooms, sliced

¾ cup peas

1 red bell pepper, seeded and
   thinly sliced

3½ oz/100 g peeled shrimp

2 large eggs

4 tbsp coconut milk

¼ cup shredded coconut

2 tbsp chopped fresh cilantro

1 Place the rice noodles in a large bowl, cover with boiling water and let soak for about 10 minutes. Drain the noodles thoroughly, then toss with 2 tablespoons of peanut oil.

2 Heat the remaining peanut oil in a large preheated wok until the oil is really hot.

3 Add the garlic, chilies, ginger, curry paste, rice wine vinegar, and superfine sugar to the wok and cook for 1 minute.

4 Add the ham, water chestnuts, mushrooms, peas, and red bell pepper to the wok and cook for 5 minutes.

5 Add the noodles and shrimps to the wok and cook for 2 minutes.

6 In a small bowl, beat together the eggs and coconut milk. Drizzle over the mixture in the wok and cook until the egg sets.

7 Add the shredded coconut and chopped fresh cilantro to the wok and toss to combine. Transfer the noodles to warm serving dishes and serve immediately.

Curried Shrimp Noodles

Although these noodles are almost a meal in themselves, if served as an accompaniment, they are ideal with plain vegetable or fish dishes.

NUTRITIONAL INFORMATION

Calories 246   Sugars 1g
Protein ....17g   Fat 14g
Carbohydrate ...14g   Saturates 2g

5 MINS   15 MINS

SERVES 4

INGREDIENTS

8 oz/225 g rice noodles

4 tbsp vegetable oil

1 onion, sliced

2 ham slices, shredded

2 tbsp Chinese curry powder

⅔ cup fish bouillon

8 oz/225 g peeled, raw shrimp

2 garlic cloves, crushed

6 scallions, chopped

1 tbsp light soy sauce

2 tbsp hoisin sauce

1 tbsp dry sherry

2 tsp lime juice

fresh snipped chives, to garnish

COOK'S TIP

Hoisin sauce is made from soy beans, sugar, flour, vinegar, salt, garlic, chili, and sesame seed oil. Sold in cans or jars, it will keep in the refrigerator for several months.

 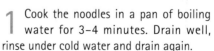  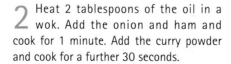

1 Cook the noodles in a pan of boiling water for 3–4 minutes. Drain well, rinse under cold water and drain again.

2 Heat 2 tablespoons of the oil in a wok. Add the onion and ham and cook for 1 minute. Add the curry powder and cook for a further 30 seconds.

3 Stir the noodles and fish bouillon into the wok and cook for 2–3 minutes.

Remove the noodles from the wok and keep warm.

4 Heat the remaining oil in the wok. Add the shrimp, garlic, and scallions and cook for about 1 minute.

5 Stir in the remaining ingredients. Pour the mixture over the noodles, toss to mix and garnish with fresh chives.

Noodles with Shrimp

This is a simple dish using egg noodles and large shrimp, which give the dish a wonderful flavor, texture, and color.

NUTRITIONAL INFORMATION

Calories 142	Sugars 0.4g	
Protein 11g	Fat 7g	
Carbohydrate 11g	Saturates 1g	

 5 mins   10 mins

SERVES 4

I N G R E D I E N T S

8 oz/225 g thin egg noodles

2 tbsp peanut oil

1 garlic clove, crushed

½ tsp ground star anise

1 bunch scallions, cut into 5-cm/2-inch pieces

24 raw jumbo shrimp, peeled, with tails intact

2 tbsp light soy sauce

2 tsp lime juice

lime wedges, to garnish

1 Blanch the noodles in a pan of boiling water for 2–3 minutes.

2 Drain the noodles well, rinse under cold water and drain thoroughly again. Keep warm and set aside until required.

3 Heat the peanut oil in a preheated wok or large skillet until almost smoking.

4 Add the crushed garlic and ground star anise to the wok and cook for 30 seconds.

5 Add the scallions and jumbo shrimp to the wok and cook for 2–3 minutes.

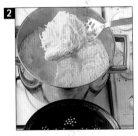

6 Stir in the light soy sauce, lime juice, and noodles and mix well.

7 Cook the mixture in the wok for about 1 minute until thoroughly heated through and all the ingredients are thoroughly incorporated.

8 Spoon the noodle and shrimp mixture into a warm serving dish. Transfer to serving bowls, garnish with lime wedges and serve immediately.

COOK'S TIP

If fresh egg noodles are available, these require very little cooking: simply place in boiling water for about 3 minutes, then drain and toss in oil. Noodles can be boiled and eaten plain, or cooked with meat and vegetables for a light meal or snack.

Cellophane Noodles & Shrimp

Jumbo shrimp are cooked with orange juice, bell peppers, soy sauce, and vinegar and served on a bed of cellophane noodles.

NUTRITIONAL INFORMATION

Calories . . . . .118 Sugar 4g
Protein . . . . .7g Fat 4g
Carbohydrate . . .15g Saturates 1g

10 mins   25 mins

SERVES 4

INGREDIENTS

175 g/6 oz cellophane noodles

1 tbsp vegetable oil

1 garlic clove, crushed

2 tsp grated fresh root ginger

24 raw jumbo shrimp, peeled and de-veined

1 red bell pepper, seeded and thinly sliced

1 green bell pepper, seeded and thinly sliced

1 onion, chopped

2 tbsp light soy sauce

juice of 1 orange

2 tsp wine vinegar

pinch of brown sugar

⅔ cup fish bouillon

1 tbsp cornstarch

2 tsp water

orange slices, to garnish

1 Cook the noodles in a pan of boiling water for 1 minute. Drain well, rinse under cold water and then drain again.

2 Heat the oil in a wok and cook the garlic and ginger for 30 seconds.

3 Add the shrimp and cook for 2 minutes. Remove with a slotted spoon and keep warm.

4 Add the bell peppers and onion to the wok and cook for 2 minutes. Stir in the soy sauce, orange juice, vinegar, sugar, and bouillon. Return the shrimp to the wok and cook for 8–10 minutes, until cooked through.

5 Blend the cornstarch with the water and stir into the wok. Bring to a boil, add the noodles and cook for 1–2 minutes. Garnish and serve.

VARIATION

Lime or lemon juice and slices may be used instead of the orange. Use 3–5½ tsp of these juices.

Sesame Noodles with Shrimp

Delicately scented with sesame and cilantro, these noodles make an unusual lunch or supper dish.

NUTRITIONAL INFORMATION

Calories	430	Sugars	.........2g
Protein	........23g	Fat	..........15g
Carbohydrate	...56g	Saturates	.......3g

5 mins   10 mins

SERVES 4

INGREDIENTS

1 garlic clove, chopped

1 scallion, chopped

1 small red chili, seeded and sliced

1 tsp chopped fresh cilantro

10½ oz/300 g fine egg noodles

2 tbsp vegetable oil

2 tsp sesame oil

1 tsp shrimp paste

8 oz/225 g raw shrimp, peeled

2 tbsp lime juice

2 tbsp fish sauce

1 tsp sesame seeds, toasted

1 Use a pestle and mortar to grind the garlic, onion, chili, and cilantro into a smooth paste.

2 Drop the noodles into a pan of boiling water and bring back to a boil, then simmer for 4 minutes, or according to the package directions.

3 Meanwhile, heat the oils in a pan and stir in the shrimp paste and cilantro mixture. Stir over a medium heat for 1 minute.

4 Stir in the shrimp and cook for 2 minutes. Stir in the lime juice and fish sauce and cook for a further minute.

5 Drain the noodles and toss them into the wok. Sprinkle with the sesame seeds and serve.

COOK'S TIP

The roots of cilantro are widely used in Thai cooking, so if you can buy fresh cilantro with the root attached, the whole plant can be used in this dish for maximum flavor. If not, just use the stems and leaves.

Oyster Sauce Noodles

Chicken and noodles are cooked and then tossed in an oyster sauce and egg mixture in this delicious recipe.

NUTRITIONAL INFORMATION

Calories	278	Sugars	.........2g
Protein	........30g	Fat	..........12g
Carbohydrate	...13g	Saturates	.......3g

5 mins · 25 mins

SERVES 4

INGREDIENTS

9 oz/250 g egg noodles

1 lb/450 g chicken thighs

2 tbsp peanut oil

1 large carrot, sliced

3 tbsp oyster sauce

2 eggs

3 tbsp cold water

1 Place the egg noodles in a large bowl or dish. Pour enough boiling water over the noodles to cover and let stand for 10 minutes.

2 Meanwhile, remove the skin from the chicken thighs. Cut the chicken flesh into small pieces, using a sharp knife.

VARIATION

Flavor the eggs with soy sauce or hoisin sauce as an alternative to the oyster sauce, if you prefer.

3 Heat the peanut oil in a large preheated wok or skillet, swirling the oil around the bottom of the wok until it is really hot.

4 Add the pieces of chicken and the carrot slices to the wok and cook for about 5 minutes.

5 Drain the noodles thoroughly. Add the noodles to the wok and cook for a further 2–3 minutes or until the noodles are heated through.

6 Beat together the oyster sauce, eggs, and cold water. Drizzle the mixture over the noodles and cook for a further 2–3 minutes or until the eggs set.

7 Transfer the mixture in the wok to warm serving bowls and serve hot.

Chicken Noodles

Rice noodles are used in this recipe. They are available in large food stores or specialist Chinese stores.

NUTRITIONAL INFORMATION

Calories 169   Sugars 2g
Protein ....14g   Fat 7g
Carbohydrate ...12g   Saturates 2g

5 mins   15 mins

SERVES 4

INGREDIENTS

8 oz/225 g rice noodles

2 tbsp peanut oil

8 oz/225 g skinless, boneless chicken
    breast, sliced

2 garlic cloves, crushed

1 tsp grated fresh root ginger

1 tsp Chinese curry powder

1 red bell pepper, seeded and
    thinly sliced

2¾ oz/75 g snow peas, shredded

1 tbsp light soy sauce

2 tsp Chinese rice wine

2 tbsp chicken bouillon

1 tsp sesame oil

1 tbsp chopped fresh cilantro

1 Soak the rice noodles for 4 minutes in warm water. Drain thoroughly and set aside until required.

2 Heat the peanut oil in a preheated wok or large heavy-based skillet and cook the chicken slices for 2–3 minutes.

3 Add the garlic, ginger, and Chinese curry powder and cook for a further 30 seconds. Add the red bell pepper and

snow peas to the mixture in the wok and cook for 2–3 minutes.

4 Add the noodles, soy sauce, Chinese rice wine, and chicken bouillon to the wok and mix well, stirring occasionally, for 1 minute.

5 Sprinkle the sesame oil and chopped cilantro over the noodles. Transfer to serving plates and serve.

VARIATION

You can use pork or duck in this recipe instead of the chicken, if you prefer.

Singapore Noodles

This is a special and well-known dish, which is a delicious meal in itself, packed with chicken, shrimp, and vegetables.

NUTRITIONAL INFORMATION

Calories 627	Sugars 3g	
Protein 44g	Fat 32g	
Carbohydrate . . .44g	Saturates 4g	

 5 mins   🕐 20 mins

SERVES 4

I N G R E D I E N T S

8 oz/225 g dried egg noodles

6 tbsp vegetable oil

4 eggs, beaten

3 garlic cloves, crushed

1½ tsp chili powder

8 oz/225 g skinless, boneless chicken, cut into thin strips

3 celery stalks, sliced

1 green bell pepper, seeded and sliced

4 scallions, sliced

1 oz/25 g water chestnuts, quartered

2 fresh red chilies, sliced

10 oz/300 g peeled, cooked shrimp

1¾ cups beansprouts

2 tsp sesame oil

1 Soak the noodles in boiling water for 4 minutes, or until soft. Let drain on paper towels.

2 Heat 2 tablespoons of the oil in a preheated wok. Add the eggs and stir until set. Remove the cooked eggs from the wok, set aside and keep warm.

3 Add the remaining oil to the wok. Add the garlic and chili powder and cook for 30 seconds.

4 Add the chicken and cook for 4–5 minutes, until just beginning to brown.

5 Stir in the celery, bell pepper, scallions, water chestnuts, and chilies and cook for a further 8 minutes, or until the chicken is cooked through.

6 Add the shrimp and the reserved noodles to the wok, together with the beansprouts, and toss to mix well.

7 Break the cooked egg with a fork and sprinkle over the noodles, together with the sesame oil. Serve immediately.

COOK'S TIP

When mixing pre-cooked ingredients into the dish, such as the egg and noodles, ensure that they are heated right through and are hot when ready to serve.

Chicken on Crispy Noodles

Blanched noodles are fried in the wok until crisp and brown, and then topped with a shredded chicken sauce for a delightfully tasty dish.

NUTRITIONAL INFORMATION

Calories 376   Sugars 2g
Protein . . . . .15g   Fat 27g
Carbohydrate . . .17g   Saturates 4g

35 mins   25 mins

SERVES 4

INGREDIENTS

8 oz/225 g skinless, boneless chicken breasts, shredded

1 egg white

5 tsp cornstarch

8 oz/225 g thin egg noodles

1¼ cups vegetable oil

2½ cups chicken bouillon

2 tbsp dry sherry

2 tbsp oyster sauce

1 tbsp light soy sauce

1 tbsp hoisin sauce

1 red bell pepper, seeded and very thinly sliced

2 tbsp water

3 scallions, chopped

1 Mix together the chicken, egg white and 2 teaspoons of the cornstarch in a bowl. Let stand for at least 30 minutes.

2 Blanch the noodles in boiling water for 2 minutes, then drain thoroughly.

3 Heat the vegetable oil in a preheated wok. Add the noodles, spreading them to cover the bottom of the wok. Cook over a low heat for about 5 minutes, until the noodles are browned on the underside. Flip the noodles over and brown on the other side. Remove from the wok when crisp and browned, place on a serving plate and keep warm. Drain the oil from the wok.

4 Add 1¼ cups of the chicken bouillon to the wok. Remove from the heat and add the chicken, stirring well so that it does not stick. Return to the heat and cook for 2 minutes. Drain, discarding the bouillon.

5 Wipe the wok with paper towels and return to the heat. Add the sherry, sauces, bell pepper, and the remaining bouillon and bring to a boil. Blend the remaining cornstarch with the water and stir it into the mixture.

6 Return the chicken to the wok and cook over a low heat for 2 minutes. Place the chicken on top of the noodles and sprinkle with scallions.

Chili Pork Noodles

This is quite a spicy dish, with a delicious peanut flavor. Increase or reduce the amount of chili to your liking.

NUTRITIONAL INFORMATION

Calories . . . . .421 Sugars 3g
Protein . . . . .27g Fat 26g
Carbohydrate . . .20g Saturates 6g

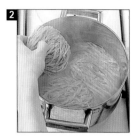

35 mins   10 mins

SERVES 4

INGREDIENTS

12 oz/350 g ground pork

1 tbsp light soy sauce

1 tbsp dry sherry

12 oz/350 g egg noodles

2 tsp sesame oil

2 tbsp vegetable oil

2 garlic cloves, crushed

2 tsp grated fresh root ginger

2 fresh red chilies, sliced

1 red bell pepper, seeded and finely sliced

¼ cup unsalted peanuts

3 tbsp peanut butter

3 tbsp dark soy sauce

dash of chili oil

1¼ cups pork bouillon

1 Mix together the pork, light soy sauce, and dry sherry in a large bowl. Cover and let the pork marinate for 30 minutes.

2 Meanwhile, cook the noodles in a pan of boiling water for 4 minutes. Drain well, rinse in cold water and drain again. Toss the noodles in the sesame oil.

3 Heat the vegetable oil in a preheated wok and cook the garlic, ginger, chilies, and bell pepper for 30 seconds.

4 Add the pork to the mixture in the wok, together with the marinade. Continue cooking for about 1 minute, until the pork is sealed.

5 Add the peanuts, peanut butter, soy sauce, chili oil, and bouillon and cook for 2–3 minutes.

6 Toss the noodles in the mixture and serve at once.

VARIATION

Ground chicken or lamb would also be excellent in this recipe instead of the pork.

Pad Thai Noodles

The combination of ingredients in this classic noodle dish varies, but it commonly contains a mixture of pork and prawns or other seafood.

NUTRITIONAL INFORMATION

Calories . . . . . . .477 Sugars 6g
Protein . . . . .26g Fat 14g
Carbohydrate . . .60g Saturates 3g

10 mins   5 mins

SERVES 4

INGREDIENTS

9 oz/250 g flat rice noodles

3 tbsp peanut oil

3 garlic cloves, finely chopped

4½ oz/125 g pork tenderloin, chopped into 5-mm/¼-inch pieces

7 oz/200 g shrimp, peeled

1 tbsp sugar

3 tbsp fish sauce

1 tbsp tomato catsup

1 tbsp lime juice

2 eggs, beaten

1¼ cups beansprouts

TO GARNISH

1 tsp dried red chili flakes

2 scallions, thickly sliced

2 tbsp chopped fresh cilantro

1 Soak the rice noodles in hot water for about 10 minutes, or according to the package directions. Drain well and put to one side.

2 Heat the oil in a large skillet or wok and cook the garlic over a high heat for 30 seconds. Add the pork and cook for 2–3 minutes until browned.

3 Stir in the shrimp, then add the sugar, fish sauce, catsup, and lime juice, and continue cooking for a further 30 seconds.

4 Stir in the eggs and cook until lightly set. Stir in the noodles, then add the beansprouts and cook for a further 30 seconds.

5 Turn out on to a warm serving dish and scatter with chili flakes, scallions, and cilantro.

COOK'S TIP

Drain the rice noodles before adding to the pan, as excess moisture will spoil the texture of the dish.

Mushroom & Pork Noodles

This dish benefits from the use of colored oyster mushrooms. If these are unavailable, plain gray mushrooms will suffice.

NUTRITIONAL INFORMATION

Calories . . . . . . .286 Sugars 3g
Protein . . . . .23g Fat 13g
Carbohydrate . . .21g Saturates 3g

 10 mins 20 mins

SERVES 4

I N G R E D I E N T S

1 lb/450 g thin egg noodles

2 tbsp peanut oil

12 oz/350 g pork tenderloin, sliced

2 garlic cloves, crushed

1 onion, cut into 8 pieces

8 oz/225 g oyster mushrooms

4 tomatoes, skinned, seeded and
   thinly sliced

2 tbsp light soy sauce

scant ¼ cup pork bouillon

1 tbsp chopped fresh cilantro

1 Cook the noodles in a pan of boiling water for 2–3 minutes. Drain well, rinse under cold running water and drain thoroughly again.

2 Heat 1 tablespoon of the oil in a preheated wok or skillet.

3 Add the noodles to the wok or skillet and cook for about 2 minutes.

4 Using a slotted spoon, remove the noodles from the wok, drain well and set aside until required.

5 Heat the remaining peanut oil in the wok. Add the pork slices and cook for 4–5 minutes.

6 Stir in the crushed garlic and chopped onion and cook for a further 2–3 minutes.

7 Add the oyster mushrooms, tomatoes, light soy sauce, pork bouillon, and drained noodles. Stir well and cook for 1–2 minutes.

8 Sprinkle with chopped cilantro and serve immediately.

COOK'S TIP

For crisper noodles, add 2 tablespoons of oil to the wok and cook the noodles for 5-6 minutes, spreading them thinly in the wok and turning half-way through cooking.

Twice-Cooked Lamb

Here lamb is first boiled, and then cooked with soy sauce, oyster sauce, and spinach, and finally tossed with noodles, for a richly flavored dish.

NUTRITIONAL INFORMATION

Calories 315	Sugars 5g
Protein 27g	Fat 16g
Carbohydrate . . .16g	Saturates 6g

 5 mins   🕐 30 mins

SERVES 4

I N G R E D I E N T S

9 oz/250 g egg noodles

1 lb/450 g lamb loin fillet,
   thinly sliced

2 tbsp soy sauce

2 tbsp sunflower oil

2 cloves garlic, crushed

1 tbsp superfine sugar

2 tbsp oyster sauce

6 oz/175 g baby spinach

1 Place the egg noodles in a large bowl and cover with boiling water. Let soak for about 10 minutes.

2 Bring a large pan of water to a boil. Add the lamb and cook for 5 minutes. Drain thoroughly.

3 Place the slices of lamb in a bowl and mix with the soy sauce and 1 tablespoon of the sunflower oil.

4 Heat the remaining sunflower oil in a large preheated wok, swirling the oil around until it is really hot.

5 Add the marinated lamb and crushed garlic to the wok and cook for about 5 minutes or until the meat is just beginning to brown.

6 Add the superfine sugar and oyster sauce to the wok and stir well to combine.

7 Drain the noodles thoroughly. Add the noodles to the wok and cook for a further 5 minutes.

8 Add the spinach to the wok and cook for 1 minute or until the leaves just wilt. Transfer the lamb and noodles to serving bowls and serve hot.

COOK'S TIP

If using dried noodles, follow the instructions on the package as they require less soaking.

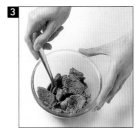

Lamb with Noodles

Lamb is coated in a soy sauce and served on a bed of transparent noodles for a richly flavored dish.

NUTRITIONAL INFORMATION

Calories	285	Sugars 1g
Protein	........27g	Fat 16g
Carbohydrate	...10g	Saturates 6g

5 mins   15 mins

SERVES 4

INGREDIENTS

5½ oz/150 g cellophane noodles

2 tbsp peanut oil

1 lb/450 g lean lamb, thinly sliced

2 garlic cloves, crushed

2 leeks, sliced

3 tbsp dark soy sauce

1 cup lamb bouillon

dash of chili sauce

red chili strips, to garnish

1 Bring a large pan of water to a boil. Add the cellophane noodles and cook for 1 minute. Drain the noodles well, rinse under cold running water and drain thoroughly again. Set aside until required.

2 Heat the peanut oil in a preheated wok or skillet, swirling the oil around until it is really hot.

3 Add the lamb to the wok or skillet and cook for about 2 minutes.

4 Add the crushed garlic and sliced leeks to the wok and cook for a further 2 minutes.

5 Stir in the dark soy sauce, lamb bouillon, and chili sauce, and cook for 3–4 minutes, stirring frequently, until the meat is cooked through.

6 Add the drained cellophane noodles to the wok or skillet and cook for about 1 minute, stirring, until heated through.

7 Transfer the lamb and cellophane noodles to serving plates, garnish with red chili strips and serve.

COOK'S TIP

Transparent noodles are available in Chinese food stores. Use egg noodles instead if transparent noodles are unavailable, and cook them according to the instructions on the package.

Beef with Crispy Noodles

Crispy noodles are terrific and may also be served on their own as a side dish, sprinkled with sugar and salt.

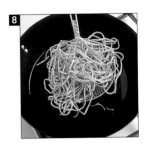

NUTRITIONAL INFORMATION

Calories	244	Sugars 9g
Protein	. . . . .20g	Fat 10g
Carbohydrate	. . .19g	Saturates 2g

🥙 5 mins   🕐 30 mins

SERVES 4

I N G R E D I E N T S

8 oz/225 g medium egg noodles

12 oz/350 g beef fillet

2 tbsp sunflower oil

1 tsp ground ginger

1 clove garlic, crushed

1 red chili, seeded and very finely chopped

1 large carrot, cut into thin sticks

6 scallions, sliced

2 tbsp lime marmalade

2 tbsp soy sauce

3 tbsp vegetable oil

1 Place the noodles in a large dish or bowl. Pour over enough boiling water to cover the noodles and let stand for about 10 minutes while you cook the rest of the ingredients.

2 Using a sharp knife, thinly slice the beef fillet.

3 Heat the sunflower oil in a large preheated wok or skillet.

4 Add the beef and ground ginger to the wok or skillet and cook for about 5 minutes.

5 Add the crushed garlic, chopped red chili, carrots, and scallions to the wok and cook for a further 2–3 minutes.

6 Add the lime marmalade and soy sauce to the wok and allow to bubble for 2 minutes. Remove the chili beef and ginger mixture, set aside and keep warm until required.

7 Heat the vegetable oil in the wok or skillet.

8 Drain the noodles thoroughly and pat dry with paper towels. Carefully lower the noodles into the hot oil and cook for 2–3 minutes or until crispy. Drain the noodles on paper towels.

9 Divide the noodles between 4 warm serving plates and top with the chili beef and ginger mixture. Serve immediately.

Beef Chow Mein

Chow mein must be the best-known and most popular noodle dish on any Chinese menu. You can use any meat or vegetables instead of beef.

NUTRITIONAL INFORMATION

Calories 341   Sugars 3g
Protein . . . . .27g   Fat 17g
Carbohydrate . . .20g   Saturates 4g

10 mins   20 mins

SERVES 4

I N G R E D I E N T S

1 lb/450 g egg noodles

4 tbsp peanut oil

1 lb/450 g lean beef steak, cut into thin strips

2 garlic cloves, crushed

1 tsp grated fresh root ginger

1 green bell pepper, thinly sliced

1 carrot, thinly sliced

2 celery stalks, sliced

8 scallions

1 tsp dark brown sugar

1 tbsp dry sherry

2 tbsp dark soy sauce

a few drops of chili sauce

1 Cook the noodles in a pan of boiling salted water for 4–5 minutes. Drain well, rinse under cold running water and drain again thoroughly.

2 Toss the noodles in 1 tablespoon of the peanut oil.

3 Heat the remaining oil in a preheated wok. Add the beef and cook for 3–4 minutes, stirring constantly.

4 Add the crushed garlic and grated fresh root ginger to the wok and cook for 30 seconds.

5 Add the bell pepper, carrot, celery, and scallions and cook for about 2 minutes.

6 Add the dark brown sugar, dry sherry, dark soy sauce, and chili sauce to the mixture in the wok and cook, stirring, for 1 minute.

7 Stir in the noodles, mixing well, and cook until completely warmed through.

8 Transfer the noodles to warm serving bowls and serve immediately.

VARIATION

A variety of different vegetables may be used in this recipe for color and flavor—try broccoli, red bell peppers, green beans, or baby corn cobs.

Cantonese Fried Noodles

This dish is usually served as a snack or light meal. It may also be served as an accompaniment to plain meat and fish dishes.

NUTRITIONAL INFORMATION

Calories 385	Sugars 6g
Protein 38g	Fat 17g
Carbohydrate ...21g	Saturates 4g

 5 mins   15 mins

SERVES 4

INGREDIENTS

12 oz/350 g egg noodles

3 tbsp vegetable oil

1½ lb/675 g lean beef steak, cut into thin strips

4½ oz/125 g green cabbage, shredded

2¾ oz/75 g canned, drained bamboo shoots

6 scallions, sliced

1 oz/25 g green beans, halved

1 tbsp dark soy sauce

2 tbsp beef bouillon

1 tbsp dry sherry

1 tbsp light brown sugar

2 tbsp chopped fresh parsley, to garnish

1 Cook the noodles in a pan of boiling water for 2–3 minutes. Drain well, rinse under cold running water and drain thoroughly again.

2 Heat 1 tablespoon of the oil in a preheated wok or skillet, swirling it around until it is really hot

3 Add the noodles and cook for 1–2 minutes. Drain the noodles and set aside until required.

4 Heat the remaining oil in the wok. Add the beef and cook for 2–3 minutes. Add the cabbage, bamboo shoots, scallions, and beans to the wok and cook for 1–2 minutes.

5 Add the soy sauce, beef bouillon, dry sherry, and light brown sugar to the wok, stirring to mix well.

6 Stir the noodles into the mixture in the wok, tossing to mix well. Transfer to serving bowls, garnish with chopped parsley and serve immediately.

VARIATION

You can vary the vegetables in this dish depending on seasonal availability or whatever you have at hand—try broccoli, green bell pepper, or spinach.

Index